THE HOLLOW KINGDOM

THE **HOLLOW KINGDOM**

ISIS and the **CULT** of **JIHAD**

EDNA FERNANDES

SPEAKING TIGER

SPEAKING TIGER PUBLISHING PVT. LTD
4381/4, Ansari Road, Daryaganj
New Delhi 110002

Published in India by Speaking Tiger in hardback 2018

ISBN: 978-93-86702-72-2
eISBN: 978-93-86702-73-9

10 9 8 7 6 5 4 3 2 1

Typeset in Sabon Roman by SÜRYA, New Delhi
Printed at SAP Print Solutions Pvt. Ltd.

For my friend John 'Mozza' Morrison (1949-2017),
one of the greatest foreign correspondents of his
generation and the very finest of men.

'Nothing is easier than to denounce the evildoer.
Nothing is more difficult than to understand him.'

—Fyodor Dostoevsky, *The Possessed*

CONTENTS

Introduction 1

PROLOGUE: The Mother of ISIS 15

1. IDENTITY

Exit from Mass Murder 29

Death Cult 47

The Grayzone 67

Blood, Gold and a Thousand Insurgencies 77

Songs of History 89

2. IDEOLOGY AND RECRUITMENT

The Line of Inheritance 103

World Wahhabi Web 127

The Eton of Islam 138

Sharia UK 155

Mindcraft 176

3. ECONOMY

Anatomy of a Terrorist Economy 195

Black and Gold 205

Death and Taxes 215

An Inhuman Trade 225

The Two-Trillion-Dollar Problem 235

CONCLUSION: The Hollow Kingdom 242

Acknowledgements 253

INTRODUCTION

> 'All of you, beware of extremism in the religion, for those before you were only destroyed because of extremism.'
>
> —The Prophet Mohammed

On 16 October 2016, the small Syrian town of Dabiq fell under the control of the Free Syrian Army (FSA). Here was a faction of Syrian armed forces defectors committed to deposing President Bashar al-Assad and ousting the Islamic State in Iraq and Syria (ISIS) to impose an alternative regime in Syria. Dabiq was home to a few thousand civilians and barely a thousand ISIS fighters. The town had no military significance and was unimportant in terms of natural resources. Yet its fall was a momentous victory in the war against ISIS, the terror network that is also known, variously, as Daesh, ISIL and Islamic State. Dabiq goes to the heart of the apocalyptic ideology of ISIS—a place where, according to the *hadith*, Muslim armies would one day fight the enemy in an epic battle that would preface the End of Times. The holy warriors of Islam would crush their enemy here, before sweeping triumphantly into Constantinople and fulfilling the prophecy to usher in the end of the world. The Islamic State believed it was the instrument of God in this matter.

So central was Dabiq to its identity, ISIS named its magazine after the town and each edition opened with the invocation, 'The spark has been lit in Iraq and its heat will intensify—by Allah's permission—until it burns the crusader armies in Dabiq.'

But Allah did not permit. Dabiq fell with ease: Turkish-backed FSA fighters advanced, ISIS black flags fluttered to earth like ash and its jihadis scarpered at the sight of a superior force. The fall of Dabiq was a humiliation and it showed there was nothing pre-ordained about ISIS's victory and that it had no God-given mandate to bring the world to an end. Just like other apocalyptic cults that went before, it espoused a false prophecy and ran headlong into the winds of defeat.

But the war was not over.

After its humiliation, ISIS insisted this was not *the* battle and that the fall of the Christian armies was yet to come. It clung to the image of the apocalypse as its leitmotif, knowing it was something that resonated deep within the psyche of the *ummah*, the universal community of Muslims. By the close of 2017, a 74-nation-strong coalition against ISIS—led by the US and including countries from the Middle East, Asia, Europe and Africa—pounded the terrorist state into submission. As its aspirant caliphate crumbled, ISIS shifted focus from enlarging its territorial writ in the Middle East to exporting its terrorist ideology directly into the lands of its enemies in the west and east. The number of terrorist attacks in cities of ISIS's so-called Far Enemies, especially in Europe and America, increased with every passing week—if apocalypse would not come to Dabiq, ISIS would take apocalypse to the enemy.

In 2015, the Centre on Religion and Geopolitics reported that 42% of jihadi propaganda referred to the End of Times ('Inside the Jihadi Mind', October 2015). But more significantly, the eschatology of the apocalypse echoed in the consciousness of the wider *ummah*, the vast majority of whom were moderate in their views. Pew Research found in an earlier (2012) survey that more than half of ordinary Muslims in Asia, the Middle East and Africa believed the End of Times would happen during their life. Out of 23 Muslim nations questioned, in nine countries, 50% or more of the Muslim residents believed this. In some countries, the number expecting to see the apocalypse in their lifetime was higher: 83% in Afghanistan, 72% in Iraq, more than two thirds in Turkey and Tunisia. The Pew Report found that the End of Times was an article of faith for Muslims, much as Christians believe there will be a Second Coming of Christ. For those ordinary Muslims, this was a matter of piety: God shall come to judge the good and the evil. It was not a signifier of sympathy with the ideological cause of jihad or Islamist extremism.

Yet ISIS took this belief and corrupted it with its fanatical vision. As with Judaism and Christianity, Islam sees the end of the world as the final conflict between good and evil, followed by salvation. Muslims believe the scene that presages this epic showdown will be Dabiq and it was this singular fact that ISIS seized upon. Another pivotal part of the *hadith* was omitted: that Jesus would return east of Damascas, to join the epic battle against The False Messiah, the Maseeh ad-Dajjal, and defeat him. The *hadith* dealing with the End of Times has been distorted by ISIS into a battle between one religion and another.

Dabiq's fall in 2016 exposed the fantastical fallacy of ISIS's claim to be the instrument of God, but one thing did have a ring of truth: the world seemed be living in an age of *fitnah*, a time of discord that the Prophet had warned of: Mohammed spoke of an epoch when *fitnah* would consume the *ummah* in a purifying fire. The word is rooted in Arabic and means to burn, a trial by fire to separate silver and gold in a spiritual alchemy that draws the impure and leaves that which is true. Throughout history Islam witnessed schisms in the faith that pitched believer against believer, Sunni against Shia, tribe against tribe as warring factions fought for supremacy. The Prophet's words were not a validation of ISIS's actions, as the terrorists professed, but prophecy of a time when men posing in the garb of faith would risk destroying it:

> 'Before the Last Hour there will be a *fitnah* like pieces of a dark night,' said the Prophet. 'A man will be a believer in the morning and an infidel in the evening. He who sits will be better than he who gets up and he who walks better than he who runs. So break your bows, cut your bowstrings and strike down your swords on stones.'

He was forewarning the *ummah* to beware of those who would subvert the peaceful word of God.

Today brings terror at home and atrocities in wars afar and it feels as if the Prophet's warning of a great violence is here. Western governments acknowledge ISIS as the greatest terrorist threat in history, greater even than Al Qaeda, which first set light to a global jihad. And it was this realization that led to the formation of the Global Coalition against ISIS in September 2014. The Coalition recognized the threat was multi-fronted, as ISIS sought to turn this into a war without frontiers, reaching out to a global army of the disaffected via every means possible, waging a war online and drawing recruits across the world.

Never before has there been such a wealth of information, propaganda and counter-propaganda on the threat that faces us. It bombards us every second of every day. The Internet has made commentators of us all, victims, witnesses and terrorists alike. Each atrocity, its cause and fallout is a part of the mosaic that needs to be pieced together if we are to understand how ISIS came to be, the rise of the jihad generation and how we can combat the threat. This book examines the founding ideology of ISIS and its birth from the fires of the 2003 Iraq war: what kind of society it wants, how it recruits, how it was financed, how it spread like a global cult, how it is being contained and defeated, and how it is opening new fronts to survive.

As 2017 draws to a close, the physical kingdom of ISIS has imploded, with the Coalition winning the battle in Iraq and Syria. But the ISIS ideology remains a viable danger that threatens to spread elsewhere.

This ideology is rooted in the minority Wahhabi sect, a set of beliefs born in the Arabian Peninsula almost three hundred years ago. The man with whom it all began was Ibn Abd al-Wahhab, born into a family of illustrious Islamic scholars and judges in the Hanbali tradition of Sunni Islam, the most conservative of Islamic jurisprudence or *fiqh*. He rejected reinterpretations of the Quran and independent reasoning, or *ijtihad*, in matters of faith. For him, the gates of *ijtihad* were closed and only the literal word of the Quran and the Prophet mattered. As the Ottoman and Mughal empires entered a period of decline, the thrones of Islamic power began to crumble after centuries of dominance and Ibn Abd al-Wahhab believed this was divine punishment for Muslims deviating from the true path of the faith: only a return to a pure sharia society could save the *ummah*.

His views might have remained a discordant voice in the desert were it not for his meeting with Mohammed Ibn Saud, an ambitious ruler from Dariyah, a small oasis town. Their encounter was the germination of a great union in religious and political history. The deal these two men made in the desert back in 1744 would echo through the centuries, leading to the eventual rise of the House of Saud as well as the global ascendancy of Wahhabism. In time, Wahhabism would evolve and become the inspiration for generations of Islamic puritans, from the sharia-governed Saudi kingdom of the twentieth and twenty-first centuries to global terrorist movements that seek to return the world to the year zero, the year of the Prophet. The inheritors of the ultra-conservative Wahhabi doctrine have included the late Osama bin Laden and his followers, as well as ISIS.

Wahhabism has always been a minority sect within Islam, with the overwhelming mainstream of Sunni Muslims believing in a more tolerant and inclusive form of the faith. In recent decades, furnished with petro-dollars, Wahhabism has been spread far and wide by Saudi Arabia, as well as other orthodox Sunni states such as Qatar. In the last few decades, Saudi alone has invested over $100 billion dollars proselytising its views in the moderate Muslim communities of the rest of the world. In this book, I explore how an ideology rooted in an exclusivist and literalist Islam that wishes for society to be governed by sharia has provided the ideological springboard for the growth of a global jihadi movement.

Islamist extremism and the spectre of international jihad are no longer confined to the wilds of Afghanistan, Pakistan or failed states of the Middle East, but have entered cities across Europe, Asia, Africa and even North America. They constitute a very real and grave threat to peace and human progress. And yet, the West—in fact, much of the democratic world—doesn't yet seem to have recognized the truth of its origin. The religious ideologies of ISIS and the Saudi regime have little difference between them, yet one is the enemy and the other an ally. In 2002, months after the 9/11 attack on America, Laurent Murawiec, an analyst with the Rand Corporation, think tank and adviser to the US military on defence matters, told the Pentagon's Defense Policy Board: 'The Saudis are active at every level of the terror chain, from planners to financiers, from cadre to foot soldier, from ideologist to cheerleader. Saudi Arabia supports our enemies and attacks our allies. It is the kernel of evil.' But his view was not endorsed by the US government at the time.

There is some hope now, in that the critics of the Saudi kingdom are becoming mainstream and vocal. In 2016, Wikileaks dumped an email cache between the then Democrat Presidential candidate Hillary Clinton and her campaign chief John Podesta. The cache dated back to 2014 when Mrs Clinton sent a plan to Mr Podesta who at the time was advising President Obama on how to defeat ISIS. The leaked documents quoted former Secretary of State Mrs Clinton saying: '...we need to bring pressure on the governments of Qatar and Saudi Arabia which are providing clandestine financial and logistical support to ISIL and other radical Sunni groups in the region.' Both the Qatari and Saudi governments denied supporting ISIS, which continued its ferocious effort to topple President Assad of Syria—a goal it shared with both Doha and Riyadh.

Whatever the denials, decades of globalization of Wahhabi doctrine has worked to erode centuries of mainstream pluralism. Those Saudi billions partly helped finance a proliferation of thousands of schools or madrassas along the Afghanistan-Pakistan border at a time when South Asia was the epicentre of global terrorism under the Taliban and Al Qaeda. Latterly, ISIS-controlled Iraq and Syria constituted the new epicentre of mass terror, and today ISIS is seeking to take its vision directly into new territories beyond the Middle East, into secular democracies in India, Africa, Europe and even North America.

But even as the West, led by America, vows to destroy these terrorist groups, its old moral ambivalence, born of realpolitik, continues to undermine these efforts. It is a paradox that is increasingly coming under the spotlight, not just in the West, but also among moderates in the Arab world.

Algerian journalist and author Kamel Daoud described ISIS and Saudi Arabia as two sides of the same coin, memorably naming them Black and White Daesh:

> The former slits throats, kills, stones, cuts off hands, destroys humanity's common heritage and despises archaeology, women and non-Muslims. The latter is better dressed and neater but does the same things.
>
> The West's denial regarding Saudi Arabia is striking: it salutes the theocracy as its ally but pretends not to notice that it is the world's chief ideological sponsor of Islamist culture. The younger generations of radicals in the so-called Arab world were not born jihadists...Daesh has a mother: the invasion of Iraq. But it also has a father: Saudi Arabia and its religious-industrial complex. Until that is understood, battles may be won but the war will be lost. (*New York Times*, op-ed, November 2015)

The threat posed by ISIS and its ideology is also effecting wider changes in democratic societies: the trade-off between security and privacy; the challenges to freedom of expression; the rise of the far right who feed on fear as ravenously as the Islamist terrorists. Unless we guard against the dark narratives of intolerance on both sides, we will be enacting the script written by the terrorists. Tragically, the American Trump Presidency seems to be fulfilling all that ISIS would wish for: division, Islamophobia as domestic and foreign policy, an attack on tolerance and co-existence.

Every few generations, there is a moment in history that signals a turn. It begins with something as imperceptible as a fruit-seller setting fire to himself in a Tunisian market in 2011, in defiance of the economic injustice he faces; or a small boat leaving the shores of Libya under darkness to cross into Europe in 2012, carrying refugees abandoning horrors; or the second-generation Muslim immigrant living in the suburban ghettos of Paris who reads the poisoned rhetoric of the fanatic on the internet and believes he's found the answer to his isolation; or the election of a US President whose opening act is to impose a ban on Muslims entering America. The direction of history is balanced upon moments like these, seemingly apart, separated by thousands of miles and yet, like pieces of the dark night, together they tell the story of our time.

The struggle against global jihad is not what ISIS and the xenophobes of the West tell us it is: a dividing line between East and West, Muslim against Christian or Jew, *them* versus *us*. What we're witnessing is a struggle between the moderate and the fanatic. It is a struggle all of us have a stake in.

From 2015 we have seen the number of terrorist attacks accelerate and ripple outwards into every region and the world is roused by the realization that this fight *is* existential and being fought on the battleground of values and identity. ISIS aims to destroy religious pluralism by burning down a common identity, whether it is in Palmyra or Paris, fashioning in its place a singular global fundamentalist Muslim identity predicated on the sharia society of the 7th century, until it has eliminated what ISIS describes in its ideological handbook, *The Management of Savagery*, as 'the greyzone'. For ISIS the 'greyzone' is the place where the moderate Muslim lives in peace with his neighbour.

In 2016-17 the West and its allies in the Middle East and elsewhere finally moved to militarily degrade and destroy ISIS's self-proclaimed Caliphate in Iraq and Syria. The Global Coalition Against Daesh includes leading regional powers such as Saudi Arabia, Qatar, Jordan, Iraq, UAE and Kuwait. Ironically, some of these are nations that have been accused of stoking the fires of fundamentalism in the first place.

Since the start of this offensive, ISIS has lost the overwhelming majority of its territory in Iraq and Syria. By the end of 2017, the Coalition's website (www.theglobalcoalition.org) was reporting that ISIS-held territory in Iraq and Syria had been cut by 95%. In June 2017, ISIS lost control of its de facto Iraqi capital Mosul, almost three years after its leader Abu Bakr Al-Baghdadi declared the Caliphate from the balcony of the 12th century mosque. Today the mosque is a ruin, blown up by ISIS to deny the Coalition its symbol of victory. 'Their fictitious state has fallen,' Iraqi military spokesperson Brigadier General Yahya Rasool declared on state TV at the time.

Raqqa fell swiftly in its wake and thus as the terrorist kingdom has imploded piece-by-piece, ISIS is finding it harder to capture fresh physical territory to replace it. On the financial front, it has been crippled. At its apogee, the terrorist state was earning $2 billion or more per annum from diversified sources, as charted under the 'Economy' section of this book. Its financial strength was the source of its promise to wage infinite war. Just as assiduously as the military effort, the Coalition has targeted this money supply. The financial earnings of ISIS had been cut by 80% by the summer of 2017, according to the respected International Centre for the Study of Radicalisation at King's College London (*Independent*, 29 June 2017).

As its money supply was choked off, ISIS struggled to pay its jihadis and suffered mass desertions. Its recruitment network on and offline is very slowly being disabled. The Global Coalition reported at the close of 2017 that propaganda output by ISIS has been reduced by more than half.

As the Iraqi military-man said, the state project is no longer viable. And yet even with this evident truth, as its territory, army and infrastructure are deconstructed, ISIS is far from finished as an ideological force.

Right now it is evolving, shifting shape and narrative

to survive. It has turned to Plan B, now that Plan A—the Caliphate—has failed. As it faces loss of territory in the Middle East, ISIS enters a new and potentially more dangerous phase in its evolution to survive: exporting its ideology of 'chaos and savagery' into new theatres—Europe, Asia, Africa and North America. The wave of terrorism outside of Iraq and Syria escalated as ISIS came under intensified attack from 2015 onwards. By 2017, major capitals around the world found themselves targeted by ISIS inspired attacks. In June 2017, Esri Story Maps teamed up with PeaceTech Lab to produce a Terrorism Map based on global crowd-sourced data. It showed that in the first six months of 2017 alone, 535 attacks had taken place across the globe, with 3,635 fatalities. That death toll has risen since. Countries hardest hit have included Nigeria, Yemen and Bangladesh. Western metropolises like Barcelona, Paris, Brussels, London, Berlin, Stockholm and New York have also seen waves of terrorist incidents targeting civilians in concert halls, train stations and on the streets.

In August 2017, a 24-page UN report prepared by a panel of experts for the Security Council affirmed the switch in strategy as it said that ISIS continued to send funds abroad in small amounts to step up its efforts internationally, 'as demonstrated by the higher pace of attacks in Europe'. Despite Coalition efforts, ISIS still has access to limited funding from oil sales and extortion of the diminished number of civilians that remain under its control. The UN report also expressed concern about the position of minors who had been radicalised and recruited by ISIS ideology and the fate of such youngsters as they left Iraq and Syria and returned home.

The EU's security chief, Julian King, told the civil liberties commission in the European Parliament in September 2017 that there was a 'real risk of influx of funding for terrorism' in regions such as Europe as ISIS lost control of its so-called

Caliphate. 'As we have success against Daesh on the ground,' he said, 'they are moving funds out of Iraq and Syria.'

Like all fanatics, the jihadis were confident they could find fertile ground anywhere.

Ten years ago I was completing my first book, *Holy Warriors*, about religious fundamentalism in four of the great faiths: Islam, Hinduism, Christianity and Sikhism. It explored how religious extremism was not the preserve of Islam or of our time alone, although it seemed so in a post 9/11 world. Instead, religion had been hijacked by the fanatical few throughout history for a deadly political cause. I found the thread that ran through every extremist doctrine was a sense of political or economic impotence at the bottom of society, exploited by the fanatical terrorist leadership. Jihad is a job for those with nothing to lose. It takes anger, nourishes it and uses it to deadly effect. The Arab Spring blossomed from the rage of ordinary Muslims living under the corrupt rule of autocratic leaders. It was a revolution born of economic failure that left many unable to get a job, to eat, to change the status quo that left them at the bottom of the economic pile.

Today the fanatic has an advantage unprecedented in history when reaching out to the marginalized: he has harnessed the power of the global social media age. Today's terrorist recruiting ground is no longer local but global, as explored in the 'Recruitment' section of this book. At its peak, tens of thousands journeyed to Iraq and Syria to join ISIS and jihad and analysts estimated that their numbers ranged from 27,000 to as much as 200,000. The highest numbers came from Saudi Arabia, home of the Wahhabi doctrine, Tunisia, Libya and Egypt, as well as European countries with large Muslim communities such as Belgium, France, Germany and

Britain, where some young people feel left behind or alienated in their new homelands.

Money to locate and reach out to the disaffected and the psychologically vulnerable, and to train and pay them, was not a constraint. At its most powerful, ISIS held one third of territory in the northwest of Iraq and the north east of Syria. It seized oil, agricultural land, antiquities and vaults of cash from the Iraqi state bank and accumulated a total of two trillion dollars of assets with a revenue stream of over two billion dollars per annum. Within a few years ISIS had become the most effective and wealthy terrorist group in history. It resurrected trade routes through the region in everything from child sex slaves to archaeological treasures purloined from some of the world's greatest museums and sites.

ISIS created an ambitious self-financing blueprint for mass terror. It operated like a multinational, with revenue-raising efforts of oil sales from plundered territory and kidnappings. It had an online recruitment and PR machine as slick as any Western corporation. It was long in foresight, with marriage bureaus matching jihadi fighters to foreign brides. In 2015 pictures of the first 'jihadi baby' were posted online, swaddled in the ISIS black flag. Children under the age of ten were trained to use an AK47 and were made to practice beheadings with dolls. Violence and hatred of the West was hardwired into the DNA of the so-called Islamic State.

The Coalition strategy was to destroy the nascent terrorist state, cut off financing and cripple its recruitment without being drawn into a full-scale ground war. The strategy has worked, but the Trump administration's more provocative stance towards Muslims threatens to play into ISIS's hands just as their focus switches overseas. The greater the divide between Muslims and everyone else, the more ISIS ideology creeps into relevance. Trump's words and deeds were 'blessed', said ISIS and Al Qaeda, within days of January 2017's bonfire of American values when Trump set out his political stall. The civilized world faces an ideological conflict and it must be fought with democratic values as fiercely as with arms. It is a struggle that must be waged by the moderate majority around the world, whether Muslim, Christian, Jew, Hindu, Buddhist, Sikh or atheist.

The emergence of nationalist populism around the world threatens to *help* resurrect ISIS and recruit new jihadis to its cause. Our best protection against fear and hatred is tolerance, our best defence against division is unity, as set out in laws and freedoms distilled over centuries in the great democracies.

To truly defeat ISIS and its inheritors we must understand what kind of world it wants, how this 21st century terrorist state was forged, financed and spread. Finally, we must expose the true legacy of their Caliphate: a hollow kingdom, more violent, venal and rapacious than any dictatorship.

PROLOGUE

The Mother of ISIS

Abu Bakr al-Baghdadi was a man who'd spent a lifetime in the shadows, especially so after taking over as leader of ISIS's predecessor, Al Qaeda in Iraq (AQI), in 2006. His life story was part apocryphal, a self-styled mythology of a man of profound belief, a scholar and leader destined for the annals of history waiting for his moment, which came in the summer of 2014. There were only two known photos of al-Baghdadi before then, taken from a US Iraqi detention camp after the 2003 invasion of Iraq. As he was handed over to Iraqi authorities he turned to the US officials and said: 'I'll see you in New York.' The next time the US authorities and the world saw him he was standing on the balcony of the Grand Mosque in Mosul on 29 June 2014, making the infamous declaration of a new caliphate. Even though he was thousands of miles away from the country of his enemy, his words had the power to unnerve them.

In February 2014 al-Baghdadi had broken the formal alliance between Al Qaeda and his group, now called the Islamic State of Iraq and Syria (ISIS). By June 2014 his fighters had unleashed the devastating 'Lion of God' campaign and captured territory in Northern Syria and Iraq, with the fall of Mosul marking the greatest victory. Three weeks later, al-Baghdadi appeared to the world for the first time on camera, dressed in the long black robes and black turban that evoked the caliphs of old: austere, commanding and unyielding.

As he presided over the assembled crowds he used the first Friday prayer of Ramadan to make a declaration. Railing against the evils of the West, he called upon the *ummah* to abandon their adopted homelands and bring their families to join him in jihad in the name of the new Caliphate. He told the crowd he accepted the *bay'ah* or pledge of allegiance and thus he stood before them as imam and Caliph for Muslims everywhere. The names of Iraq and Sham, the old name for Syria, were dead; henceforth the land would be known as the Islamic State.

Grandiose, theatrical, wearing a newly stolen large gold Rolex watch and speaking of himself in the third person, the terrorist posing as a man of religion told the assembled crowd and, he imagined, the world's 1.6 billion Muslims, that he was the natural inheritor of the Prophet:

> ...the Islamic State represented by the ahlul-halli-wal-'aqd (its people of authority), consisting of senior figures, leaders and the shura council, resolve to announce the establishment of the Islamic khalifah, the appointment of a khalifah for the Muslims and the pledge of allegiance to the shaykh, worshipper, the leader, the reviver, descendant from the family of the Prophet, the slave of Allah, Ibrahim ibn Awwad Ibn Ibrahim Ibn Ali Ibn Muhammad al-Badri al-Hashimi al-Husayni al-Qurash.

The man who started life as a firebrand insurgent against the US invasion of Iraq in 2003, and had been a prisoner in Camp Bucca, was reincarnated as the self-anointed Caliph Ibrahim, who wished for Muslims everywhere to wage jihad for Allah and only then would the Islamic kingdom see the return of its 'dignity, might, rights and leadership'. He believed Allah had granted the mujahideen victory on the battlefield and now the Caliphate had returned after centuries.

It proved to be the birth of a nascent terrorist state and a cry for others to join and build upon its sphere of influence: al-Baghdadi sought fighters as well as administrators, judges, engineers, accountants and doctors—people who would build the infrastructure of a lasting nation. Already his eye was on the next phase. The message must be spread, he told his followers, across jihadi websites and in all tongues. And as he fully expected, the news led the bulletins around the world; it was depicted as an audacious and stunning defeat of the US-backed Iraqi regime and a taste of what was to come. The call to arms was powerful and in the months that followed it led to a migration of foreign jihadis from countries as far afield as Canada, America, Europe, Asia, Africa and the Middle East. They numbered tens of thousands, perhaps as many as 200,000.

Abu Bakr al-Baghdadi had turned jihad into a global phenomenon. He had succeeded in uniting disaffected and angry Muslims on a scale even Osama bin Laden, the founder and first leader of Al Qaeda, had failed to do.

What was the catalyst? Quite simply, he leveraged the fallout from the biggest foreign policy mistake of recent history: the 2003 invasion of Iraq, where the dark spectres of Abu Ghraib and other human rights abuses ignited a sense of grievance in Muslims worldwide. Without that invasion, ISIS might never have been born.

When President George W. Bush ordered the American invasion on the fake premise of Iraqi weapons of mass destruction (WMD), his aim had been regime change, pure and simple—to redraw the Middle Eastern map. He claimed it was about planting the seeds of democracy, but in truth it was an illegal invasion of an oil-rich country that posed no direct threat to the US and had no link to 9/11. On paper it seemed a simple calculus for the American neo-cons: American forces and their allies, like Britain, would topple the dictator and potentially begin a chain reaction of change in the region which would be more closely aligned to American interests. Brutal Arab dictators would wither, supplanted by pro-American stooges; Iran would be held in check by the new order; the West's prominent ally, Israel, would feel safe in the neighbourhood for the first time in its modern history. So much for the plan.

There were no WMD of course. Saddam Hussein fell, but what followed was a great unravelling of the region. The invasion placed the Shia (who are a minority in Islam and a majority population in Iraq) into power in an Arab heartland for the first time since the fall of the Shia Fatamid dynasty in 1171. The history of the Sunni-Shia divide would prove crucial in all that followed.

Since the death of the Prophet, for 1400 years Islam has been a divided house between these two rival sects. When Mohammed died in 632 CE he did so without formally appointing a successor, which led to a split in the nascent religion over who would lead the fledgling Islamic state. The larger number of Muslims chose Abu Bakr, a Companion of the Prophet, as their Caliph. But another group believed that the Prophet's true successor was his son-in-law and cousin Ali. However, Abu Bakr was appointed the first Caliph and on his deathbed he was succeeded by Umar ibn al-Khattab as the Second Caliph, who in turn was followed by Uthman ibn Affan. This third elected Caliph was eventually murdered and only upon the death of Uthman, did Ali succeed as the fourth Caliph and move the capital of the Islamic state from Medina to Kufa in Iraq.

But Ali's succession was a troubled one, disputed by Aisha, the most favoured wife of the late Prophet who was also the daughter of Abu Bakr. Aisha accused Ali of not doing enough to bring justice upon Uthman's killers and this was the beginning of a schism between the two rival factions.

Ali was challenged for the Caliphate in a battle by Uthman's kinsman, the governor of Damascus, Mu'awiya. In the end Ali settled that dispute through arbitration, feeling morally conflicted about killing fellow Muslims. Not everyone was happy with the outcome and a renegade group of Ali's followers, angry at what they saw as Ali's betrayal, broke away and turned hostile, maintaining that Uthman deserved death and by agreeing to arbitration Ali had sinned; he had rejected God's judgement. (This group would later start the Kharijite movement.) In 661, one of these rebels stabbed Ali with a poisoned sword while he was praying at the mosque in Kufa.

After the death of Ali, Mu'awiya assumed control of the Caliphate, moving the capital from Kufa to Damascus. He was succeeded by his son, Yazid. But the dispute over the succession remained unresolved as Ali's son Hussein was invited by the people of Kufa to come to Iraq and become their leader. Before he would reach them, Hussein was met at Karbala by Yazid's huge military force and killed. Hussein was to become the first in a long line of Ali's descendants to be murdered by their rivals.

The Muslims who believed that Ali's descendants should have ruled became known as Shia or 'Shiat Ali', meaning 'partisans of Ali'. Those who followed the line of chosen caliphs from Abu Bakr became known as Sunni, or 'the ones who follow the Sunnah (the ways of the Prophet)'. The Sunnis' persecution of the bloodline of Ali through this early history cast a shadow that would shape relations and conflict between the rival factions through to modern-day in Iraq and the West Asian region.

A *hadith* forewarned of the divide by quoting the Prophet

as saying: 'My ummah will be fragmented into seventy-three sects and all of them will be in the hell fire except one.' Both the Shias and Sunnis insist they are the one and represent rival religious and political power blocs in the region; Iran being the dominant Shia power and Saudi being the dominant Sunni power.

For much of Iraqi history, the Shia had often been the dominant people and yet for centuries Iraq has been ruled by Sunni leaders, first under the Umayyad (661-750 CE) and Abbasid (750-1258 CE) caliphates and then under the aegis of the Ottoman Empire (1301-1922), followed by Iraqi Sunni monarchs and political rulers right up to Saddam Hussein's rule which began in 1979 and ended in 2003. Saddam was a secular dictator, but his government was dominated by fellow-Sunnis and the Shiites were treated with brutality.

While Saddam ruled Iraq, the minority Sunnis maintained political supremacy in the country. Once he was toppled and a Shia dominated US-backed government came into power, the old order was destroyed. On Iraq's liberation from Saddam, Shias saw it also as liberation from centuries of tyrannical Sunni rule. Under Sunni dominance, they had seen 11 of their imams killed or die unnatural deaths, starting with Ali. Iraq was a place redolent with the history of this persecution of the Shias and it was here that many of the shrines to their most important martyrs lay. Saddam's removal re-opened old historical wounds dating back to the beginning of the Muslim faith and offered Shias a chance to reassert themselves. By 2006, a full-blown civil war began between the Sunni and Shia factions after a new Iraqi prime minister was appointed—Nouri al-Maliki, a Shia. This reinforced the violent frustration and anger of Sunni hardliners and former members of the Saddam regime, who stoked the Sunni insurgency.

But the repercussions were wider still. The removal of Saddam had regional implications, in that Shia Iran now had a bulwark in the form of a new Shia-led government in Iraq, thereby providing a counter-balance against the dominant Sunni power in the region, Saudi Arabia. The Sunnis already felt the last centuries had been of heavy losses after the fall of two of the world's mightiest empires, both Sunni—the Mughal empire in South Asia ended in 1857 and then with the onset of the First World War, the Ottoman Empire was carved up and the British took control of swathes of what had been another great caliphate. Additionally, in the new order that followed in the Middle East, in many countries like Lebanon, Syria and Jordan, there was non-Sunni rule. And now Iraq was run by a Shia-dominated government as well.

For all his terrible flaws, Saddam Hussein had maintained equilibrium in Iraq. But he had done this as a dictator, with an iron fist. Thus, when he was deposed, ancient grievances on both sides were unleashed and Iraq descended into a sectarian bloodbath where chaos, not democracy, bloomed.

'Iraq's "liberation" unleashed a profusion of local, regional and international hatreds, as thousands of suicidal Sunni jihadi recruits flowed into Iraq with the desire to kill an American and die a hero's death,' wrote Malcolm Nance, a former CIA operative and counter-terrorism expert, in his book *Defeating ISIS*. He believed 2003 achieved what even 9/11 could not: it galvanized a global army of jihadists: 'In one day, the entire balance of power in the Middle East shifted. It would enter a very new phase in the global war on terrorism that was not only entirely predictable, but wholly made from one historic geopolitical error: the American invasion of Iraq.'

What followed was years of asymmetric warfare between the occupying force of the US and its Iraqi allies against thousands of Iraqi Sunni insurgents. These insurgents had not risen overnight; most had been trained for just such an eventuality.

Saddam Hussein knew his people and had prepared for

a possible American attack and invasion. His generals had predicted that many of the regular army units would run from American military might, so he had raised an elite paramilitary force, Fedayeen Saddam or 'Saddam's Men of Sacrifice'. It was a group of between 30,000 and 40,000 hardened fighters committed to Saddam's Ba'athist party regime. The Ba'athists were Saddam's powerbase, hard line devotees made up of spies, intelligence agents, paramilitaries who would eventually orchestrate the fightback. They already had a plan, called 'Mogadishu on the Tigris' or Project III, whereby the US would meet an insurgent force after invasion.

In April 2003, all these fighters were invisible, hiding in the shadows of villages and cities across the country. To the US and its allies, it seemed as if victory was in the bag: the statue of Saddam was toppled and a bravado-filled Bush announced it was 'mission accomplished'. In fact, it had only just begun.

In May 2003, Saddam gave the word from his hideout to unleash the insurgency and from that day forth until the American forces quit in 2011, the US would lose thousands of troops. In the red-mist of suicide attacks, IEDs and daily attrition of terrorism, 4,493 Americans were killed, 32,000 wounded. On the Iraqi side the toll was vastly higher: the UN estimated conservatively that 155,000 people, including civilians, died in the aftermath of the invasion.

While Saddam lit the match that started the insurgency fire before he was captured in December 2003, other powerful actors were waiting to exploit what would follow. From his hiding place, as he remained the world's most hunted man after 9/11, Osama Bin Laden ensured it would become a conflagration that would burn not just Iraq, but eventually engulf the region. The godfather of modern Islamist terrorism encouraged jihadis from around West Asia and nearby areas to travel to Iraq to fight the Americans. The growing Iraqi insurgency would give birth to what would evolve into

ISIS—an organization with a globalized appeal to jihadis everywhere.

Bin Laden saw Iraq as another Afghanistan and just as the mujahideen had defeated the Soviet superpower on the battlefield and precipitated its demise, so he believed that fighting the Americans in Iraq could be the path to bleeding her dry, economically and militarily, weakening her until she too was defeated. Iraq had the makings of the new Islamic kingdom, as he saw it. His new Iraqi division came to be known as Al Qaeda in Iraq (AQI). And it birthed ISIS.

AQI started out under the leadership of a bin Laden supplicant, Abu Mussab Zarqawi, who began his career as a Jordanian petty criminal. Zarqawi, a school dropout and ex conman, evolved into a terrorist mastermind who orchestrated hundreds of bombings, kidnappings and beheadings in Iraq. He created a terrorist group made up of multiple cells across the country and became the single most wanted man in Iraq by the Americans and their allies. In early June 2006, the Americans got their man, dropping two 500-pound bombs on a safe house where Zarqawi was meeting fellow insurgents. He was killed and yet even as the US hailed the victory, they also cautioned that this was not the end of the threat by any stretch.

By then, AQI had developed into a sophisticated terrorist outfit and installed a dual command structure: an Egyptian called Abu Ayyub-al-Masri and an Iraqi, Abu Umar al-Baghdadi. They were killed in another US strike, leaving their deputy, the Iraqi Abu Bakr al-Baghdadi in control.

Known mainly by his *nom de guerre*, after the first Caliph of Islam, Abu Bakr, this self-styled Islamic leader had various other names that he went by: Dr Ibrahim, Dr Abu Dua, Caliph Ibrahim. To the Americans, he was detainee US9IZ-

157911CI. His real name was Ibrahim Awwad al-Badri al-Badri bin Armoush.

This former US Army prisoner was born in Samarra in 1971 and according to his declassified file hails from the Bu Badri tribe. Beyond a few basic facts, the rest is difficult to verify and may well be a tapestry of lies to transform the man into legend: his claim to be a professor in Islamic studies and descended from the bloodline of the Prophet himself. His transformation into the world's premier terrorist threat happened when he became involved in the insurgency against the Americans and in 2004 he was arrested whilst visiting a friend in Fallujah and jailed at Camp Bucca on suspicion of being an Al Qaeda supporter.

Camp Bucca, known by US intelligence as the Jihadi War College, was the place where he met professional terrorists who used their imprisonment as an opportunity to radicalize and recruit others. For the one year he was in jail there, al-Baghdadi ate, slept and breathed jihad, embroiled in endless discourse with imprisoned terrorists and former Saddam loyalists. Many of these fierce fighters were formerly of the Fedayeen Saddam or Special Republican Guard and the intelligence agencies. They became his men in time.

Within a year he was released: at the time he was classed as a 'civilian detainee' and not deemed a high ranked threat. 'He was a street thug when we picked him up in 2004,' an anonymous Pentagon official told *The New York Times* in 2014. 'It's hard to imagine we could have had a crystal ball then that would tell us he'd become head of ISIS.'

By 2007, the Iraqi insurgency had become so devastating that American soldiers could not go to the toilet without wearing full body armour. The fanatical ardour of the militants had been intensified by the leaking of the Abu Ghraib photos showing Muslim prisoners being humiliated and tortured by their American captors. The images told the world the 'liberators' were no different to the dictator Saddam; there was no illusion of American moral ascendancy any more. It was exploited by the terrorist groups and used to incite young men in the global *ummah*. The insurgency was gaining ground and the calls for American withdrawal intensified.

In December 2011, US convoys pulled out of Iraq and the incumbent Prime Minister Nouri al-Maliki sought to assert authority over Sunni and Kurdish minorities. The Shia partisan nature of al-Maliki's governance brought fresh unrest, and he responded to protests with a brutal security crackdown. Thousands of Sunnis were detained without charges and this further nursed the sense of grievance and fuelled the anger that would feed the terrorist insurgencies of AQI and others within Iraq.

Sunni nationalism grew with a vengeance yoked to the religious fanaticism of AQI. The terrorist organization had become a haven for Sunni hardliners, ex-paramilitaries and intelligence and espionage operatives from Saddam's regime. Together, they created a formidable alliance that was able to execute the ambition for a Sunni-based Islamic caliphate.

The withdrawal of US forces in 2011 and the emergence of the Arab Spring provided expansion opportunities for AQI in Iraq and then Syria. In January 2011, al-Baghdadi sent fighters to join rebels in Syria and radicalize Sunnis in the country. In 2012 and 2013 in Iraq, the terrorist group launched Operation Breaking the Walls, whereby it raided Iraqi prisons and freed hundreds of battle-hardened fighters, enjoining them in the coming conflict. In 2013, Abu Ghraib prisoners were freed—these were the most wanted men in Iraq, embittered and vengeful.

By early 2014, al-Baghdadi had broken free of Al Qaeda, killing its envoys to send the message emphatically that any alliance was over. His progress thereafter was merciless and swift: by June 2014 he had realized his 'Islamic State' (IS, or ISIS); in July 2015 his fighters had captured the largest oilfield in Syria and terrorism had a source of self-financing, as this opened up a black market in oil; by the summer of 2015 ISIS's ascendancy in the pantheon of terrorist groups was complete, as 35 global terrorist groups swore allegiance, starting with Nigeria's Boko Haram. ISIS's physical territory now covered northern Iraq and Syria, but its realm of influence also reached into Europe, Africa, the Middle East, Asia and beyond. Bush's ill-conceived fantasy of an American-sponsored, American-controlled pan-Arabian democracy movement had instead spawned a globalized terrorist movement that posed an existential threat to secular democratic values everywhere in the world. ISIS wished to spread its brand of savagery and chaos into new territories both in the west and the east, creating fissures in society that would lead to the Muslim becoming an outcast in his adopted land. Only when the Muslim was humiliated and rejected would he join the 'Caliphate'.

In the binary world of ISIS, there could be no religious co-existence—indeed, no co-existence of any kind. The only acceptable face of Islam was a militant Islamist identity fashioned in their image and predicated on fear and violence. The first step in al-Baghdadi's ambition of a global Caliphate was clear: destroying the enemy from within. They would target the disenfranchized, the dispossessed, the criminal, the disturbed and simply violent, to forge a coalition of terror. It had worked in Iraq, it had worked in Syria and this was the model they would seek to export elsewhere.

1

IDENTITY

EXIT FROM MASS MURDER

Canary Wharf, London in the wake of the 2008 financial crisis

It was rush hour in London and the worker bees of the great metropolis swarmed out of the Tube onto escalators that soared into the light-filled brilliance of the glass and steel atrium of Canary Wharf station. In the piazza, a swirling mass of commuters filed to their offices in marble-lobbied skyscrapers, including the world's biggest financial institutions. American banking giants JP Morgan and Morgan Stanley sat on prime waterfront plots, surveying London's skyline like the masters of the universe they were. The iconic HSBC tower, visible across the capital, formed the architectural heart of a multi-billion-pound office-and-shopping complex with gourmet coffee houses where a cappuccino cost four pounds a pop. London vied only with New York for the title of financial capital of the world, and Canary Wharf was its heartbeat. The Reuters headquarters was directly opposite the station, with a digital ticker tape of news scrolling around the building's curved facade: global financial meltdown, market lows, blue chip corporates going under; these were the stories that commanded the headlines and the workers of Canary Wharf were in the eye of the biggest financial storm since the American Great Depression. Iraq and the Middle East could not have been further from their minds.

Amid the hustling throng of suits and briefcases, stood a young man. He *alone* was still. He was in no rush to go anywhere, with no office manager waiting for him, no desk to man. He was exactly where he needed to be. The man was small and birdlike, wearing glasses and sporting a wispy beard. He looked like nobody and if you passed him you would not remember him. It was as if he were invisible.

Sohail Ahmed had been building up to this moment almost his entire life. Since he was a child he had been taught to hate the *kaffirs* and all that their world stood for. 'They hate us,' Sohail's father would tell his kids repeatedly.

Over seven years later, in the corner of a quiet café Sohail would tell me his story word for word, how he learned from his father that he would never be one of *them*, or be accepted for what he was. He would tell me how he grew up to become an advocate for Salafist Wahhabi ideology, how he believed in time it was his duty as a Muslim to overthrow the West and impose sharia law and even kill. His belief was a mirror image of the ideology that was growing each day in insurgency-torn Iraq—the uprising that spawned ISIS and led to the creation of a terrorist kingdom ruled by their violent interpretation of sharia.

Sohail had learned from the imams at his mosque in east London that his duty as a Muslim was to defend and protect the *ummah*. In private viewings with friends he watched film footage of his co-religionists being slaughtered in Iraq, children ripped to shreds by explosives, and believed this was what Americans, British and their allies were doing to defenceless Muslims around the world. He had seen news photos of abuses of Muslim honour at Abu Ghraib prison and then Guantanamo Bay and decided the dishonour must end. Before 2008, Sohail described himself as a non-violent radical Muslim. But slowly over the years, almost imperceptibly, like a shift in the atmospheric pressure on a heavy and hot day, something changed within him. He felt a great storm coming and he knew he would be part of it.

For months he told nobody of his plan. He went onto the Dark Web, the off-grid internet where one could access the criminal underworld, and there he found many sites giving him the information and sources for materials he required. His plan was to plant multiple explosive devices at a single location with the aim of mass casualties. As an aspirant doctor gifted in science, the young man was confident of executing his plan. He selected Canary Wharf as his target. If he was successful, *Inshallah*, he would be responsible for Britain's 9/11.

At a time when ISIS was still in its infancy, Sohail was looking at the chaos unfolding in Iraq and was inspired to bring jihad to the *kaffir* in their own backyards.

'I was a boy planning and researching how I would carry out a lone wolf attack in a public place,' he recalled to me in our interview. 'I wanted to target as many civilians as possible. I wanted to terrify the British public and in the end I considered Canary Wharf a good choice—Britain's Twin Towers. That was my thinking.'

His objective was mass murder, to teach the British people a lesson they would never forget: no longer would the Muslim tolerate opposition to his ideology, militarily or otherwise. Being careful, being an A+ student, he knew not to give himself away. He knew he must leave no online footprint. Nobody would know until the attack was imminent, unstoppable. At college, he later recollected, everyone knew him to be the gentle one, the sensible one, someone who was *not* political or extreme in his views. His teachers said British security agencies had warned them to look out for extremists within the student body and report back, they even said he was on a watch list. Yet here they were, confiding in him.

The trip to Canary Wharf that day was one of the final

reconnaissance missions. He described to me how he looked about him, considering the best places to plant bombs. And then he imagined the moment of impact.

Recalling the moment, he said what he saw was not the fantasy of martyrdom but the impact on human lives, the carnage it would unleash as shrapnel shredded flesh. It played in his mind like a video clip on a loop, over and over. And in that moment of uncontained imagining, as ordinary people rushed by him anxious to get to work, there was the beginning of an unravelling of an identity that had been formed decades earlier.

All his life, Sohail's parents and the imams at his local mosque had told him that he and everyone he was related to by blood and faith were living among enemies. He grew up in Walthamstow, and for 20 years the main mosque there had been seen as a recruiting ground for terror, first under the Syrian-born preacher Omar Bakri Mohammed, who was one of the first clerics to openly preach jihad in Britain, and then his protégé, the now-imprisoned Anjem Choudary. The latter would evolve into Britain's most notorious hate preacher, a man charged with being the chief recruiter for ISIS in Europe, connected with the perpetrators of at least 30 terrorist attacks around the world ('Hope not Hate' report, 2015). Together, the two preachers set up Al-Muhajiroun, an organization that aimed to radicalize young men in London, and it was in this orbit of extremism that young Sohail moved as a child. It was against this backdrop that he devised his plan to mount his own terrorist attack.

But when confronted with Londoners face-to-face at Canary Wharf that day, and the coming moment of his part in their violent deaths, he finally understood that these people were *real*. The blur of the crowd was broken down into hundreds of ordinary lives and it was as if he had seen them for the very first time: he told me he stood there stupefied as he examined the lines upon their faces, the anxiety in their eyes; he looked upon their clothes and discerned a daily struggle to commute to jobs to support families at home.

'There in Canary Wharf for the final recce, I stood alone and watched all the workers walking around. It was surreal. All through my upbringing I'd been told by the imams this is what God wants me to do. But then I remember, I started to *really* look, look at these people and consider their lives and the details of those lives, their faces. Unexpectedly, I found myself thinking, "I don't want to do it. I can't hurt these people." Suddenly after all the years of anger and hate I realized I *couldn't* do this. I had changed my mind.'

In his head he pressed the abort button. He told me of that moment all those years ago as if it were yesterday. He described taking the Tube back home to Walthamstow where he abandoned all plans to kill, to exact revenge. To the outside world, none of it had ever happened. But for Sohail Ahmed, everything had changed.

When I met him seven years later, Sohail told me he was a reformed man. After that fateful morning, he suffered a crisis of belief. First, he abandoned violent radicalism and then he began to openly debate his former friends who espoused terrorism at university, at cafes, at student debating groups. He began to work for anti-radicalization and even started to question the basic tenets of Islam. The struggle for belief led to a mental breakdown and when he emerged it was as if he were a butterfly transformed in the chrysalis of his despair: he was ready to tell his violent and orthodox father he was an 'agnostic deistic Muslim', one who believed God created the universe and did not intervene after that. He also told his family he was gay. Coming out, he recalled in our interview, was important, because the secret had formed the core of his self-loathing that led him down the pathway to radicalization. He broke away from his parents, from his mosque, from his faith, For the first time in his life, Sohail felt free.

I first saw Sohail in the summer of 2015 on stage at an anti-terrorism fundraiser, about to make his most public declaration yet of what he called his 'exit from mass murder'.

The stage was at a grand ballroom somewhere in the City of London. The lights dimmed; the tinkle of crystal abated as wine glasses were downed, plates of smoked salmon and main courses consumed were pushed aside, and a spotlight hit the stage. It was an event that can only be described as a spymasters' ball.

Such was the secrecy and such the security concerns for the guest list that included the cream of Britain's security and anti-terrorism agencies, the invitation citing the exact location had been released only hours before the fundraiser. Warnings were issued to the 700 or so guests not to tweet about the ball or its location. We were told we could not take notes or record anything. It all added to the frisson of the evening, which would begin with dinner, speeches about the fight against terrorism and end with a disco.

Ladies twiddled with their gown straps, while men loosened their bow ties as a host from the anti-terrorism think-tank, the Quilliam Foundation, introduced Sohail. The guests were an eclectic lot: former terrorists turned informers and government allies, bearded imams and their impeccably neat families, academics specialising in intelligence and security matters, Arab historians, young researchers, journalists, stiff-backed military men, neo-con commentators and the spymasters like the conductor in the pit, directing the sweeping music of the evening.

The mood was ebullient, optimistic even, as each speaker told the story of their fight against terrorism and the various successes. There was less talk of the failings, the spectacular gains of ISIS that had culminated in the declaration of a self-ascribed caliphate, the first nascent terrorist state since the Taliban's Afghanistan. Tonight was a time to have an optimist's eye and a steel spine for the battle ahead. Wallets would be opened and money raised for the cause of fighting jihadi ideology. Quilliam, with the financial support of the British government and other backers, was at the forefront of that ideological counter-offensive. Theirs was a battle for young Muslim minds.

Sohail was one of the last speakers. He took the mike and under the glare of the spotlight high on stage, he seemed fragile as a bird trapped in a room with no way out. He was lightly bearded, wore glasses and appeared uncomfortable in his hired black tuxedo. He began to speak, hesitantly at first but then clearly, in a thin, high voice, all the while smiling in nervousness. He told the audience he'd been part of a terrorist network once, one who had advocated that British Muslims should fight the West in holy war, one who radicalized others, a person steeped in the very Salafist ideology of jihad that everyone was fighting to defeat.

This in itself was not shocking: many of the founders of the Quilliam Foundation, which was the recipient of hundreds of thousands of pounds of government funding, were ex-jihadists now committed to the cause of anti-radicalization. Some had even fought alongside Al-Qaeda in the war in Afghanistan against the Soviet empire before turning.

But Sohail's battle had not been waged in the distant mountains and plains of Central Asia or the Middle East. It was in the heart of London he'd grown up, it was here he'd been radicalized, where he in turn had tried to indoctrinate others, and it was here he had planned to launch a mission involving multiple explosive devices. He told the audience he had researched and made plans for a devastating act of lone wolf terrorism of the kind that had become the hallmark of

ISIS in the Middle East and now in Europe, with the aim of killing as many people as possible. They were acts of terror either orchestrated or inspired by ISIS, using all available means, turning everyday objects into instruments of jihad.

At the final moment, he had turned away. He told them: 'I changed course, I repented before I could do harm." His speech ended awkwardly. There was no ovation for Sohail, nor was there applause for him changing his mind. A smattering of hand-claps greeted him as he left the stage. Still the outsider, looking in.

Had Sohail gone ahead with his plan, he would have been the first lone wolf terrorist in Britain and his name would have joined the pantheon of other notorious killers: the London 7/7 bombers, now dead; Mohammed Emwazi, or 'Jihadi John', the British ISIS high executioner 'evaporated' in a US drone-strike in 2015; the murderers of Fusilier Lee Rigby—Michael Adebolajo and Michael Adebowale—who reside in jail for what *was* Britain's first lone wolf attack in 2013. And yet more recently: Khalid Masood, a middle-aged convert to Islam from Kent, who staged the attack on Westminster and the Houses of Parliament, killing five people on 22nd March 2017; then in subsequent months Britain saw attacks on London Bridge commuters which killed eight people, on the Arianna Grande concert in Manchester which killed 22 and an IED (Improvised Explosive Device) attack on the London metro, which failed to explode properly.

Weeks after the 2015 Quilliam ball, I met Sohail in the basement café of the National Portrait Gallery in London. I wanted to know what radicalized him and, more importantly, what brought him back from the brink. He arrived with a friend, a fine-boned Somali student called Said. The two joined me at a corner table, overlooked by elegant black-and-white photographs of classical English actors.

Here was a man desperate to unpack his past. Sohail's

chatter was loud and quickly drew troubled looks, with tourists and visitors turning to see a huddle of dark faces in a corner talking of holy war over pots of Earl Grey. I told him to speak softly, to relax. His friend stroked his arm and instantly calmed him. He nibbled on a corner of frosted icing like a nervous child and as I watched him settle down, I found it incredible that global jihad is built upon such fragile young minds.

'I was born in east London, in Walthamstow,' he began simply. 'In Waltham Forest, the place named the terror capital of London. Two of the 7/7 London bombers came from there.' That was the introduction he fashioned for himself, an identity in tweet-sized proportions. As he ate velvet cake and sipped tea, he peeled back the years to reveal a boy trapped in a strict Salafi Wahhabi household that banished freedom and individuality and sowed the seeds of hate against Britain, against the west, against a world where Muslims like them felt excluded and under siege.

Sohail was the oldest of five children in the Ahmed family. Both his parents were from Pakistan. His father hailed from Mirpur in Pakistan-held Kashmir and had spent his late childhood in Libya before marrying and coming to England in one of the first waves of migration after Partition in 1947. From the outset his father experienced casual racism and it led him to construct a wall of isolation around his family as they set up home in Walthamstow's Hornbeam Tower, one of London's most deprived and violent council estates. It was far removed from the orthodox Muslim communities of their homeland: gun crime, gang culture, drugs and murder were features of everyday life here. Hornbeam was a mixed public housing development, with all ethnicities and faiths. Yet for Sohail's father, already bitter after the barely concealed, constant racism, integration was anathema to his beliefs.

The difficult social conditions of the Hornbeam estate

mirrored the economic position of many Pakistani migrants to England in the early 1950s and 60s. In 2009, a government report—'The Pakistani Muslim Community in England'—said that decades on from the first community settling in Britain, the community remained 'one of the most economically disadvantaged ethnic groups in the UK'. Despite being a third-generation immigrant community, the report also detected a disconnect among some young people due to lack of economic advantages, increasing Islamophobia, the perceived 'terrorism label' placed on their community, and the lack of positive news about Muslim identity. All of these issues combined with the erosion of culture and tradition that had underpinned their parents' generation.

The Ahmeds clung fiercely to their traditions and faith when they first arrived, these being their only link to a lost life. They were law-abiding citizens, hard working, focused on building a family, and yet they did not integrate, as Sohail recalled. It was typical of many immigrants, of all religions, who sought comfort among their own. His family mixed only with other Muslims and eventually became friends with a Mauritian family who would introduce them to a new, more hardline Islamist ideology. 'My parents started to become radicalized when I was around four and I clearly remember a change in them, in our lives. That was the turning point.'

The other family were Salafi Muslims who believed fiercely in a return to the literalist faith that they believed had existed in the time of the Prophet. This faith said the gates of *ijtihad*, or independent reasoning and reinterpretation for a modern world, were closed. The family told the Ahmeds that jihad was permissible under Islamic law in certain circumstances, and that circumstances in Britain were bad for devout Muslims. Sohail remembers how his father feared that the modern ways of life in London would seep into their lives and spoil their piety. To the Ahmeds, religion provided a continuum with the past in a new world that seemed alien and hostile. Retrenchment into an Islam rooted—or so they believed—in the seventh century promised to safeguard their Muslim identity.

The Ahmed's began to learn about Salafist beliefs through their new friends: Sohail recalled how he grew up believing that all westerners were the enemy, that their world needed to be toppled and replaced with sharia society, that some sins must be punished with stoning or even the death penalty, that to be gay was an abomination in the eyes of God. Sohail's parents learned to accept and welcome the technological advances of computers, engineering and medicine, but the values of democracy, freedom, equality and tolerance that unleashed such creativity and intellectual discovery were identified only with the West and were, therefore, deemed unIslamic. 'I grew up in an ideology that accepted the technological advances of the West, but rejected its morals. This is what makes it so dangerous,' Sohail explained. 'It creates people willing to use a nuclear weapon in the name of a medieval cause.'

At no point in this early childhood did Sohail learn about violence or terrorism. Yet the ideology was like a trail of breadcrumbs leading him to the house of violent radicalism that would soon come to dominate his life.

'I clearly remember my mum started wearing the *hijab*, then the *niqab*. That was a sign of how things were changing—suddenly she wished to cover her hands and feet. My dad grew a long beard. In our house music, TV, games were banned. Instead we were told we must spend our time helping the *ummah*.' The prohibitive nature of their version of Islam effectively cut them off from the world they inhabited and went out into every day.

Neither parent was politically active, Sohail said. Yet the ideological extremism was deeply ingrained in everyday life. His father was an Islamic teacher for small children and allowed only Islamic and Arabic books in the house. English reading was banned. This pained the young Sohail in particular and for a while he resorted to inventive methods to keep up his love of books:

'As a child, I liked normal books: Agatha Christie, teenage novels, that sort of thing. I had to smuggle them up to my bedroom and hide them, often reading by torchlight under the sheets. If my parents found me reading such things they beat me up.

'I felt alienated and soon it began to infect my school life. I was banned from swimming trips. On non-uniform days when we were asked to give 50p for charity, my parents told me, "We won't give 50 pence for no *kaffir* charity." This led to me being treated differently at school and that would become a self-fulfilling circle—the more different I became, the more the *kaffir* hated me.

'As I got older, our parents would say to us, "Why aren't you kids leaving this country?" They'd come for the NHS, for welfare, for jobs, but they hated the values her, entirely.' It was only later that Sohail understood the tragic contradiction—his father believed that it was his children's duty to leave England and return to their religious roots, with no thought for their future, even though he had himself come to Britain for its economic opportunities.

At secondary school, Sohail relied more and more on the views of the imams in east London to shape his world-view and it was then he began to become radicalized. The preachers would say that foreign policy in the West was an attack on Islam and their very beliefs. It was an attack on the Quran, they told him. The faithful understood they must never question the imams and anyone in the community who tried to do so was either attacked or ostracized.

Against a backdrop of the Afghan and Iraq invasions

post 9/11, Sohail became attuned to this message. He didn't read the newspapers, or follow news bulletins on mainstream TV and radio. Instead, his staple diet of information was fed to him by preachers with views in line with local hard line leaders such as Omar Bakri. Men like Bakri became role models for young people like Sohail.

By 2009, Sohail was on the watch-list of the security services, which alienated him further. 'My anger was building, building, building. My teachers told me: "Careful. *They* are watching you." The police, the authorities, the security services—they were watching many Muslim students at the time.' Surveillance connected to mosques and colleges in the east end of London was high in the aftermath of the London 7/7 bombings that killed more than 50 people in 2005—Walthamstow was where some of the bombers had come from.

'I was never the one who was angry, or a loner,' Sohail told me. And yet clearly he was on a watch list, like many of his friends. His anger may not have been obvious, but his firebrand rhetoric among his fellow students couldn't have escaped the notice of authority figures around him. But Sohail believed they never saw him as an immediate danger. 'At the time I was studying for 4 A levels and 2 A*s. Though I wore a full beard and Muslim dress they thought because I was clever I couldn't be radical. But all these terrorist leaders are doctors, scientists, engineers. We must never underestimate the enemy.'

Sohail described himself as 'popular, liked by everyone' and drew comparisons between himself and Mohammed Emwazi, the British ISIS executioner who became known as Jihadi John after being filmed decapitating hostages in the terrorist group's numerous propaganda videos. When he was finally identified and killed, Emwazi's former friends painted a very different portrait of the man they once knew: '(Emwazi) was described as a caring, loving and gentle person,' said Sohail. 'There're lots who join the groups and their intention is this—in the beginning they think they're doing something just, helping humanity. I was like that too. That's how it begins, the brainwashing.'

I asked if anyone suspected when he finally shifted from non-violent radical to a man with violent terrorist intent.

'Those closest to me might have suspected, but nobody *knew*. Had I gone through with it, I'd have given no sign. I was a real lone wolf in that sense. I might never have been stopped. Terrifying, isn't it?'

He told me he plotted in the privacy of his head, a place no phone tap could eavesdrop on or intercept. 'I planned the planting of a series of explosive devices. I started to research where I would get these without being noticed. It's very easy to get access to such things. Even now. Security is so lax... it's easy to do.'

'How far advanced was your plan?' I asked.

'Advanced, ready to go.'

'How did you research it?'

'I didn't research mainstream sites myself. I found out how to access the Dark Web and which sites had this information available. I was careful to avoid leaving a trail. I didn't want a trail until the attack was imminent, unstoppable.'

'Who helped you?'

'I acted alone.'

I thought he was lying. How did one learn to access the Dark Web without help, to research explosives and decide what devices were most deadly? How did one learn, with no help at all, how to avoid leaving a trail? After all, he had also told me that he personally encouraged others to go to Iraq and wage jihad, he claimed to have friends who had gone to fight for ISIS. So he was part of a wider radicalized fraternity.

Why did Sohail change his mind at almost the last

minute? He said the reasons were more complex than just guilt: first he was becoming increasingly aware of his own homosexuality and second, as a scientist, he had growing doubts about Islam's position on topics such as evolution. So the final turning way, that morning at Canary Wharf, was not the result of just a brief moment of seeing the true face of horror. It had a longer history.

And then, having stepped back from the abyss, he was desperate to find a moral justification for it within his Salafist paradigm. To the non-radicalized person, the morality of such a decision is self-evident, but for those like Sohail it would go against all that they have been taught from childhood. Part of Sohail felt that his final refusal to carry out his plan was a betrayal—of the *ummah*, of the wider cause of exacting revenge for the dishonour of Muslims around the world. For months he grappled with his conscience and for a time it felt as if his mind were torn in two. In the end, he told himself, he had a duty to his country, not just his faith.

'This was my exit from mass murder. Suddenly I really wanted it, I wanted an excuse to be free of all of it,' he told me, his eyes wide with a desperation to be released. His friend Said whispered in his ear, offering words of encouragement as Sohail gulped down the cold tea. I asked Sohail why someone who saw himself as a moral and religious person, as a man who wanted to become a doctor, would consider murdering innocents at all, and his answer perhaps illuminates why so many terrorists are described by those who once knew them as 'gentle' or 'kind' or 'compassionate' in their formative years.

'I'm the kind of person who sees someone with special needs, someone disadvantaged, who needs help, and I want to help them and defend them. I feel their pain. It was a kind of excessive empathy for Muslims in places like Iraq that brought me to the point where I was ready to kill other innocent people here in London. I cannot explain it better than that. Yet in that one moment at Canary Wharf, seeing those people's faces, I wanted out. I needed to honour my religion but also my duty to humanity.'

He turned back, but he didn't turn himself in. Nor did he confess. By 2010, he was ready to argue against those who espoused violence, but he never disclosed then that he'd been one of them.

Who or what did he blame for the rising tide of terrorism?

'It's the ideology, never blame the religion. Islamophobia, racism, it wasn't this that turned me into a violent radical. It was the ideology in the end. I'm blaming the militant Islamist extremist.'

Did he doubt his faith? He told me he did and even now he believed he would suffer damnation for that doubt. 'I'll burn forever for this. During this period after the aborted attack, I felt as if my mind was split in two. I suffered depression and anxiety. I tried to re-educate myself. I read the mainstream news and saw many people in this country care for Muslims, care about the Iraq war. Had I become a doctor, the NHS would have trusted me with its most vulnerable. So how could this country hate me?'

As I listened to Sohail's story, I wondered if he had really avoided detection and changed course of his own volition or if he had been intercepted by security agencies and co-opted to the anti-radicalization cause. By 2011, he had sought out a former imam and reformed terrorist, Usama Hasam. Hasam had also travelled the road of radicalism and exited the other side and now worked for Quilliam, the anti-radicalization group that has significant funding from the British government. Hasam put his life on the line by challenging Islamic orthodoxy. Now, he was helping others like Sohail to reform and rehabilitate.

'Usama Hasam helped me. I've known him from the age of 6—he played a big part in radicalizing me in the first place. He studied physics at Cambridge and he was a senior religious figure for us. But in 2011, he was the first imam to say "I believe in evolution." He said it in the mosque and it went like wildfire around the community.

'Hasam received death threats and Al Shabaab [a jihadist group based in East Africa] put him in a video and said he was an open target. He went into protection and it was in this context that I examined the issues.'

Having changed his views on radical Islam, Sohail began to question everything, including his identity. Could he reconcile his faith with his country? Once he had rejected the exclusivist, violent version of his faith, he realized anything was possible: 'For the first time in my life, I felt British.' In time, as we know, he would also accept his sexuality as a gay man, which had for so long fuelled a sense of isolation and a need to justify himself as a devout Muslim.

Sohail's struggle for identity goes to the core of the fight against global Islamic jihad. Identity is the battleground on which this war is being waged. In the past, as this book will show in later sections, politicians and Western governments have been guilty of allowing the forces of Islamist radicalism to spread into the legal system, into schools, into universities, into the homes of the next generation of immigrant Muslims. They llowed the advocates of hate and violence to speak unchallenged on the streets, in the mosque and market square, and those unchallenged apostles of jihad turned freedom of expression into a weapon to use against the society in which they lived. The result over decades has been the emergence of a hard-line anti-Western Salafist ideology amidst certain sections of the Muslim community. It has led to the infiltration of a rival set of values that challenge the cornerstone beliefs of tolerance, freedom and equality.

'The public doesn't realize the full gravity of the situation,' Sohail told me. 'The government does. But it can't say it because it could rip the social fabric apart. If people knew the full truth, attacks against Islam and Muslims would rise…In recent decades we've seen political correctness gone crazy, I call it liberalism on steroids. We've allowed the high priests of extremism—people like Anjem Choudary, like Omar Bakri—to spread their poison. These people are incredibly smart, and we need to find ways to stop them. As we attack them, they'll adapt just as they've been adapting all the while. Look at the history: the ideology has never changed, only the methods have.'

Indeed, the ideological inheritance that runs from the extremely puritanical Salafi Wahhabism through to many terrorist movements in South Asia, Afghanistan, Iraq, Libya, Syria and now Europe has not changed for over three hundred years. This ideology drives Al Qaeda and its inheritor, ISIS, and all the terrorist groups that operate like satellites orbiting around them. At the root of this belief system is violent jihad, the overthrowing of order and topping of governments everywhere in order to install a caliphate based on an unyielding system of sharia—to hijack the faith of 1.6 billion believers in order to wipe out 1400 years of Islamic heritage, history and culture and take the world back to an imagined 'pure' order of the seventh century. This is the script that ISIS and its like have written, and they expect everyone to play a part in it. Absolutely everyone must bend to their will.

Among the peaceful majority of Muslims, the terrorist only needs to succeed in recruiting one troubled person: the one who will turn into the homegrown jihadi, the wolf in our midst, who will threaten not just our physical safety, but the values and harmony of civilized life.

DEATH CULT

> 'You are fighting men who look into the barrel of your gun and see heaven.'
>
> —Dzhokhar Tsarnaev, one of two American terrorists behind the 2013 Boston Marathon bombs

In 2013, two other young British Muslims travelled down a path of radicalization similar to Sohail's. But this time, they played out the violent narrative to the end. It was Britain's first lone wolf attack and marked the beginning of a new era in the history of Islamist terrorism in the West: the emergence of a cult of jihad. Like any cult, it preyed on the weak, the vulnerable, the mentally unstable, the disaffected and the marginalized. For those second- and third-generation Muslims suffering alienation and a kind of identity crisis, the cult of jihad offered a false utopia where the price of entry was death.

Around 2pm on 22nd May 2013, 29-year-old Michael Adebolajo and 22-year-old Michael Adebowale pulled over in a blue Vauxhall Tigra to purchase a parking ticket for £1. It was just enough to see them through, expiring at 2.53pm. In the boot of the car was a knife sharpener, a five-piece knife set costing £44.98 purchased the day before, a meat cleaver and a 90-year-old Dutch KNIL 9.4mm revolver that did not work. They parked by the Royal Artillery Barracks in Woolwich, south London, turned off the ignition and waited.

Lee Rigby was off duty that day and on his way to the barracks where he was a soldier in the Second Battalion of the Royal Regiment of Fusiliers. Lee was a drummer and machine gunner from Greater Manchester and already, so early in his career, he'd served in Cyprus, Germany and Afghanistan before coming home to take up duties in the Tower of London. With his easy smile he was a popular figure and in his spare time raised funds for the veterans' charity Help for Heroes. He was wearing one of their hoodies as he returned home from duty that day and it was this fateful choice that marked him out as a soldier.

As he approached the shops in Wellington Street, a blue car came towards him at high speed, hitting him head-on shortly before 2.20 pm. Adebolajo and Adebowale jumped out armed with knives and a cleaver and rained blows upon his head and body. After hacking Lee to death and attempting to behead him, they dragged his mutilated body into the open road like a hunting trophy and calmly stood over him as they awaited the arrival of the police. A group of passers-by gathered and it was at this time that Cub Scout leader Ingrid Loyau-Kennett got off a bus at the scene and went to give first aid, thinking this was the scene of a car accident. Adebolajo, still gripping the knife, his hands slippery with blood, explained to her in an even voice: 'The reason we killed this man today is because Muslims are dying daily by British soldiers. By Allah, we swear by Almighty Allah we will never stop fighting you until you leave us alone.'

The raw footage captured on a mobile phone was aired on teatime news bulletins and people across Britain sat in their living rooms and witnessed a scene as terrifying as it was surreal. 'You people will never be safe,' he spoke directly into the camera, his bloodied hands flailing in the foreground. 'You think politicians are going to die? No, it's going to be the average guy. Like you and your children.'

He handed a bystander a letter explaining the reasons for their actions that day. Written in blue pen over two A4 pages, the letter was addressed to his 'beloved children' and urged others to seek what he called martyrdom in retaliation for what was happening in the Muslim world. Armed police arrived at 2.34pm and fired shots at the killers before taking them into custody. Lee Rigby was pronounced dead and his post-mortem showed he died from 'multiple incised wounds'. In the months that followed his murder, his mother Lyn Rigby was tormented by visions of the final moments of her boy who had dreamed of being a soldier since he was four years old. The images would not leave her and one time, driven by a mother's infinite sorrow, she went to his grave in Middleton Cemetery where she lay on the ground in the pouring rain and spoke softly to him through the earth. 'I wanted to claw away at the grass and get into the grave to hold and cuddle my son to bring him some comfort,' she wrote in her memoir.

Her son's killers were found guilty of murder on 19th December 2013 and sentenced to life imprisonment. During the trial, a recording of a police interview with Adebolajo was shown in which he explained, without emotion or remorse, that Lee Rigby died because he was 'the soldier that was spotted first'. This was not murder, he said, but war between Muslims and the British people. He was not a killer but a 'soldier of Allah'.

Both killers were British men of Nigerian descent. Both had been raised as Christians, both were described as happy children and both at some point in their adult years had deviated into a life of crime before converting to Islam and coming under the sway of the notorious East London imam, Anjem Choudary, the man widely seen by security services as a leading recruiter for ISIS and other jihadist groups in Europe. In 2013, ISIS was yet to burst into global public consciousness. It was a full year before it would achieve a series of victories that culminated in the declaration of a caliphate. In the spring of 2013, the international cult of jihad required mediators like Choudary to reach out to vulnerable, disconnected and disenchanted young men and women in cities across Europe, drawing them with a siren call of religious duty, holy mission and vengeance. Especially young immigrant men like Adebolajo and Adebowale, who lived on the margins. In September 2016, at the Old Bailey court in London, Choudary was finally held to account for turning as many as 100 young British men towards ISIS. He was jailed for five and a half years and kept in solitary confinement after the jury convicted him unanimously for terrorism charges. The hate-preacher was accused of ordering his followers to obey the ISIS leader and support the caliphate in its war on the west.

Like Sohail, both of Lee Rigby's killers espoused the terrorists' narrative of demanding atonement of the West for abuses of Muslim honour around the world, a narrative learned at the knee of men like Choudary. They believed this was blowback: the wars of the East were being repaid on the streets of the West.

The murder of Lee Rigby was the first example of lone wolf terrorism in Britain of the kind that had been unleashed in Iraq and then Syria through lone suicide bombings, IED devices made of everyday materials, targeting of ordinary civilians. This was the clear modus operandi of the kind of new terrorism being waged by the Islamic State. The aim of such attacks was not an Al Qaeda style terrorist extravaganza, taking years in the planning, but a series of Iraqi insurgency style strikes by individuals that created a paralysing fear among the public of an enemy within. In the aftermath, the UK's domestic intelligence service MI5 set up a 'lone wolf' terror unit which aimed to 'manage individuals judged to present a risk of carrying out violent acts of terrorism alone or in small groups'. Its renewed focus on lone operators was coupled with better communications with police to identify and monitor threats. The House of Commons Intelligence and Security Committee said in a report that British intelligence could not have prevented the murder, despite one of the killers, Adebolajo, being on MI5's radar. Adebowale was never ranked before as a high threat.

Fusilier Rigby's murder was a game changer. For intelligence and security services across Europe, it marked a new era of attacks by individuals using crude methods that required no or little pre-planning and no forewarning of what was coming. In the years to follow it would become the new normal. In June 2016, a 19-tonne cargo truck was hijacked and driven into crowds of people walking along the seaside promenade in Nice, France, killing 86 people; that same method was used at London Bridge and Barcelona's La Rambla, killing 8 and 13 people, respectively, in 2017; in October 2017, a man drove a pick-up truck into pedestrians on West Street in Manhattan, New York, killing eight people; armed knifemen have mounted random attacks on civilians in cities across Europe—from the killing of a priest in 2016 after storming a church during Mass in Normandy to an assault on security guards at the Louvre Gallery in Paris in 2017. Suicide bombings involving IEDS have also been used to deadly effect in London, Paris, Berlin, Barcelona and many other places.

For ISIS, the lone wolf attack is the hallmark of a new form of terrorism that lengthens its geographic reach. Each successful attack has helped ISIS grab the media spotlight and build a brand that would eventually draw tens of thousands of foreign recruits from countries across the globe into the conflicts of Iraq, Syria and Libya. Whereas Al Qaeda had recruited through stealth an army of battle-hardened mujahideen, ISIS issued an open invitation to *anyone* to join their cause, offering a homeland, training, weapons, adventure and a cause. It welcomed men, women, children, extended families. Here was a jihad where one could sign up online, be assigned a mentor within days and join a holy war within weeks. Recruiters like Anjem Choudary worked with others across Europe to target and lure young men and women to the cause of ISIS, to pledge allegiance to the Caliphate and, in around 100 cases, to be part of terrorist plots.

The network entailed not just firebrand preachers talking to audiences in Islamic centres and mosques but online chat forums to groom people into the cause, as well as Twitter and SnapChat accounts boasting of Five Star Jihad where a recruit could get to kill with an AK47 and return to home comforts in the new caliphate. The image, of course, was a lie. But this architecture of terrorist propaganda helped awaken a generation of violent adventurers from countries around the world, a force larger than the one that fought the Soviet Union in Afghanistan in the 1980s. This time, war was not focused on one country and one enemy; now the mission was to spread chaos and savagery across the Middle East, North Africa, Asia, Africa and Europe. In this way, ISIS and its cohorts believed they would bring down the capitals of the 'infidels' themselves: London, New York, Rome, Paris, Delhi and more. Turning immigrant Muslims—or persecuted, angry citizens—into weapons against their own country lies at the heart of this strategy. Rewiring their sense of identity was the way ISIS would achieve this.

Within a matter of years, the scale of the home-grown jihadi problem has evolved into the greatest security challenge of modern times and poses the gravest terrorist threat in history. At the close of 2015, estimates of the size of ISIS's army of foreign jihadis ranged from almost 30,000 to as high as 200,000, depending on which analysis you believed. The greatest momentum for recruitment came between the summer of 2014, when the 'Caliphate' was declared, and December 2015. But 2016 marked a turning point in the fightback by the US and its allies: aerial attacks, a clampdown on terror financing and support for anti-ISIS fighters on the ground all succeeded in rolling back ISIS-held territory, killing its leaders and high-value fighters, as well as disrupting its funding (as detailed in later chapters). By April 2016, Pentagon officials said US air strikes alone had killed 25,000 militants and that the number of ISIS fighters had fallen to a two-year low. In addition, ISIS had lost 40% of its territory in Iraq and 20% in Syria. The former US president Barack Obama declared, 'The ISIS core continues to shrink. Their ranks or fighters are estimated to be at their lowest levels in about two years and more and more of them are realizing that their cause is lost.'

Yet a beast is most dangerous when cornered. As it has lost ground in its heartlands, ISIS has been expanding elsewhere and stepping up terrorist attacks globally. In June 2014, The Soufan Group, a New York based security intelligence group that advises governments around the world, published a report ('Foreign Fighters in Syria') that said around 12,000 fighters from 81 countries had travelled to wage jihad in the region. Despite an international effort to staunch the flow of foreign jihadis travelling to the region to fight for ISIS and their like, the numbers had more than doubled in just over a year. At the close of 2015, Soufan and intelligence agencies such as the CIA believed up to 31,000 people from 86 countries around the world had gone to Syria and Iraq to join ISIS and other terrorist groups.

Other reports have suggested the number could be much higher. Even in 2014, before the huge coalition assault on ISIS strongholds began, Fuad Hussein, the chief of staff to the Kurdish President Massoud Barzani, said the CIA was massively under-estimating the problem of foreign jihadi recruits, indicating the real figure was closer to 200,000: 'I am talking about hundreds of thousands of fighters because they are able to mobilize Arab young men in the territory they have taken.' (*The Independent*, 16 November 2014). Mr Hussein said he believed US intelligence figures of 31,500 foreign jihadis referred only to 'core' fighters and warned that as fighting had spread, ISIS had matured into a greater challenge: 'We're talking about a state that has a military and ideological basis,' he said. 'So that means they want everyone to learn how to use a rifle...have training in their ideology. In other words, brainwashing.'

This cult-like approach to spread their message and draw in converts had greatest effect in the Arab region. But even outside this region, the rise in those numbers is most alarming. In Western Europe, foreign fighters have more than doubled. In 2015, Russia and central Asia saw a 300% leap in foreign jihadis from June 2014 (Soufan Group/CIA). The flow of recruits fuelled the wars in Iraq and Syria, swelling the ranks of terrorist armies on the ground, enhancing the capability of ISIS to win territory and assets to finance their nascent terrorist state. It is in these theatres of conflict that the US and the anti-Daesh coalition of 74 nations has made the greatest advances in killing ISIS fighters and recapturing territory since 2015, destroying the terrorist group's financial earnings base, making it difficult to pay its recruits. As a result, many foreign jihadis are deserting and returning home, all of them trained to kill and many of them still dangerously radicalized. By the close of 2016, up to one third of these fighters had gone home, raising unprecedented challenges for security agencies across the world. As the Caliphate crumbled by the end of 2017, that figure accelerated sharply.

With the number of jihadis who abandon ISIS and return home increasing, governments are beginning to question their motives: are they deactivated terrorists or ticking time bombs? For this reason, it is imperative to understand where the foreign jihadis came from and who they are.

If we take the base figure of 31,500 foreign fighters in ISIS given by the CIA and Soufan at the close of 2015, the largest contingent comes from Tunisia that accounted for more than 6,000 jihadis. Next is Saudi Arabia, with 2,500, then Russia with 2,400, Turkey with 2,100 and Jordan with 2,000. On a regional breakdown, Western Europe accounted for 5,000 fighters, the former Soviet Republics for 4,700, the Maghreb for 8,000, the Middle East for 8,240, Southeast Asia for 900, the Balkans for 875 and North America for 280.

But growth areas are being developed by ISIS all the time, and the blueprint for expansion is the same everywhere: seek out allies, recruit experienced commanders plus raw recruits and find sustainable local sources of terror financing. For example, in South Asia, it is believed that ISIS has been organizing in the region since 2014. By September 2014, 200 militants had left Pakistan to join ISIS and five regional Pakistani Taliban commanders had switched allegiance to Abu Bakr al-Baghdadi, the ISIS head. More leaders switched allegiance in January 2015 and the group branded itself Islamic State of Khorasan, embracing Afghanistan, Pakistan and parts of India. As well as winning fealty among local terrorist leaders, Khorasan is fighting Taliban militants for control of the Nangarhar Province drug trade that affords a source of revenue. In large Pakistani cities like Peshawar, they have been openly handing out propaganda leaflets. From this stronghold, the problem has emanated outwards. The luxury tourist hotspot of the Maldives islands off the west coast of India has 100 ISIS members. India itself has recorded that around 90 of its citizens have joined ISIS, with evidence of recruiters operating in places like Hyderabad and Christian-dominated Kerala, which until now has not had a problem with Islamic radicalization but has a large workforce that travels back and forth from the Gulf states. The Islamic State has also made it clear it wishes to attack India, which has the second largest Muslim population in the world at 150 million. ISIS wishes to mount those attacks via Pakistan and Bangladesh, where it has existing strongholds.

Also, there is emerging evidence that Saudi financed Salafism has targeted the Kerala youth. In November 2016, a report in the *Guardian* (UK) documented the problem in India's most educated, affluent and hitherto peaceful state: 'Salafism is not new to southern India, but an influx of Saudi Arabian money in the past decades—partly detailed in Saudi diplomatic cables released by Wikileaks—has produced a harder-edged Islam in the region, says Ashraf Kaddakal, a professor at the University of Kerala. "It is a very narrow, very rigid, very reactionary kind of ideology," he says. "And it has attracted many youngsters, especially students."'

Up to now, India's main security threat has been from Pakistan-based terrorist groups like Lakshar-e-Taiba and Jaish-e-Mohammed, both of which have been active in attacks in the disputed territory of Kashmir and in Mumbai, Delhi and other cities. Radicalization of Muslims in southern India is a new and developing front. But other regions are also in the sightlines for an attack. In an interview with the ISIS magazine *Dabiq* in 2016, Shaykh Abu Ibrahim Al Hanif, the self-appointed Amir of the Caliph of Bengal (Bangladesh), warned he planned to launch raids into eastern and western India: 'Having a strong jihad base in Bengal will facilitate performing guerrilla attacks inside India from both sides and create a condition of fear and chaos in India,' he said.

The approach is being rolled out elsewhere in the world. Libya is an example in North Africa, where ISIS took advantage of the post-Gaddafi vacuum and instability to target the country, set up training camps for terrorists and recruit fresh blood to its cause. Libya is developing into the third frontline after Iraq and Syria for the ISIS, and from here it is just a boat ride into mainland Europe across the Mediterranean.

The reach of the cult of jihad is truly global with close to 100 countries affected. Within those countries, particular 'hotbeds' of radicalism and recruitment stand out: for example, Norway's Lisleby district of Fredriksta, Molenbeek district in Brussels (Belgium), Libya's Derna, Tunisia's Bizerte and Ben Gardane and Georgia's Pankisi Gorge. All have been identified as close-knit communities where radicals have used personal invocation to recruit others.

Evidence of recruitment hotspots shows that even with the sophistication of ISIS's social media infrastructure, the local advocate remains the most powerful weapon in the arsenal of terrorist recruiters. In less than a year, 8 men left Fredrikstad to go to Syria, for example. This is a place with a population of 6,000, meaning the per capita rate of recruitment is astonishingly high. Terrorist clusters have also been seen in areas such as Molenbeck that was the base of the cell that attacked Paris on November 2015. Indeed, this district of Brussels is the place where most of the country's foreign jihadis come from. Molenbeck is known for poverty, crime and a mixed ethnic population. One third are Muslim immigrants who, as a community, have suffered from low educational and economic opportunities. One young man summed up the lure of extremism thus to a *Le Monde* newspaper reporter: 'Please understand that if lots of young people have left for Syria, it's above all because no one's ever paid them any attention, until these fanatics gave them the impression that at last they were going to truly exist.'

Such has been the success rate in channelling fighters from these places, that they have been dubbed the 'ISIS Pipeline to Jihad' (*New York Times*, 4 April 2015). Like South Asia and

Libya, Europe is proving to be a new growth market for ISIS, and this has become a priority as the terrorist group suffers losses due to attacks by the anti-ISIS coalition. The opening up of new fronts has become increasingly important to restore the lustre of success.

Therefore, the battle against ISIS and terrorism of its kind is entering a new and perhaps more volatile stage, whereby the group is taking its attack directly to its enemies. Looking at the peak recruitment figures in October-November 2015, out of Europe's 5000 foreign fighters for ISIS, 1,800 were from France, 760 from Germany, 760 from the UK and 470 from Belgium. These four countries made up the majority of ISIS's European army of fighters. Of the four, France, Germany and Belgium have borne the brunt of terrorist attacks by ISIS and its supporters, whether orchestrated and multiple strikes upon cities, such as those in Paris, or lone wolf attacks by individuals sympathetic to the cause, such as the truck attack in Nice in 2016.

All four countries have large Muslim immigrant populations, some of which have for decades felt marginalized or economically disenfranchized. All four countries are secular nations that are witnessing a section of Muslim society being targeted by extremist ideologues offering identity; a sense of belonging. Many of the individuals involved in terrorist activities began their journey on the road to jihad not as committed radicals but as minor criminals, gang members or those with experience of prison. The Salafist ideology has proved to be a way to channel their anger and offer these men and women a cause, imbuing violence with a sense of religious mission and personal empowerment.

Whether one looks at those countries in the Middle East that saw the greatest numbers leave to become jihadis, or those from countries in Europe originating from the Muslim immigrant populations, there is a pattern that seems to indicate that economics plays a key factor in their feelings of marginalization. Poverty, unemployment, lack of education or lack of opportunity to get a job and rise up in society contribute to a sense of disconnect from their country, making them vulnerable to the revolutionary jihadi message.

Among Middle East and North African countries, Tunisia and Saudi Arabia are two countries that saw the most people leave to join ISIS. Tunisia has a population of 11.1 million people, of which 99% are Sunni Muslims. This was the birthplace of the failed Arab Spring in 2011. There, youth unemployment is close to 38% (CIA Country Fact File), with joblessness particularly afflicting educated youth and women. This level of unemployment has created huge social strains in the labour market, education and healthcare. And if it is not addressed it could fuel future domestic unrest. Against this backdrop, 6000 Tunisians left to join the Islamic State, a disproportionately large number given the size of the country. When Tunisia's Arab Spring movement began in 2011 and overthrew Zine Al-Abidine Ben Ali's dictatorship, it led to a greater freedom for hardline Islamists to organize and recruit once the old security and intelligence apparatus was gone.

Saudi Arabia also has a major problem with youth unemployment. It saw an estimated 2,500 of its nationals join ISIS at its peak (Soufan). Saudi Arabia has a population of just over 28 million, 85-90% Sunni and 10-15% Shia. The population aged under 25 is just over 45% and the unemployment rate for those aged 15 to 24 is 30.4% overall and 58% for women (CIA Fact File). Economic challenges lie ahead: namely, a large fiscal deficit, lower oil prices, the need for restructuring of the economy to move away from oil dependency. There is a political backdrop of rising civil unrest as cuts in government spending impact on a population that has long been cushioned by generous state benefits and subsidies funded by oil wealth. Luay al Khateeb, a nonresident Brookings Institute fellow specializing in the GCC, wrote in December 2015: 'Saudi Arabia needs to increase public-private cooperation to absorb millions of unemployed youth and avoid rendering them to the abyss of terrorism or civil unrest.'

In Europe, France has seen an estimated 1800 nationals (Soufan/CIA) join the jihad and it has the largest Muslim migrant community in Europe, at around 7.5% of its population (Pew Research Centre, July 2016). Most its Muslim residents are of North African origin, from the former colonies of Morocco, Algeria and Tunisia, and for years they have faced high unemployment and often lived in poor suburbs. Late 2005 saw widespread and prolonged rioting among mainly immigrant communities across France.

The Brookings Institute released a survey in 2004 ('Being Muslim in France') of how well integrated France's Muslims were. Its report said: 'Immigrants have experienced higher unemployment than the rest of the population; a higher incidence of accidents on the job; housing problems, such as being isolated in large, high-density housing projects on the outskirts of big cities that were slowly deserted by native French families; problems at school; and high levels of crime and unrest...Unemployment, however, remains the biggest obstacle to integration and the biggest impediment to advancement for immigrants and their children and grandchildren, whom it affects disproportionately.'

The report said immigrants, most of them from the Muslim community, were also much lower skilled than native French workers and thereby commanded lower wages, which impeded social mobility. A January 2014 Al Jazeera report ('Is France failing its Muslim youth?') said: 'In the suburbs of Paris, where millions of first- and second-generation Arab and African immigrants live, unemployment is over 50 per cent. A paper from the Migration Policy Institute concluded that even after a decade of living in France, immigrants are still highly vulnerable on the labor market because of ongoing discrimination and the lack of resources to help them integrate into society.'

In the UK, 3% of the population is Muslim, with the overwhelming majority coming from Pakistan and Bangladesh, and in recent years also from India. Britain saw an estimated 750 of its population join ISIS (Soufan). The Muslim population here is a young immigrant community, with the 2001 Census showing that one third of British Muslims were under the age of 16—the highest for any religious or ethnic group. The census also highlighted high levels of unemployment, low level qualifications and low home ownership for this group. As the 2009 UK government said, this was the 'most economically disadvantaged ethnic group in the UK'. In August 2016, a parliamentary committee found that Muslim unemployment was more than double that of the general populace: 12.8% of Muslims are unemployed, compared to 5.4% of the general population. Also, 65% of unemployed Muslims are women. 'The report "Employment Opportunities for Muslims in the UK" raises concerns that not enough is being done to ensure British Muslims are afforded the same employment opportunities as the rest of society,' said a write-up in the *Independent* newspaper.

To the Muslim youth facing lack of economic opportunity and social mobility and thus feeling marginalized, the terrorists offer an alternative narrative. Their sales pitch is: excitement, belonging, identity and power—the promise of a life less ordinary. It is an adrenalin shot to the heart to those adrift in their adopted countries, living out what they see as meaningless or diminished lives.

This call has resonated and beyond a few broad strokes of similarity, the army of foreign fighters has come from all walks of life. In March 2016, a vast cache of ISIS documents was leaked online (BuzzFeed News) giving the personal registration data of thousands of recruits to the terrorist group. The minutiae of the personal records of fighters put faces on a black-masked army: the Tunisian baker without work, the sports coach from France, the bookseller from England, the engineer from Germany, the Indonesian businessman with six children, the Uzbek who listed 'mafia' as his profession. As if applying for a job in the civil service, they filled out forms, mainly online, provided by the terrorist caliphate, giving names, date of birth, blood type, marital status, country of origin, education and employment histories and date of arrival.

In an exercise of box ticking, they were asked to choose: 'Do you wish to be a fighter, suicide bomber, sharia judge or bureaucrat?' All those who filled the forms provided emergency contact details and, tellingly, most gave the numbers of their mothers. Many were not battle-hardened mujahideen, but ingénues in the business of war. Few were deeply religious and the forms sought to categorize this by asking for a declaration of the applicant's 'sharia level' as well as the 'obedience level'. The data cache referred to people arriving in the second half of 2014. The source of the leak of 22,000 documents was a Syrian activist with contacts in Raqqa, ISIS's Syrian capital. The information in the leaked cache was deemed credible by governments and analysts alike.

The question of our time remains: what motivates a young man or woman or even an entire family to abandon the security and safety of home to plunge themselves into a conflict that clothes itself in the language of the apocalypse? While there are few certainties, the key word in all this seems to be *home*. What makes people abandon home? Feeling as if they are *not* home, that they *don't* belong, that they have no stake in their country. Theirs is a disturbed and conflicted identity. There are a few common identifiers in the army of global jihadis: young, male, urban, unemployed, underprivileged, minorities or immigrants. In the Middle East's failed Arab Spring of 2011 that swiftly turned into a winter of repression and counter-revolution, the anger and desire for change was born of economic hardship, political disenfranchisement and years of tyranny. Look to Tunisia, Libya, Saudi Arabia, Iraq and Syria, which together provide the largest numbers of jihadis in the Middle East.

In the West, there has developed another kind of isolation and disconnect. In the relatively rich and democratically progressive capitals of Europe, there are second- and third-generation immigrants who have grown up in a migrant ghetto mindset. They look upon the bounty of opportunity and modernity and yet feel like the outsiders looking into windows of beautiful houses that will never belong to them. Their immigrant parents fought to come to a new world, crossed continents to cast off the old life and its failings and for their children there was tremendous pressure to reap the rewards: fit in, assimilate and succeed. While the world became ever more interconnected, transient and economically divided, some felt they did not fit. Theirs was a legacy of mourning for a lost identity and ancestral land abandoned long ago.

Now ISIS is looking for fresh recruits in places like India. Its belief is that some of India's 150 million strong Muslim population feel a sense of grievance not only over issues like poverty, education, lack of opportunity and human rights abuses that have taken place in states such as Kashmir, but also, in recent years, criminal violence, threats and abuse by Hindu right-wing extremists who feel empowered by the majoritarian discourse of the ruling Bhartiya Janata Party (BJP). The BJP has also given the impression that in its vision of Indian democracy, the Muslim vote is irrelevant. In the national elections of 2014, only 7 of its total 482 candidates were Muslim—that is 1.45%; while Muslims are 14.2% of India's population. In the February 2017 assembly elections in Uttar Pradesh, India's largest state which has a Muslim population of 19.3%, the BJP did not field a single Muslim candidate, and it did the same in Gujarat—with a Muslim population of 9.6%—in December 2017. For a community with one of the lowest rates of employment and education in the country since Independence in 1947, this perceived political insignificance has only added to a historic sense of insecurity. Always contemptuous of democracy and secularism, ISIS believes it has a better chance than ever of finding young people in India disaffected or angry enough to join its army of jihadis. In 2016 it released a video mocking Muslims living in harmony with Hindus and urging them to join the 'Caliphate' (*Independent,* 22 May 2016); in 2017 a 10-minute audio clip in Malayalam surfaced on the messaging application Telegram, calling for lone wolf attacks at religious congregations like the Kumbh Mela and Thrissur Pooram (News18, 14 November 2017).

Like any abuser, the terrorist recruiters are attuned to those who are most vulnerable: the disconnected, the lost, the criminal and mentally disturbed among us. In October 1993, the psychologist J.M. Curtis published a paper called 'Factors related to susceptibility and recruitment by cults' which cited nine factors that made people join: 'Generalized ego-weakness, emotional vulnerability, propensities towards dis-associative states; tenuous, deteriorated or non-existent family relations and support systems; inadequate means of dealing with exigencies of survival; history of severe child abuse or neglect; exposure to idiosyncratic or eccentric family patterns; proclivities towards or abuse of controlled substances; unmanageable and debilitating situational stress and crises; intolerable socioeconomic conditions.'

ISIS is no different from other cults that have gone before:

it preys on those who live on the margins, whether due to poverty, crime, drugs, mental health issues or abandonment by family, society or the state. These are the ones who are targeted, cherished through instant and deep friendship, groomed to understand the necessity of fundamentalist ideology and sacrifice, until finally they believe they are 'home'. One of the clearest examples of how they target schoolchildren is the case of three London schoolgirls. In May 2015 three schoolgirls from east London, Shamima Begum, Amira Abase and Kadiza Sultana, fled their homes to fly to Turkey to enter Syria. They were known as the British 'jihadi brides' in the media.

They were groomed online by a female mentor figure and ISIS commander, Um Asmah, who told Sky News: 'IS is not stupid, they have educated people who know how to deal with [the] psychology of others, how to deal with the human being...They have ways to attract people, especially foreigners. Otherwise young British people wouldn't come and say they will change the flag on Buckingham Palace. IS have the ability to manipulate the minds of young people. If they can convince foreigners, it is even easier to convince Arabs and Syrians.'

Today this recruiter wants to escape and the three girls are on the run from ISIS.

Recruiters have one goal: to make a person believe in something *more* powerful than family, friends or country, something sacred and eternal. ISIS gives them an identity, a cause and the power to avenge everything that ever rejected them. No longer the outsider looking in.

At the heart of the terrorist message lies the story of the Prophet Mohammed's *hirjah* or migration from Mecca to Medina to found Islam. In 622 CE the Prophet migrated from Mecca in order to seek sanctuary from persecution and strengthen the position of the faithful by making a nation that would spread the faith outwards. The story has been corrupted and transplanted to modern times by ISIS to urge all Muslims to recreate this epic journey by casting off the modern world, family, friends, nation and bind their future to ISIS's version of a sharia based kingdom. The formation of the so-called Islamic State's caliphate in 2014 sent out a powerful invocation of the past: to join the true believers in a land where the prophecy of the End of Times would be fulfilled. With the conviction that he hastens the coming of Allah, the would-be-jihadi is willing to commit any abomination, make any sacrifice, to cast off his very identity as easily as he takes another's life.

THE GRAYZONE

> 'The grayzone is critically endangered, on the brink of extinction. Its endangerment began with September 11.'
>
> —*Dabiq*, the ISIS magazine, February 2015

My first experience of Ramadan, the Muslim holy month of fasting and prayer, came when I lived in Delhi many years ago. My friend Ashraf, a Kashmiri carpet seller, arrived unexpectedly at my house at dusk. That night he was to celebrate the end of the holy month with a banquet at his home for Eid-ul-Fitr, the feast of the breaking of the fast. As I was unable to join him and his family, he arrived at my door with five or six boxes of tiffin, each one carrying a different and fragrant dish. And all before he had broken his own fast. There was too much delicious food, I said, but he insisted. For Eid was a time for sharing one's blessings with others, Muslim and non-Muslim alike. It was about thanking God, showing compassion, praying for loved ones who had passed to the other side. Muslims visited family graves on Eid, honouring the tradition of the Prophet who was said to have visited his mother's graveside where he was moved to tears as he prayed for her soul. Ashraf's Eid gift of an array of shining tiffin boxes was one of the finest moments of friendship I have experienced and it will forever symbolize for me what Ramadan is about.

On 22 May 2016, the now deceased ISIS spokesman Abu Muhammad al- Adnani appeared in a grainy promotional video to talk to the group's followers about the forthcoming month of Ramadan that was due to begin on 6 June. 'Ramadan, the month of conquest and jihad,' he said. 'Get ready to make it a month of calamity everywhere for the non-believers...Make it, with God's permission, a month of pain for infidels everywhere.'

While devout Muslim families around the world marked the four weeks with fasting, prayer and charitable giving much like my friend Ashraf and his family in India, ISIS celebrated Ramadan with blood. It began on the first day of Ramadan in Mosul itself, when 65 people, including university students, were executed as the sun rose.

It would be a month of the slaughter of innocents.

On 12 June, an ISIS inspired gunman opened fire with a machine gun at a gay club in Orlando, Florida, killing 49 clubbers on a Saturday night out. It was America's worst terrorist attack since 9/11. The very next day, French policeman Jean Baptiste Salvaing and his wife Jessica Schneider were killed by another lone wolf attacker outside Paris.

A fortnight on, three suicide bombers attacked Istanbul's Ataturk Airport, unleashing machine-gun fire before blowing themselves up. They killed 44 people and left 17 fighting for their lives. Days after that, terrorists allied to ISIS stormed a café in Dhaka, Bangladesh and murdered anyone who could not recite the Quran. Twenty-two were left dead, including a pregnant woman and her unborn child. In Raqqa, footage was released of a crowd watching the beheading of a man in the town square by a masked executioner wielding a curved scimitar.

Then the day before Ramadan ended, in the holy city of Medina in Saudi Arabia, suicide bombers mounted a multiple attack on the complex of the Prophet's Mosque, the second most holy place in Islam that includes the shrine of the Prophet. Millions around the world saw photographs of the mosque enrobed in black smoke that rose from behind the dome into the skies like a prayer of mourning, as security forces men lay dead on the ground nearby, felled by the explosion. It was to Medina that the Prophet first fled in 622 AD and where his body was returned and buried. It was a place beloved to him, flanked by two mountains, Jabl Ayr and Uhud, described as the Gates to Hell and Heaven. In one particular *hadith*, the Prophet warned that he who did evil in this sacred place would be cursed: 'Whoever terrorizes the people of Medina with oppression, then Allah will terrorize him. The curse of Allah, the angels and the people altogether will be upon him.' (Source: Musnad Ahmad, 6498).

The attack was described as an assault on Islam, traumatising and uniting Sunni and Shia in condemnation. There were rare words of solidarity from across the sectarian divide and Medina's grief was the grief of all Muslims. 'There are no more red lines left for terrorists to cross. Sunnis, Shias will both remain victims unless we stand united as one,' said Iran's foreign minister Mohommed Javad Zarif.

And yet there *was* more.

On the last evening of Ramadan 2016, the city of Baghdad prepared for the breaking of the fast and the highlight of the Muslim year, Eid-ul-Fitr. The bazaars of the packed Karrada neighbourhood on this Saturday evening were thronging with families preparing for days of celebration. Parents with elderly relatives and young children were buying gifts, new clothes, last-minute foods and sweets for the holiday parties that lay ahead. Men and boys languished in cafes telling jokes, sipping tea and watching the football in the shopping malls and streets.

Shortly after midnight, hours after the breaking of the

last fast and when Karrada was at its most teeming, a truck ploughed into the heart of the shopping district packed with explosive. The explosion ripped through the multi-storey arcade, blowing the sides off the building and unleashing a firestorm that incinerated those inside. Eye witnesses were left reeling by the horrors of those moments, even in a city whose history had taught them all there is to know of suffering. Karim Sami, a 35-year-old street vendor, who had been on his way home from the market, recalled: 'I wrapped up my goods. I was heading home when I saw a fireball with a thunderous bombing. It was like an earthquake.'

A second smaller IED went off in the northern Shaab area. In total almost 300 people died in the city that night, including many children. Most perished in the inferno that engulfed the shopping complex, others from smoke inhalation. Once more, Muslims from around the world expressed raw anguish as they took to Twitter and social media to grieve with Baghdad. Raza Ahmad Rumi tweeted that he would not be celebrating Eid that year. 'People came to buy clothes...they're buying coffins,' he said. Amir Taki shared a photo of a beautiful little girl, perhaps no more than five years old. 'She was supposed to celebrate Eid today. Now her family are mourning her death.' And there were very many more, montages of those lost in Baghdad, with the admonishment from one tweeter: 'These are not just faces. Each victim has a story and has left family and friends who are grieving.'

The outpouring of anger and sorrow from *ummah* around the world was a measure of how far removed ISIS is from the religion of the world's 1.6 billion Muslims. For those who would indulge in Islamophobia, it is a reminder that most of ISIS's victims have been Muslim. The terrorist group released a statement claiming responsibility for the attacks.

Later that month, ISIS issued a graphic online boasting it had killed or wounded 5,200 people during the most violent

Ramadan in history, with the aim of starting a holy war. The graphic showed a callous breakdown of the victims: they included 2000 Shiites, 1,000 Kurds, 600 Syrian Alawites and 300 Christians. It made no mention of the Sunnis killed, or tiny children blown apart as they shopped for Eid, or the white-robed pilgrims at Medina who witnessed the sacrilege of their shrine.

In the aftermath of the massacre, new shrines sprung up in Baghdad, in Medina, in Orlando, in Istanbul, in London, in Paris: solidarity flowed through culture, race, religion, nationality and sexuality. Mourners and those who stood with them held night vigils and lit candles for the dead in the streets, until the flames shone as a carpet of light in the darkness. They shed tears and prayed to whichever God they believed in. And to those with no God, one grief-stricken young man offered the words of the 13th century Persian poet Jalal-ud-Din Muhammad Rumi, translated by the 20th century American poet Coleman Barks:

Out beyond ideas of wrongdoing and rightdoing,
there is a field. I'll meet you there.
When the soul lies down in that grass,
the world is too full to talk about.
Ideas, language, even the phrase 'each other'
doesn't make any sense.

I am a woman born in Africa, of Indian heritage, raised in Europe. I am Catholic and my circle embraces Jews, Muslims, Hindus, Christians, Quakers, atheists and red-socked octogenarian revolutionaries. And those who tick none of the above. The summons of church bells holds a particular beauty, as does the haunting call of the *muezzin*. My bookshelves are home to everything from Marx to the Bible, the Ramayana and the Quran. I listen to Sufi qawwalis and Ravi Shankar's sitar, Mozart's Requiem and Prince, and occasionally the Swahili jazz of my dad's vinyl collection. My identity is not singular. I'm the product of one faith, three continents and a world with more connections than the snapping synapses of the human brain. I am composite. I am grey. Like most of us.

Grey is anathema to the terrorist.

On 7 January 2015, two gunmen armed with Kalashnikovs entered the offices of the Paris satirical magazine *Charlie Hebdo* and gunned down 12 people on its editorial staff, including the editor and cartoonist Stephanne Charbonnier. The mass assassination was carried out in revenge for the magazine publishing cartoons of the Prophet. It was the first of several attacks, with a police officer also gunned down and hostages seized and killed at a Jewish grocery store. Between 7 and 9 January a total of 17 people were killed and in the aftermath France was put under a state of emergency that remained in place for months.

In February 2015, ISIS released the latest edition of its magazine *Dabiq*. The cover photo could have been taken from the front page of the *New York Times* or *Paris Match*, portraying two elderly Muslim gentlemen, neat in white *thawb*, skullcap and trimmed beards. Each held a small placard bearing the globally trending legend: 'Je suis Charlie'. The photo spoke of a shared humanity with those who had been murdered in Paris on 7 January. Yet in *Dabiq*, beneath the photo was a headline that travelled to the core of the terrorist group's belief system: 'From Hypocrisy to Apostasy: The Extinction of the Grayzone'.

The imams in the photo lived in this 'Grayzone', a space of tolerance and co-existence. *Dabiq* told its readers the men were hypocrites, apostates to their faith, and ISIS intended to wipe them out. In the inverted moral universe of ISIS, two old Muslim men of faith calling for peace were now on a kill list.

The editorial was arid as the desert with its religious

references and could have been missed as just another fanatical rant. Yet it is pivotal to our understanding of the existential threat we face and how we may defeat it. The *Dabiq* editorial set out a vision for its newly born Caliphate: that a day will come when all Muslims take sides in the defining battle that lies ahead, an apocalyptic struggle between believer and unbeliever, holy warrior and apostate. Those who remain on the sidelines of the battle represent the Grayzone, a place ISIS has vowed to destroy. It will erase all sanctuaries of tolerance from the map, rend the fabric of multiculturalism and feed the flames of Islamophobia until the Muslim is a stranger in his adopted land. At this point, faced with isolation and estrangement at every turn, ISIS believes every Muslim will choose jihad.

The attack on *Charlie Hebdo* and the supermarket was just the beginning. Far from hiding its true intentions, ISIS used the editorial to stake out its territory with nihilistic intent; it warned Muslims to choose sides or face death themselves and served notice on the Islam of peace. All whilst invoking Osama bin Laden and George W Bush in a single breath: 'Ibn Ladin said, "The world today is divided into two camps. Bush spoke the truth when he said, *Either you are with us or with the terrorists.*" Eventually the Grayzone will become extinct and there will be no place for grayish cells and movements.'

The Grayzone is the place where Muslims and non-Muslims live together, the grey cells ISIS speaks of like a cancer waiting to be excised are those of us who reject their creed. Grey is what makes each of us unique: allegiance to God, loves, family, friends, country, football club, hockey team, the orchestra we play in, the neighbourhoods we live in—pieces of the mosaic that compose identity. Grey is the colour of the music we listen to, books we read, ideas that fire our mind.

Yet ISIS wants to paint the world black, like the flag that has come to symbolize its tyranny. In the times of the Prophet, it was said he and his followers rode under a black flag as he sought to expand the reach of the new faith into fresh territories. His was a unifying banner for an emerging and fragile faith in a fragmented world almost 14 centuries ago. Today ISIS flags of conquest swarm like dark moths over the rooftops of Syria and Iraq as well as the territories of Al Qaeda in the Arab Peninsula. They lay claim to parts of Somalia in East Africa under Al Shabab and on the West Coast in Nigerian provinces controlled by Boko Haram. The flag is a call to all Muslims to join the global jihad and return to a violent variant of the faith. So it has come to pass, that in the new millennium, in an era of unimagined freedom defined by globalization and the Internet, ISIS seeks to distil human identity into a single question: Whose side are you on?

The 11th of September 2001 was the lighting of this ideological torch, an act of mass murder that kindled chaos, terror and division across the globe. In the years up to that point, the world had lived in a relative age of innocence that followed the end of the World War and the Cold War. Much of the world realigned on the values of economic liberalization and interconnected global trade, seeing the rise of new economic powers in the East coupled with financial stability in the West. The events of 9/11 challenged the prevailing order and in its wake we saw their declaration of a 'them and us' divide, followed by the war on terrorism in Afghanistan and Iraq that proved to be the start of a conflagration that would consume the region.

Al Qaeda remains responsible for the one act of terrorism with the most devastating consequences in modern history. But its aim of establishing an Islamic State was never expected in the lifetime of its leadership. And yet, a little over a decade after 9/11 and the ill-conceived invasion of Iraq in 2003,

Al Qaeda's inheritor had turned bin Laden's distant dream into a reality. The global business of terrorism witnessed a quantum evolution from Al Qaeda's model of autonomous cells operating out of the caves and mountains of failed states into a defiant nascent terrorist state, with self financing, a slick propaganda machine and global reach into the minds of disconnected, disenfranchized, violent youth around the world, via smartphones and laptops.

The 'Caliphate' was declared in the summer of 2014 and its advance was swift and merciless, taking a sweep of territory across Iraq and Syria the size of the United Kingdom and at its peak with more than eight million souls under its control. At its apex, it built up an economy with revenues of well over $2 billion a year.

Of course today, that physical kingdom, at least, is turning to dust but the question remains: in those initial years, how did ISIS move so fast so quickly? The answer lies in its very savagery. The world has been transfixed by the horrors of mass beheadings, crucifixions and the burning of caged captives. It is a manufactured rage that is pre-medieval, sanctified by a barbarous distortion of the words of the Prophet. At times the violence seemed the work of mad men. Yet from the beginning, savagery has been the heart of a deliberate, cold and logical military strategy, set out word-for-word in a document first published in 2004, ten years before ISIS declared its Caliphate, ten full years before *Dabiq* promised to eliminate the Grayzone.

If 'Extinction of the Grayzone' is the manifesto, then the jihadi text *Idarat al-Tawahush* or *The Management of Savagery* is its modus operandi. The book was written in 2004 by a jihadi going by the name Sheikh Abu Bakr Naji. In the history of modern Islamist terrorism, this is jihad's version of *Mein Kampf* and Sun Tzu's *The Art of War* rolled into one and is required reading for all of the group's commanders.

To read *The Management of Savagery* is to enter the minds of founders and ideologues of ISIS, see what kind of society they wish to fashion from the dust and bones and how they intend to do it. Their ambition is not to deliver a single spectacular act of terror. Nor are they a traditional terrorist movement in the sense that a negotiated settlement is not what they seek. Instead, they spearhead a Wahhabi-inspired jihad that has global ambition. They will sow chaos and cruelty to reap harvests of division and power. What was once theory is today fact across the Middle East, Africa and now Europe.

ISIS seeks to provoke its enemies into a ground war that inflicts a toll of blood and treasure, bleeding its enemy to the point of defeat. The history of jihad taught the group that even empires crumble: the mujahideen fought the Soviet Union in the decade-long Afghan War that ended in 1989 with military defeat and financial pain for Moscow, helping to topple a superpower. Al Qaeda in Iraq, the earliest incarnation of ISIS, paralysed Western forces in a terrorist insurgency after the ill-fated invasion of 2003. To this day America, Britain and their allies pay the price.

Today ISIS has taken the age of jihad into a new phase and its ambition is bolder still. The target is no longer limited to landmarks and civilians, but democratic values and identity. This is its vision of the future. Only one thing stands in its way: the colour grey.

BLOOD, GOLD AND A THOUSAND INSURGENCIES

'The most likely way to defeat the strongest enemy is to drain it militarily and economically.'

—*The Management of Savagery*, 2004

'Last week, the Pentagon told you the costs of the war on terror had eclipsed $1 trillion. Wednesday morning, a panel of academics experienced in war accounting says that's only a down payment and that its real, total cost is around $5 trillion. Five trillion dollars: that's $16,000 per American.'

—*Time*, 29 June 2011

And counting…

By the close of 2014, the US Congressional Research Service issued a report putting the total cost of America's War on Terror, encompassing Afghanistan, Iraq and other operations, at an official $1.6 trillion. A respected military think-tank, the Royal United Services Institute (RUSI), estimated that Britain, America's main military partner in these wars, had spent around £29 billion ('Wars in Peace', RUSI, 2014). Both wars were deemed by RUSI to be 'strategic failures'.

By June 2015, according to the Institute for Economics and Peace, the economic impact of wars around the world, many of which were related to the fight against Islamist extremism, amounted to $14 trillion. That is 13% of global GDP, or the combined value of the economies of the UK, Germany, France, Canada, Brazil and Spain.

Yet the economic cost is nothing compared to the human cost in terms of deaths, displacement and injuries, both physical and psychological. In 2015, the International Physicians for the Prevention of Nuclear War issued a report called 'Body Count' which put the total number of casualties in the wars on terror in Afghanistan, Iraq and Pakistan between 1.3 million and 2 million. Looking at Iraq in particular, the report noted that there were casualties that could not be quantified easily—those caused by the collapse in healthcare and the degradation of living conditions: '(After) June 2006 living conditions in Iraq worsened drastically once again. While the healthcare system largely collapsed, diseases spread because of the lack of access to drinking water and the contamination of rivers.'

The report said almost 3 million people became internal refugees. It catalogued 'the long-term consequences through the poisoning of the environment brought about by the war' and cited that in many areas of Iraq 'the number of occurrences of various forms of cancer, of miscarriages and abnormal and deformed babies multiplied. A major reason for this is likely to be the massive use of ammunition containing depleted uranium. On impact, this material combusts into extremely fine, highly toxic and radioactive uranium dust, which is able to spread very widely and can enter the body not just through the air but also via water and food.'

'Body Count' also referenced a study (2005-2009) by the International Journal of Environment Research and Public Health, which said child mortality multiplied in the following years, the number of occurrences of cancer quadrupled, and the number of cases of leukaemia increased by a factor of 40.

But the report did not make global headlines on the scale it should have done, as the world was preoccupied with the latest front in the war on terror—against ISIS in the newly declared Caliphate.

These and other studies on the battle against Islamist extremism, whether of the Al Qaeda or ISIS brand, demonstrate that the provocative ideology that has inspired jihadis in both groups has worked. The economic burden to the world's superpower and its allies, together with a mounting civilian death toll, has long been part of a deliberate strategy by these and other terror groups to draw their enemies directly into costly wars, sow division at home and abroad through mass casualties, and alienate some Muslims within their adopted land until they are driven into the arms of the fanatics. The impact of the West's assault in Iraq had a huge impact on civilian lives, which in turn helped fuel the fanatics' campaign for infinite war.

The story of what unfolded in Iraq is pretty much by the terrorist textbook, Naji's manual of jihad, *The Management of Savagery: The Most Critical Stage Through Which the Ummah Will Pass*, which was first published by Al Qaeda in 2004. If we are to understand why ISIS has been successful, where it wishes to go next and how to avoid playing into its hands, this is a good place to start. This textbook is required reading for all ISIS recruits and it sets out the operational goals to form a caliphate and the cruel tactics that must be deployed in order to achieve this. The book's premise is this: a purity of faith will emerge from the haze of blood: 'Thus, we need to massacre...if God should give us power and we take control and justice spreads, how tender the people of faith will be at that time and they will say to the people: "Go, for you are free."'

According to the manual of jihad, it is better for the world to be destroyed than for a single Muslim to live amongst the unbelievers: 'The increase in savagery, which may result from failure, is not the worst thing that can happen now or in the previous decade and those before it. Rather, the most abominable of the levels of savagery is less than the stability under the order of unbelief.'

It tells its followers that active holy war can surpass mere spiritual jihad: '...despite the blood, corpses and limbs which encompass it and the killing and fighting which its practice entails [it] is among the most blessed acts of worship for the servants, if not the most blessed in reality.'

Naji's manual begins with a warning: the global Muslim community, the *ummah*, must pass through a time of 'chaos and savagery' to see a return of the Caliphate. The ISIS strategy is to create regions of 'savage chaos' across the world by launching a series of multiple attacks against the interests of America and its allies. The manual notes that the fastest way to defeat even the strongest enemy is to draw it into the quagmire of one or *many* unwinnable wars: death by a thousand insurgencies.

There are three stages on the road to an Islamic State, Naji predicted back in 2004:

Stage 1: Vexation and Exhaustion. This stage is about mounting multiple 'vexation operations' or terrorist attacks that weaken the enemy and lay the groundwork for a global conflict. The primary target is economic, whether the oil industry or tourism—to destroy the 'opulence and worldly pleasures which societies thirst for'. Once an economy is crippled, the stage is set for the rise of social unrest followed by 'savage chaos'. After 9/11, Naji named the priorities for Stage 1 as: North Africa, Nigeria, Pakistan, Yemen and lastly *Haramayn*, meaning the two sanctuaries of Mecca and Medina, the Islamic holy cities.

The choices were careful and deliberate, targeting countries suffering economic hardship and weak governance and those that would give the jihadi movement geographical depth. Other factors included the availability of weapons, a ready supply of sympathizers and safe houses, as well as remote locations that make it harder for governments and their Western allies to exert control. For example, in the aftermath of Gaddaffi's fall, Libya became a vortex of chaos in the region, drawing in jihadis and criminals. There was no proper governance, allowing ISIS and groups like Al Qaeda to operate with impunity and use it as a base to fan outwards.

Stage 2: Administration of 'Regions of Savagery'. While the first step involved establishing a domain, stage two was all about governance and the imposition of sharia. The manual warned that no movement could survive unless it secured internal security—that means food, water, medical and power supplies and the infrastructure of government. The attention paid to the mundane functions of everyday civil governance shows that from the outset ISIS was focused on enlarging and defending a *sustainable* terrorist nation state. Its mantra is 'The Islamic State will remain', which captives are forced to chant until the very moment of their execution.

The objective was not mere existence and expansion, but endurance. To do this, ISIS knew it would require not just fighters, but hundreds of thousands of others—professionals of all kinds—to govern their terrorist state. Through their communications forums, through WhatsApp, through other messaging platforms, the group sent out the word for doctors, civil servants, technicians, construction workers, spies and administrators. Once ISIS had established a functioning terrorist state with all the apparatus of government in place, it could 'pluck the fruits of jihad'. This was the plan that unfolded in northern Iraq and Syria, once ISIS had declared its Caliphate and sought to build a lasting nation.

Stage 3: A lasting global caliphate, or theocratic state, the fruit of jihad, was portrayed as the apogee of ambition. In this phase, the jihadi manual offered no room for negotiated settlement, of the kind that the West made with the Taliban. It offered only a binary choice to Muslims and non-Muslims alike: 'fight us and die' or 'join the jihad'. In the end, said Naji, '[We will] unite the world through Sharia governance.' It was an invocation that was taken in the literal sense by jihadis around the globe who boasted openly of the day the ISIS black flag would fly above the White House, above 10 Downing Street, over the flat rooftops of the Middle East, Asia and Africa. In October 2014, ISIS went further, releasing a photo-shopped image of the flag flying over the Vatican. It was positioning this as not only a battle of ideals but a war of religions, between Islam and Christianity.

These goals set out back in 2004 offered the millennial jihad generation a political roadmap, military strategy, history and governance, all within 200 odd pages. Its vision of lighting the fires of extremism and terror across the world seemed at the time unrealistic, a fantastical nightmare. And yet by 2015, many of the targeted territories first cited in 2004 were under the sway of ISIS or its affiliates: Libya, Nigeria's northeast, Yemen, parts of Pakistan, as well as Iraq and Syria. The 'savage chaos' then spread beyond the Middle East and South Asia, infecting European countries through multiple terror strikes that happened, as they still do, on an almost daily basis. And ISIS *has* succeeded in plundering its enemies' assets for its own economic use, as has been seen in both Iraq and Syria, where it took over parts of the oil industry, as well as agriculture and transportation. Although, those gains are now being effectively reversed by coalition strikes.

ISIS had also established a low-level government administration before the Coalition assault, although that clearly had funding shortages and many failings in meeting the demands of the millions of people captive or living under ISIS. But most importantly, in the summer of 2014 it *declared* the return of the Caliphate itself.

The so-called Islamic State was the centerpiece of a long-term strategy—offering recruits a physical homeland, a reason to renounce the West and fight. It is central to the group's prophetic mythology of building a kingdom that will lead the battle in the End of Times and rule the globe. Despite the successes of the coalition against ISIS, the group remains a threat across the world, having brought the war directly to enemy territory, and we are still faced with the fulfillment of what *The Management of Savagery* described as the marrying of political vision with military action: 'During our long journey through victories and defeats, through the blood, severed limbs and skulls, some of the movements have disappeared and some have remained. If we meditate on the factor common to the movements which have remained, we find that there is political action in addition to military action.'

Here was a prophecy of how the global threat would evolve, and bloodily so. Al Qaeda enacted terrorist strikes that took years in the planning, then retreated to its caves, and failed to deliver on the political vision of the Caliphate. It was usurped in the end by a more brutal, ruthless and ambitious successor that quickly moved to enact the stages set out in *The Management of Savagery* almost word for word. Unlike Al Qaeda, ISIS was comfortable with killing not just civilians but Muslims as well, both Sunni and Shia, as well as other religious groups, such as Christians, and minorities in the Middle East, like the Iraqi Yazidis.

ISIS has killed tens of thousands of Muslims in Iraq alone, according to the United Nations ('UN Report on the protection of civilians in armed conflict in Iraq', September 2014). While much of the Western press coverage has focused on terrorist attacks and kidnappings and beheadings of Western victims, the overwhelming majority of victims are Muslim. The savagery of those executions was not born of individual freelance depravity but part of a scripted and orchestrated violence to instil terror in everyone not aligned with ISIS: whether it meant crucifixion, beheading or death by fire. In other words, these acts were part of the jihad manual.

Where there is a political vacuum, chaos and savagery have entered and engulfed entire regions. ISIS has, at different times, declared provinces in Algeria, Libya, Egypt, Syria, Iraq, Saudi Arabia, Yemen, Afghanistan, Pakistan and Nigeria. But its *sphere* of influence is wider than this when one examines ISIS-led attacks or ISIS-inspired attacks around the world. Between October 2014 and January 2016, there were 16 major ISIS-inspired attacks globally, ranging from Australia and Canada and the US to Germany, Bangladesh, Turkey and Algeria. Of ISIS-directed or ISIS-linked major attacks around the world, there were 64 in total, including in the following countries: Belgium, France, Germany, Libya, Bangladesh, Saudi Arabia, Tunisia and Yemen. This list is far from exhaustive and added to almost daily. The attacks dramatically stepped up in frequency from January 2015 onwards, months after the Caliphate was declared and the bombing by the Global Coalition Against Daesh commenced. The atrocities ranged from an ISIS affiliate in the Sinai downing a Russian passenger jet on 31 October 2015, killing 225 people, to the multiple bomb blasts in Paris on 13 November 2015 that killed more than 130 people and injured hundreds more.

Then there are the smaller scale operations in diverse locations. Whether directly, through affiliates or through lone wolves it indoctrinates or inspires, the fires of insurgency are being lit across the world. By February 2017, ISIS was reportedly responsible for 140 terrorist attacks in 29 countries other than Iraq and Syria, killing 2,043 people and injuring thousands more. ('ISIS goes global', CNN, 13 February 2017). The level of terrorism has continued to escalate into 2017, with a renewed focus on Europe, Britain and Spain in particular.

It is impossible to list all the atrocities, to name all the people who have died and draw the circles of grief and loss that emanate from each of those deaths: children, husbands, wives, sisters, brothers, fathers, mothers, lovers, friends, colleagues.

This war of a thousand insurgencies aims to draw not just the West and its allies but the entire civilized world into a direct ground war, to levy upon us an unbearable toll of blood and gold and begin the battle for identity that culminates with the destruction of the Grayzone. It is a trap the West has been careful to avoid this time, following the failings of 2003. 'We should not be drawn once more into a long and costly ground war in Iraq and Syria. That's what groups like ISIL want us to do,' former American President Barack Obama said on 6 December 2015 in an address to the nation from the Oval Office. Lessons had been learned, he said, and the jihadis recognized that another US invasion meant 'they can maintain insurgencies for years, killing thousands of our troops, draining our resources and using our presence to draw new recruits'.

Instead, the last US administration and its allies under the 74-nation anti-Daesh Coalition focused on aerial strikes on ISIS targets and strongholds, backed by on-the-ground support for their proxies who are pushing back ISIS positions with alacrity. Allies have offered training, supplies and intelligence support to the Iraq army as well as the Kurdish military—a strategy that has proved effective.

Similarly, the US and its alliance has bombed ISIS positions in Syria and sought to arm and train Syrian rebels, although its efforts were seen to be deficient in saving civilian lives. America is putting pressure on allies in the Gulf region to stem the flow of funding to ISIS and take part in the coalition to break it. There is evidence that early funding and assistance from supporters in Sunni countries like Saudi Arabia, Kuwait and Qatar helped ISIS to become what it is today in a bid to provide a counterbalance to Shia and Iranian influence. ISIS soon moved beyond their control and has evolved into the Frankenstein of terrorist movements, now threatening to turn on its paymasters too. Witness the attacks within Saudi itself, even at Medina.

Although not universally successful, America and its allies' war and cutting ISIS's sources of funding have paid serious dividends. ISIS today faces being routed from almost all of its strongholds in Iraq and Syria. The US 'destroy and degrade' campaign is reaping dividends in Iraq, as ISIS is coming under sustained pressure from the Peshmerga from Iraqi Kurdistan who have been defending their autonomous territory. In Syria, its de facto capital Raqqa fell in October 2017. ISIS has lost most of its territory, seen fighters desert the cause and recruitment dissipate as financing has been hit. The question is, how will this strategy evolve under President Trump?

One thing Trump can be sure of is that ISIS is evolving already to survive. With its finances being frozen and supply lines to the so-called Caliphate being targeted (as detailed in the Economy chapters that follow) ISIS is renewing its focus on expanding 'savage chaos' to new areas and into fresh minds. Weeks after ISIS suffered its biggest loss of territory in the caliphate in two years, its supporters decapitated a priest on the altar of his church in St Etienne and then drove a truck through the promenade of Nice on Bastille Day, mowing down and killing 84 people. The message was clear: nowhere is safe, not your beaches, not your cities, not your airports, not your churches. In Britain in 2017, within one month there was one lone wolf attack at Westminster which killed five civilians, and another attack by a man armed with a bagful of knives was foiled shortly afterwards in the same area. In the case of the former attack, ISIS claimed responsibility. The terrorist surge in Europe and the multiple global attacks during the Ramadan 2016 massacre demonstrated that ISIS's imperative to destroy the Grayzone as described by *Dabiq* is stronger than ever.

There are 1.6 billion Muslims in the world. This is the second biggest religion after Christianity. Islam remains the dominant faith in the Middle East, North Africa, Horn of Africa and parts of Asia including Indonesia and Pakistan. There are large Muslim communities in China, India, Russia and the Balkans. In Europe, the Muslim diaspora is almost 4% of the population, according to Pew Research, and in countries like Germany and France it is higher. Every one of these is a target. Every one of these is a Grayzone. The assault on ISIS strongholds means the greatest danger may lie ahead as the group becomes more desperate to expand its sphere of influence in order to survive. After Iraq, Syria, the Maghreb and parts of Africa, Europe and Asia are next in its sightlines.

The political climate across Europe is ripe with disaffection in a way not seen since World War Two. Post-recession Europe is weakened by slower growth, an enfeebled Euro and growing inequality of wealth, within countries as well as between EU nations. The rise in debt and unemployment coupled with the greatest refugee crisis since the Second World War has put the EU under pressure unprecedented in modern times. Britain's Brexit in June 2016—the referendum decision to exit the European Union due to fears among many of a failing European project and rising migration—is one manifestation of the political uncertainty in the region once clothed in the robes of stability and prosperity. We are in a new era of political instability with the emergence of far right and anti-immigration politics in countries ranging from America, Britain and France to Germany and Denmark. In America, Trump's anti-immigrant nationalism has set the tone in the free world, leading to the emergence of a so-called alt-right or fascist political movement. In France, presidential elections in May 2017 saw the far right Front National candidate Marine le Pen defeated by centrist Emmanuelle Macron, but Le Pen still achieved the highest vote ever for an anti-immigration and anti-EU party whose campaign was accused of indulging in blatant racism and xenophobia. In Germany in September 2017, the EU's leading politician and liberal voice on migration, Chancellor Angela Merkel, clung on to power but had to fight off a surge in votes for the far-right party Alternative for Germany that won more than 12% of the vote. The surge in votes for them came after major public criticism of Merkel's handling of the refugee crisis in Germany, following a wave of refugees from the Middle East as a result of the war on ISIS.

At a time when Europe is weakened and the far right smells the cordite whiff of opportunity, ISIS will no doubt seek to exploit fear and division, just as its handbook set out.

SONGS OF HISTORY

> 'The deliberate destruction of our common cultural heritage constitutes a war crime and represents an attack on humanity as a whole.'
>
> —Ban Ki-moon, UN Secretary General, March 2015 after the destruction of Nimrud in Iraq

The video footage was edited down to a sharp seven minutes, ideal for YouTube. First the jihadists used sledgehammers and drilling equipment to remove and deface sculptures and carvings that were some 3,000 years old. With each slab that toppled and shattered to the ground, the militants shouted an ecstatic '*Allahu Akbar*'. Faces of vast reliefs of Assyrian kings and gods were sliced off, walls strafed with AK-47 gunfire and buildings bulldozed into rubble. The militants filled barrels with explosives and positioned them to blow up three separate sites in controlled explosions. The video showed each site obliterated amid billowing clouds of brown dust, leaving craters and debris behind. Music played in the background and the voice of an anonymous jihadi intoned: 'God has honoured us in the Islamic State to remove all idols and statues worshipped instead of Allah.' The group promised it would do the same wherever it seized land, in order to spread its singular vision.

Thus was the great Assyrian capital of Nimrud destroyed

by ISIS in April 2015. One of the world's finest archaeological treasures, it was first excavated in the mid-19th century and hailed as a window into the hinterlands of Iraq's history. In a modern era when Iraq had been reduced so greatly by war and bloodshed, Nimrud was a testament to the wealth and greatness of what had been and hope of what might be again. In the early second millennium BC, it became an important trading centre in everything from copper, tin and bronze to textiles. It rose to become a great power in the Near East and the capital of the empire itself. Under the expansionist rule of Ashurnasirpal II (883-59), Nimrud underwent a transformation as its ruler and then his descendants invested in magnificent palaces and temples described in lyrical detail in sandstone stele inscriptions that told of a sophisticated city with canal irrigation, orchards and scented palace gardens. 'The canal cascades from above into the gardens,' reads one stele. 'Fragrance pervades the walkways. Streams of water numerous as the stars of heaven flow in the pleasure garden.'

It was during this prosperity and evolution that the city saw the emergence of colossal statues of human-headed winged bulls, gods and kings that became the emblem of one of civilization's greatest empires. Thousands of years of Nimrud's stories were blown apart by ISIS in 2015, robbing future generations of their wonders.

It provoked a worldwide reaction from academics across borders and disciplines. Here was one aspirant power erasing evidence of what came before. 'Empires rise and fall and ISIS, who want to found a new one, will surely fail,' said Mark Ronan, an honorary professor of mathematics at University College London, writing on the news in *History Today*. 'In the meantime, the remains of Nimrud leave a hole in history, vandalized for the sake of nothing.'

There is a history of such destruction by invading powers and historians and archaeologists are at pains to emphasize that this is nothing new. 'There's been destruction of heritage as long as we've had conflict,' said Dr Emma Cunliffe of Oxford University, one of the experts working alongside people in the region to protect what is left. 'The destruction of a city wall is symbolic of taking a city. Look at the pictures of Jerusalem 70 AD, the Sacking of Baghdad 1258. Destruction followed by looting is age old. As for iconoclasm, during the Reformation we saw faces hacked off statues. During and after the Second World War, there was widespread looting of artefacts and artwork. The Taliban blew up the Buddha statues of Bamiyan valley in March 2001 with dynamite. The difference here is the sheer scale of the looting and the destruction.'

The UN's cultural agency UNESCO said the attacks by ISIS on Iraqi and Syrian heritage had reached 'industrial scale'. At its apex, the group had control over 2,000 heritage sites across Iraq alone and thousands more were under threat if one considered Syria. Nine out of ten UNESCO world heritage sites in the two countries are in danger, it said. Palmyra and Nimrud are just the tip of the iceberg, warned Amr Al Azm, former Director of Scientific Conservation at the Department of Antiquities and Museums in Syria.

The professor of Middle East history and anthropology now works in America but was once one of Syria's leading cultural figures at the University of Damascus and the Department of Museums and Antiquities. Today he is part of a team working through a global network to protect what remains.

'You cannot put a price on what has been lost. We're talking about not just archaeological sites but whole complexes. The ancient city of Aleppo was decimated. Sites like Palmyra. In Iraq you have seen what happened to Nimrud. There is almost nothing left. I look at the satellite images from 2011-12 in Syria and compare them to those from 2015 and the scale of change is catastrophic.'

Like others he said ISIS is not the only one behind the damage. Prior to 2011, there was piecemeal looting. But the collapse in governance and the civil war in both countries have left the states unable to function in entire regions. ISIS has stepped into the vacuum and, just as *The Management of Savagery* advised, it has monetized heritage and exploited it for terror funding as well as propaganda.

Now if the looters want to pillage a site before it is levelled, they offer to pay a tax to ISIS on any profits. 'The money goes back into helping build the Caliphate. IS gets 20%, sometimes as much as 70%,' said Al Azm in an interview in early 2016. 'It took over control of the trade. Today it offers crews for hire, equipment, earth moving machinery that can excavate, in return for a fee and a share in the profits. The more help IS affords to the looters, the bigger the tax. It controls the trade routes. It is industrialized. What is not sold is destroyed in the name of their war.'

The terrorists know where the treasures are buried and their true worth thanks to a simple truth: history has been betrayed by a few local archaeologists. Not all are sympathizers but they are those who have seen livelihoods ebb to nothing, their loved ones placed in danger and penury, and fear for their own lives every day. To survive they have struck a Faustian pact with ISIS.

'These members of our profession are helping ISIS identify the sites. They know where to find them and their value. They may even know of customers who want to buy. The sales network can be eBay, auction houses, but mostly it is happening through middlemen and dealers. The trading network extends far beyond the territory that ISIS controls,' Al Azm told me in the interview.

The routes used to sell what is not destroyed are the same smuggling routes that have been in place for as long as there has been a need for contraband trade. Into Lebanon and through the Middle East is one route, while the porous Turkish border has provided a boon for trading into Europe. Items for sale range in value from a few hundred pounds to half a million dollars.

The Kurdish People's Protection Units (YPG) showed Reuters a document in March 2016 from ISIS's Department of Artefacts. One note advises checkpoint patrols to allow a Turkish antiquity seller into Syria: 'To the brother responsible for the border, please assist the passage of brother Hussein Hania Sarira through your post along with the man from Turkey, the artifacts trader, for the purpose of working with us in the department of artifacts in the Ministry of Natural Resources. May Allah bless you, Loving brother Abu Uafa Al Tunisi.'

It remains a valuable source of income, especially after coalition air strikes against ISIS's oil facilities. The spoils of cultural cleansing of the region's history have been ploughed into the Caliphate's coffers, to buy arms, pay soldiers, fund the infrastructure of a cash-constrained nascent terrorist state. Markets like London and New York have seen a steady flow of precious objects and their source is almost indisputable. Mark Altaweel, a Near East specialist from the UCL Institute of Archaeology, observed that pieces of early glass, fragments of bone inlay and statuettes from the second to fourth century BC were just some of the items being offered on the black market. They are freely offered for sale, sometimes a mere stone's throw from the British Museum itself ('Looted in Syria and sold in London', *Guardian*, 3 July 2015).

Efforts have been made by European and Middle Eastern governments to tighten controls on the sale of what is known as 'blood antiquities'. But the academic fraternity is refusing to take a passive role and doing far more in direct action. Middle Eastern academics like Al Azm have linked up with major museums around the world like the US Smithsonian to establish the Day After Project. Backed by major funding, it aims to protect what heritage is left from being blown up or broken up and sold piecemeal to fund terrorism.

'We're a loose-knit community of archaeologists, curators, archivists and we document, we protect, we report,' he told me. These are the modern inheritors of the Monuments Men who fought their own cultural war against the Nazis by embarking on dangerous rescue missions to save Europe's treasures during World War Two. A purist, Al Azm dislikes the comparison. The work is unglamorous, meticulous and dangerous, he explained, not exactly Indiana Jones meets Mad Max. In one case, his people on the ground knew of a mosaic that had been uncovered in a village where they had good connections. They went to the village and persuaded the locals to bury it. After all, it was their history. There were other times when his people argued directly with the religious hierarchy in formal meetings with local imams.

'We used religious arguments to say this is our heritage and it should be preserved, not stolen or destroyed. In other cases we've sent covert teams in to remove items from museums that are at risk from ISIS. We bury them at secret locations which are then recorded or we sandbag mosaics or items that could face aerial attack.'

'The people on the ground are the real heroes. There's a cost to what we do. In the past summer we lost many people. Some fled the danger to Europe, others died. I lost one of my men who was the cornerstone of this work. His village was bombed with chlorine gas and we lost him,' he said quietly, pausing for a moment as he counted the many losses among his group. 'In the summer of 2015, we had 40 men. Now we have half that. Just by continuing to live in Syria they're taking a risk. They could be killed by a bullet or a barrel bomb or the enemy. This is our frontline.'

I asked him why they took these risks or chose this

work rather than addressing the wider humanitarian crisis. He agreed it was baffling perhaps to those who had not dedicated a lifetime to the study of these ruins. Yet the logic was unshakeable for one reason: 'So much humanitarian assistance is needed, I agree. Food, medicine, soldiers. Cultural heritage may be secondary to lives. But it takes a special kind of person to do what is not obvious. My people are looking beyond conflict, towards a time of post-conflict stability, a time for reconciliation. Edna, one day we will need ways to reconnect our broken society. A common history is one area where both sides can be united. And this is why protecting history is so important. It says there was a time when people of all religions were together.'

As his children slipped in and out of the background, their yelps of happiness cutting through the darkness of the conversation like shafts of sunlight, the professor was mindful that he was one of the lucky ones, living safely in America. From this position of safety he felt compelled to help those left behind and protect a heritage that had been his life's passion.

I asked him what message he had for those who purchased blood antiquities believing they were 'saving' it from destruction, even if it paid for guns and bombs used to slay the innocent.

'I tell these people, by buying from ISIS you're not saving it from ISIS, you are perpetuating this destruction and trade. Which would I choose—for it to be sold illegally or destroyed, you ask? I say the binary way isn't acceptable. We're finding other ways to stop them.'

His thoughts turned to his former colleague, the world-renowned archaeologist at Palmyra, Khaled Al Assad, who was beheaded by ISIS for refusing to cooperate and show them where the treasures were buried. The two men had known each other well and yet he was unsentimental, his words startling in their directness: 'A lot of people made a big issue of his death. It shone a light on the cause. But his death wasn't an isolated atrocity. Dozens of people, dozens of archaeologists are taken away by Daesh and tortured in order to answer the standard question: "Show us where the gold is buried." Khaled al Assad's treatment was no different to the many.'

He was tormented by the loss of all such men in Syria's time of need and accepted that the elderly archaeologist had come to represent all the unsung heroes: 'He was brave, like so many of our people. Despite his allegiance to the Assad regime, he was involved in the removal of items to protect them. He stayed behind knowing he would be killed by ISIS. In many ways he *was* Mr Palmyra, with his vast deposit of knowledge, knowledge that comes not from books, but living and being a part of this environment. He wasn't a man in the ivory towers of Oxford or Harvard. He lived his passion every day, with the dust of the ground in his hands. This is what makes his loss all the more unbearable.'

The Day After project and others like it are not the first intellectual resistance movement against an evil that threatens to demolish civilization and impose a new order upon the rubble. Like the Monuments Men of the Nazi era, today's academic community knows the past is the pathway to the future. While the United Nations and the American FBI and its counterparts elsewhere warn that the looting and sale of antiquities is helping finance terrorism to the tune of millions of dollars, historians believe we are also witnessing the beginning of a cleansing of a pluralistic identity, wiping out an inheritance that has led to people of different faiths and cultures co-existing for centuries and millennia.

When ISIS raids the tombs of ancient gods and kings, it's not merely for buried gold. The Islamic State is in the business of rewriting history and destroying identity. To destroy the *other*, first one must destroy their identity. Who we are is inextricably linked to where we came from. History is dangerous for demagogues, for the evidence of the past is capable of exposing the false prophecies of today. The men and women of history believe that when this war is done, the past can help rebuild the peace: shared stories, shared glories, shared identity carved in grey stone.

---

5 May 2016, Palmyra, Syria

Against powder-blue skies, the haunting voice of a solo violin playing Bach's Chaconne soared over the desert city of Palmyra. For its composer it was a song of profound grief, written three hundred years ago after the death of his wife. On the stage of the Roman amphitheatre in 2016, the violin sang of another loss. A year before, surrounded by surging heaven-bound columns, ISIS had executed Syrian soldiers with a bullet to the back of the head when it took one of the greatest cities of ancient civilization. It destroyed the once iconic temples of Bel and Baalshamin as well as the Arch of Triumph. It looted graves and used the amphitheatre to stage executions that it filmed and broadcast to the world.

At the time, CNN and many others reported on one such video that began with images of the aftermath of the capture of Palmyra, overlaid with the Quran. Captives with heads bowed were taken single file onto the ancient arena's stage. A man read out a document to the assembled crowed who sat on stone seats. Some ISIS supporters waved black flags, while others wept. The cue for execution was given and within seconds young ISIS militants shot all 25 captives.

Since the Syrian civil war began in 2011, more than 470,000 people have been killed and much of Syria's cultural inheritance has been laid to waste. The fightback is happening in many ways: with guns against the enemy, through the humanity one stranger shows another. But as we have seen, one of the most unexpected battles is that of archaeologists risking their lives to protect a shared history that they hope one day will form the basis of peace. It may seem reckless to risk a life and future to save what is past, especially in the midst of so much suffering and bloodshed. Yet the stand of civilization against barbarism is fought every day in the villages and towns of Syria and theirs is a battle just as perilous and necessary as the one on the frontline.

Dr Khaleed Al Assad was an octogenarian archaeologist who had devoted his life to the preservation of the UNESCO World Heritage Site of Palmyra. When the iconoclasts came in the summer of 2015 and demanded he reveal the city's treasures, the old man refused. He had lived there and loved the ruins like children and it become apparent that he would not trade what remained of his time on earth for all of Syria's past glories. He was an Assad regime loyalist, and unpopular among some people because of that—Assad has been accused of human rights abuse, rigging elections, detaining or killing dissidents and using chemical weapons against his own people. But Dr Khaleed commanded respect despite his support of the dictatorial president. Foremost, he was a man of history who had devoted a lifetime to making the stones of the past speak to the present. The place where ISIS hanged Dr Khaleed Al Assad's body was not far from the Roman amphitheatre. In a final theatre of mockery ISIS placed his spectacles back atop his head after they were done.

Ten months after his execution, the Syrian Arab Army (SAA), supported by Russian airpower, took back the city in March 2016. The Islamic State's victory turned to rout and its reign over the golden-columned citadel was another chapter archived in the memory bank of Palmyra's long history. The operation had required six months of fierce desert combat, with the SAA and its ally retaking mountainous terrain and the stretch of Syrian Desert around the city. The Syrian Army estimated that 450 militants from ISIS were killed in the offensive to retake Palmyra.

The concert at Palmyra's Roman Amphitheatre was meant to symbolize the restoration of civilization as much as the lowering of the black banner. The spirit of Dr Khaleed Al Assad endured in a place where blood had flowed once, and Bach filled the skies. The orchestra of St Petersburg's Mariinsky Theatre played for an audience that included foreign dignitaries, Russian and Syrian soldiers, flint-faced in Ray-Bans on the terraces of the amphitheatre, approved foreign journalists bussed in especially, and those who represented culture and its preservation. Against a tableau of ruin, Russia's foremost conductor, Valery Gergiev, spoke to the assembled audience of what this concert signified: 'We protest against barbarians who destroyed wonderful monuments of world culture. We protest against the execution of people here on this great stage.'

Russian president Vladimir Putin, tight-faced and triumphant, appeared on a huge screen beamed in live from Sochin, to pronounce that the world must unite against the 'terrible evil'. And then the musicians played, just 15 km away from ISIS-controlled territory. One likes to imagine that the desert winds carried the music far and wide that day, a sublime riposte to the madness. No Western powers attended, repulsed by the idea of showing any solidarity with the blood-soaked regime of Syrian president Bashar al-Assad and his complicit Russian ally.

Russia made a propaganda feast of ISIS's worst defeat in two years. The act of staging a concert upon the sands of victory showed that Putin understood the brutalist language of his enemy: we shall play music upon your fields of death.

At the time it was presented as a rare moment of hope, conjured for the cameras to tell the world that the forces of civilization had been restored and here was a concert to prove it. Or had they? ISIS had fallen for now, yes, and while Putin had spoken of restoring the forces of beauty, civilization and democracy, President Assad's bombs continued to pound civilians in Syria elsewhere, aided by the Russians. 'Liberation' from ISIS was paid for with the blood of ordinary people who had exchanged the tyranny of ISIS and their kind for the tyranny of Bashar al-Assad and his Russian friends from the skies.

By December 2016, Russian fighter jets and Assad's army had turned their focus to eastern Aleppo. This time, the world watched in real-time how 'victory' over Assad regime rebels was purchased—with daily civilian bombardment by Russian and Syrian regime planes, backed by Iranian ground support. And after months of siege, the city was crushed into the silence of surrender. The world was shamed by its incoherent response to photographs of dead children lined up for burial, killed by Assad's barrel bombs of chemical weapons. This was what victory looked like to Assad and Putin and their allies. For the Syrian people, 'triumph' tasted the same as defeat. On the day Aleppo fell in December 2016, 131 miles away Palmyra returned once more to ISIS control. The inference from the Islamic State's indomitable fight for an already ruined land was clear: the songs of history will be silenced at all costs. He who owns the past, owns the future.

2

IDEOLOGY AND RECRUITMENT

THE LINE OF INHERITANCE

'ISIS is a true product of Salafism and we must deal with it with full transparency.'

—Sheikh Aadel Al-Kalbani,
former imam of the Grand Mosque, Mecca

'A doctor cures millions of people over many years. Is he to be blamed if a few patients die?'

—Dr Makhdoom,
London Director of the Muslim World League

The tolerant and peaceful Islam of the vast majority of the world's Muslims has been permeated in recent decades by an austere literalist branch of the faith called Wahhabism that was born in Saudi Arabia three hundred years ago. Similar to Salafism, which believes Muslims need to return to the ways of the earliest faith, the Wahhabi ideology was founded by Muhammed ibn Abd al-Wahhab (1703-1792) and was born of the belief that Muslims would not be rewarded by God until they purged their faith of all modernity, rejected all reinterpretations of the faith and reverted to the very beginning. Wahhabism seeks to impose an unyielding vision on the *ummah* everywhere: a vision where society is ruled by sharia. In Wahhabi-based societies like Saudi Arabia, homosexuals and adulterers are stoned to death, theft is punished by amputations or lashings, murderers or apostates are beheaded or hanged and women have inferior rights to men. The ideology began as a tiny minority sect within the Arabian Peninsula yet it has become a global force in the last few decades. Today it is a formidable voice within the global Muslim world, its message spread around the globe by the petro-dollars of the Saudi government: it is propagated in Saudi-funded mosques and madrassas from East to West, and in the sharia courts that have spread from sharia-ruled theocracies to democracies like Britain, France and India. It is being propagated in social media online and it has become the ideological lodestar for terrorist groups like Al Qaeda and ISIS, who have taken it one step further and fused it with violent jihad. ISIS and its fellow travellers believe that Muslims who do not adhere to its singular vision of Islam are apostates, worthy of death, whether they are Shia or moderate Sunni believers. Today we see a schism within Islam as it becomes the battleground between the moderate and the fanatic.

To understand how ISIS and terror groups like them have recruited so many foreign jihadis to their cause, it is necessary to examine the ideological lineage of their movement and its spread around the world. This is a story that takes us from the *idea* to the mosque, to the law, to the final invocation online to join jihad.

Three centuries past, in the year of 1703 in a village called Al-Uyaynah in the Najd region of the Arabian Peninsula, Mohammed Ibn Abd al-Wahhab was born into a family of illustrious Islamic scholars and judges in the Hanbali tradition of Sunni Islam, the most conservative of Islamic jurisprudence. Ibn Abd al-Wahhab proved to be a prodigious intellect: by the age of ten he had memorized the entire Quran and by his teens he had travelled to the holy cities of Mecca and Medina. Quickly, he developed a reputation for uncompromising piety and controversy as he rejected the interpretations and teachings of the powerful body of imams, the *ulama*, in favour of looking directly to the Quran and the *hadith*. He shuttled between the holy cities and during this time met Muhammad Hayat al-Sindi, a scholar from what is now Pakistan's Sind province, who came to Medina after witnessing the beginnings of the disintegration of the Mughal Empire.

The decline of the Mughals had begun during the reign of Emperor Aurangzeb, who ruled much of the Indian subcontinent from 1658 to 1707. A puritanical and devout Muslim but, by most accounts, a man without compassion, Aurangzeb is remembered largely for his autocracy and religious persecution of non-Muslims and Sufis who did not follow orthodox Islam. By the end of his reign, rebellions—by the Marathas, the Sikhs and other groups—were taking root, and became full-blown revolts after his death. It was against this backdrop of political unrest and the decline of Islamic rule in India that Muhammad Hayat left for Arabia to continue his studies. He believed the Mughal Empire was failing not due to religious intolerance and unjust rule, but because Muslims were deviating from the true path—Aurangzeb, like Muhammad Hayat, subscribed to the forbiddingly austere Naqshbandi order of Sunni Islam, but his son and successor, Bahadur Shah, identified as Shia.

Muhammad Hayat al-Sindhi's beliefs shaped young Ibn Abd al-Wahhab. He too saw the fraying of a powerful Sunni empire—the Ottoman Empire—and attributed it to the rotten heart of its religious and moral leadership. He loathed the Egyptian and Ottoman nobility who came to Mecca to pray while flaunting back home a lifestyle of luxury and excess, smoking, dancing and imbibing hashish. The hedonism of these self-styled pashas appalled the ascetic scholar who believed their dissolute lives were in defiance of the Prophet.

Muhammad Hayat encouraged the young Ibn Abd al-Wahhab to reject the prevalent reinterpretations of the Quran. He believed the gates of independent reasoning or *ijtihad* should be closed if the Islamic world was to regain past glories. Only what literalists like him believed to be the word of the Quran and the Prophet mattered. He considered the worshipping of tombs, prayers to Muslim saints and modern lifestyles to be *haram* or forbidden. Only sharia could save the *ummah*.

This was to be the formative first step in the development of the ideology called Wahhabism that would continue to resonate in the Arab world and across the globe almost three hundred years later.

The Quran puts the *ummah*—the entire community of Muslims in the world—at the heart of its message. It is the duty of every Muslim to strive for a just society, and a world where any part of the *ummah* suffers poverty, persecution or oppression is intolerable to all Muslims. Islam also views religion and politics as entwined. The sacred and the state are one, therefore, 'political fragmentation of society was not just a political challenge but also a religious problem'. (*Fields of Blood*, Karen Armstrong.) As the 18th century Islamic world witnessed its standing diminish, with thrones of power crumbling after centuries of dominance, many believed the cause was a loss, or corruption, of faith. It was in this time of tremendous introspection among Muslim scholars and thinkers that Ibn Abd al-Wahhab was formulating his religious philosophy.

He went to the city of Basra, in Iraq, where he completed his studies and calibrated his thinking. By the time he returned to his birthplace, the 37-year-old preacher was adamant the Muslim people needed to be reoriented to the true path. He perceived the veneration of Sufi saints and worship at their graves, and worship of trees and other inanimate objects—

which were prevalent and accepted in Sunni Islam at the time—as heretical. He was also against indulgences like the wearing of fine robes, smoking, singing and dancing. Ibn Abd al-Wahhab, 'Son of the Worshipper of the Giver', denounced these practices and called upon believers such as Sufis to abandon their shrines to saints, which he saw as tantamount to idolatory. He wanted them to give up their poetry and music, to silence what he saw as their revelry and submit to humility. In a way, his message was the Reformation moment of Islam and proved to be a dangerous provocation to the political and religious status quo of leading religious scholars of the day, many of whom rejected his work, including his own father and brother who believed it was a message that would divide the Muslim people. Many political leaders in the region also disliked his message as it was seen as an inherent critique of their rule and privilege. Indeed, some of his opponents plotted an assassination attempt that failed.

Local scholars in Al-Uyaynah mounted a campaign to exile Ibn Abd al-Wahhab, saying he advocated violence against those who did not submit to his version of Islam. When this news came to the attention of the leader of the powerful local Bani Khalid tribe, it led to Ibn Abd al-Wahhah being expelled into the desert.

Like a scorching breeze, his words and notoriety blew through the Arabian Peninsula, but he may have remained a discordant voice in the desert were it not for his meeting with Mohammed Ibn Saud, an ambitious ruler from Dariyah, a small oasis town near Riyadh. Their encounter was the germination of a great union in religious and political history, leading to a partnership that would see the eventual rise of the House of Saud and Saudi Arabia as well as the global ascendancy of Wahhabism. In time, Wahhabism would evolve and become the inspiration for generations of Islamic puritans, from the sharia-governed modern-day

Saudi kingdom of the twentieth and twenty-first century, to global terrorist movements that seek to return the world to the year zero, the year of the Prophet, but under their aegis. The inheritors of Wahhabi doctrine included the late Osama bin Laden and his followers, as well as ISIS, who believe the world must burn to purify the *ummah* in the fires of faith in preparation for the End of Times.

The line of inheritance can be traced to 1744 when two men made a deal that would echo through the centuries. Muhammad Ibn Saud agreed he would protect and spread the Wahhabi doctrine that stated that the Quran and sharia should be the basis of governance. Ibn Abd al-Wahhab, in turn, would support the ruler and give him a religious legitimacy and thus his kingdom would be bestowed with 'glory and power'. At a time when Ibn Abd al-Wahhab had no other powerful local patrons, Ibn Saud offered him a unique opportunity for an alliance that would protect the fledgling religious reform movement. In turn, Ibn Saud's quest for territorial expansion was lent a religious sense of mission by the alliance and his armies began to fan out into surrounding towns and villages on the pretext of ridding them of Shia and other practices prohibited by Ibn Abd al-Wahhab.

The preacher vowed he who abided by the true message of the Quran would 'rule lands and men'. It was a union of the sacred and the state and it proved to be enduring—indeed it remains the basis of the modern-day theocracy of Saudi Arabia. It was sealed through a marriage alliance: Muhammad Ibn Abd al-Wahhab's daughter married Abdul Aziz, the son and successor of Ibn Saud, and their descendants would safeguard that legacy.

The preacher saw his role as reformer, not ruler, so he sought to lead by example. He undertook three acts of faith to demonstrate the nature of his beliefs. In the first, he instructed his followers to cut down a grove of palm trees which was worshipped by some residents of Al-Uyaynah. In particular there was one tree deemed particularly sacred: maidens prayed there for husbands, widows for their lost loves and barren wives for a child. Ibn Abd al-Wahhab announced he would take the axe to this particular tree himself.

The second act was for hundreds of his followers to destroy the tomb of an early associate of the Prophet—a place visited by many, but Ibn Abd al-Wahhab believed this violated the teachings of the faith that there must be worship of none other than the one God.

The third act was over a woman who confessed adultery. When she admitted that she had repeatedly 'sinned', he sentenced her to death by stoning rather than any lesser punishment that would have been deemed acceptable at the time. The preacher believed stoning was what was required under the *hadith*. He cast the first stone, and then performed prayers over her dead body. It was the first such stoning in a century and so news of it spread rapidly across the region.

In such ways, his fame grew. He saw himself confronting the corrosive morality of modernity to defend Muslim virtue. He was becoming a charismatic figure, one unafraid to challenge the corruption of the ruling powers and promise a new and absolutist version of the faith. He began to attract a growing number of young men, who moved to Dariyah. The nomadic Bedouin tribes also joined his cause as it offered opportunities for looting and brought the spoils of holy war. They paid a religious tax to Ibn Abd al-Wahhab who sent out armed tax collectors to collect a share of the plunder, whether crops or livestock.

Three centuries on, this ideology that combines puritanism, exclusivism and violence has blossomed once more among some young people alienated from the world around them. Boundless freedom has not been liberating for all, plunging some into confusion and a crisis of identity.

Wahabbism claims to offer a refuge from the modern world and an answer to Muslim decline in an age of Western, not Islamic ascendancy. Then as now, the 'reward' for piety and atonement was a new golden age, belonging and paradise. And when one looks at ISIS, it is clear that the opportunities for adventurism, for plunder, for expansion and control were all elements that inspired followers to join the Islamic State and its Wahabbi-based society.

As if fulfilling the prophecy that he who lives the message will rule lands and men, Muhammad Ibn Saud's allegiance to the Wahhabi doctrine in those early days began to pay dividends. The preacher proclaimed jihad and under Muhammad Ibn Saud, Wahhabi-inspired armies conducted a series of successful military campaigns capturing a sweep of territory.

Ravenous ambition fed upon each success and Ibn Saud's appetite for expansion and plunder was never sated. His band of holy warriors devoured land and gold and in time tension emerged between the patron and his preacher. Muhammad Ibn Saud believed in spreading the religious message via the sword while reaping the spoils, whereas the cerebral Ibn Abd al-Wahhab envisioned a more classical interpretation of jihad—rooted not just in battle but an internal struggle through dialogue, study and prayer. There is no doubt Wahhabism spread by the sword of jihad but some scholars note that contrary to the actions of ISIS and others today, Ibn Abd al-Wahhab was against the killing of prisoners of war, the slaughter of civilians, especially women and children, on the battlefield. Crucially, he never claimed that those who died as martyrs would win the highest honour in heaven: jihad was a selfless struggle for higher faith, not a quick ticket to paradise and virgins. Despite the differences, the alliance endured—cemented by intermarriage—and remains the basis of Saudi today.

The run of conquest continued over almost three decades until in 1773, Ibn Saud took Riyadh. The ruler also consolidated his other territories and the wealth and power of his family increased. Ibn Abd al-Wahhab disliked the growing climate of excess in the court of the Saud family and urged the payment of the tax to charity, as demanded by the Prophet.

After the preacher's death in 1791, the ideology turned ever more violent under the Saud dynasty and became an instrument of the ruthless state machine. Abd al-Azizi Ibn Muhammad, Ibn Saud's son and successor, declared *takfir* on whole populations—the controversial practice of declaring someone an unbeliever. *Takfir* was followed by the slaughter of those who resisted. In 1801, his army sacked the holy Shia city of Karbala and plundered the tomb of Imam Husain, killing thousands of Shias, including women and children. The Wahhabi-allied tribes looted and carried off plunder of gold, jewels, carpets and weapons—enough to load 4,000 camels. By April 1803, the holy city of Mecca was captured and the writ of Saudi rule eventually extended from the Persian Gulf to the Red Sea. It was seen as a major act of defiance to the ruling Ottoman Empire that had retained control over Mecca and Medina since 1517. The result of this was the Ottoman-Saudi war (1811-18). Abd al-Aziz died in 1803, killed by an assassin, and was replaced by his son Saud.

The Ottoman Empire sent the allied Egyptian army to crush what they saw as a dangerous rebellion—one that challenged their religious legitimacy by calling them apostates for not believing in the Wahhabi way. It was a military offensive that would take years to effect and the Egyptians finally crushed the Wahhabi armies, razed their capital of Dariyah and retook the holy cities. In 1818, the Wahhabi kingdom's leader Ibn Saud was taken to Constantinople for justice to be dispensed. He had dared to call the Ottoman Sultan an unbeliever and brought jihad to the holy cities for over a decade. The Ottomans, mindful that the Wahhabis forbade music, forced their prisoner to listen to the playing of the lute before executing him and throwing his head into the Bosphorus river. The captured Wahhabi religious leaders were stuffed into canons, which were then fired, blowing them to smithereens.

In the aftermath of this emphatic defeat, the descendants of Ibn Saud lived in exile. Their time would not return until the rule of another Abd al-Aziz who managed to recover most of the first Saudi first kingdom and turn it into the beginnings of a modern state by fully exploiting the religious zeal of Wahhabi doctrine once more. Abd al-Aziz had a ferocious army of Wahhabi Bedouin at his command, known as *Ikhwan* or The Brotherhood. They were militant zealots, fierce in battle but difficult to control.

The Saudi leader mounted his people's comeback by first leading a surprise attack on Riyadh in 1902. The mission proved successful and allowed him to take the city and establish himself as the Al Saud leader and the Wahhabi imam. From this strategic foothold, he made alliances with tribal leaders while winning the support of religious leaders. Thus safely entrenched, Abd al-Aziz, still in his twenties, mounted an extended offensive across the region and in in 1905 he retook his ancestral homeland of Najd. Then in 1921 he defeated the Rashidi clan at Hail and finally he conquered Hijaz three years later. However, Abd al-Aziz and his followers did not retake the holy cities of Mecca and Medina until 1924, in the aftermath of the First World War and the collapse of the Ottoman empire

In all of this, the *Ikhwan* were central to Abd al-Aziz's success, his sword-arm in battle as they fanned out into the deserts and brought more nomadic tribes to their cause by demanding obeisance to the Wahhabi way. They called on the nomads to leave their desert life to join agricultural settlements or *hirja*, an echo of the Prophet's migration to Medina in 622. The *hirja* signified a physical move from a place of unbelief to true belief. By 1915, they had established 200 settlements and there were around 100,000 *Ikhwan* allied to Abd al-Aziz's cause and committed to enforcing the Wahhabi system: they believed in gender segregation, abhorred technology, music, smoking and alcohol. They demanded Muslims follow public prayer and regular attendance of the mosque. Those who defied the Wahhabi doctrine were killed.

Ikhwan had some similarities to ISIS—zealots seeking to break up traditional settlements and govern people in communities rooted in Wahhabi Islam. The *Ikhwan* traded traditional nomadic desert raids for the Wahhabi way and jihad, brandishing swords and lances, fancying themselves to be like the Prophet's men. They killed women, children and civilians in massacres of the so-called apostate and enforced the strict practices of Wahhabi Islam at point of death wherever they went. Their merciless reputation was such that towns would surrender rather than risk slaughter on seeing the *Ikhwan's* approach on the horizon, the hooves of their camels and horses throwing up clouds of dust.

The Brotherhood were ambitious and wanted to extend their religious writ even further and were making political trouble when they went on to raid territories under the British protectorate. This posed a threat to the Saudi political leadership as it sought to consolidate its territorial gains in the geopolitical fall-out from the First World War. The *Ikhwan* eventually became ungovernable even by their own ruler, before finally turning on Abd al Aziz himself for allowing modern devices such as telephones, cars, music and smoking in his kingdom. Their rebellion was quashed by Abd al-Aziz when in March 1929 the Saudi king drove north from Riyadh with a convoy of cars mounted with machine guns and faced off the camel-borne *Ikhwan* on the plains of Sibillah. They were asked to surrender and on their refusal, he ordered open fire. Hundreds of the warrior brethren and their camels were felled. The leadership of the *Ikhwan* was decapitated.

After this defeat of the *Ikhwan*, the official Wahhabi movement of the Saudi Kingdom jettisoned militant jihad and expansionism for arch religious conservatism and continued to be governed by Wahhabi doctrine. It has remained so to this day. The historic tension between the violent and militant strain of Wahhabism, as represented by the *Ikhwan*, and the ruling religious establishment would endure as a feature of life in the Kingdom, however. In a way, Osama bin Laden was another modern-day inheritor of *Ikhwan*, seeking to depose what he saw as the religious decay of Saudi rule and replace it with a purist religious austerity.

It showed that the death of the *Ikhwan* leadership did not kill the dream of expansionism through violent jihad: instead, it was merely in incubation until its moment came again.

Three events are pivotal in the resurgence of the religious doctrine of Wahhabism globally in the twentieth century and beyond. The first came on 3 March 1938 when an American-owned oil well in Dhahran, Saudi Arabia, discovered what would become the largest source of petroleum in the world. The oil strike shook the geopolitical order, putting Saudi Arabia and the Middle East at the heart of the world's and America's future energy and economic security. Saudi Arabia was now central to US strategic interests in the region. Prior to this, Saudi's economy had relied on religious tourism to Mecca. Today, it has 16% of the world's proven petroleum reserves and ranks as the number one exporter of petroleum. Petroleum accounts for 90% of its export earnings and 92% of the Saudi budget. From that moment in 1938, Saudi Arabia had a superpower on its side and one day it would have the financial firepower to export Wahhabism globally, thereby launching a religious offensive that lasted decades.

The second pivotal event happened on 18 May 1962, when the General Islamic Conference in Mecca adopted a resolution to found the Muslim World League (MWL), a global body with the aim of propagating Wahhabi Islam, persuading Muslims worldwide to adhere to strict sharia law. Saudi Arabia continues today to be governed by the most conservative of Islamic laws: imposing the death penalty for apostasy, homosexual activity and adultery. It also enshrines in law inferior rights for women. The Muslim World League would go on to establish operations in 56 countries worldwide, with its reach extending from the Middle East to Asia, to Europe to the United Kingdom to America and Africa. It has funded and established tens of thousands of mosques, schools, Islamic cultural centres and women's centres.

Controlled and largely funded by the Saudi government, MWL is composed of eight distinct bodies, including the International Islamic Organization for Education, International Islamic Relief Organization, the Makkah al-Makkarahmah Charity Foundation for Orphans, the World Supreme Council for Mosques and the Fiqh Council, which states in literature from MWL that its objective is to 'Project the supremacy of the rules of Sharia over man-made laws.' That means for purist Wahhabi Muslims, sharia takes precedence over the law of their country, wherever they may be. It puts faith before nation and, in many cases, over modern ideas of equality and justice.

In 1964, when King Faisal came to the throne, he wholeheartedly championed the work of the MWL to fund and spread Saudi Arabia's brand of the faith globally. Two events in the 1970s made it possible for Saudi to do this more aggressively than ever before. In 1973, oil prices jumped as the Organization of Petroleum Exporting Countries (OPEC) announced an oil embargo in retaliation for American support for Israel in the 1973 Yom Kippur War, and the Saudi Kingdom, with its vast oil reserves, benefitted greatly. Then, in 1979, came Iran's Islamic Revolution. Shah Mohammad Reza Pahlavi was toppled in what started as a pro-democracy movement, not unlike the Arab Spring, but swiftly turned into a coup by the country's mullahs and Shia hardliner Sheikh Khomeini took over as the Grand Ayatollah of the Islamic Republic of Iran. The price of oil rocketed soon after, as a decade of war ensued between Shia-majority Iran and neighbouring Sunni-led Iraq, following a miscalculated invasion by Saddam Hussein. With the Middle East in flames and the fires of Shia Islamist revolution unleashed, US alliance with Sunni Arab powers became ever more critical. The Saudi Kingdom with its Sunni Wahhabi doctrine was viewed by the US and its allies as a counterbalance to the threat of rising Shia radicalism. Saudi Arabia was effectively given a free pass by the US to propagate its version of Islam in a bid to contain Iranian influence.

Fortified by petrodollars and its American ally, Saudi Arabia began to mass export Wahhabi Islam. As Evenii Noviko of the Jamestown Foundation observed in a 2005 study, 'In the mid 1980s...anxious to contain Iranian ambitions, the Saudis embarked upon the most extensive missionary campaign in history, exporting Wahhabism to the four corners of the globe.' Slowly, the Saudi funded MWL eroded centuries of influence of a more dominant and tolerant form of Islam. Some saw it as a form of mass conversion to the new doctrine.

A majority of Muslims around the world have no time for violent fanatics. As recently as 2017, a Pew study found that most respondents in all countries with significant Muslim populations had an unfavourable view of ISIS. Few outside of arch-conservative countries like Afghanistan and Pakistan wanted sharia law to be the official law of the land. The vast majority of Muslims—whether Sunni or not—did not subscribe to Wahhabi doctrine, and yet its spread was being financed by Saudi Arabia for its own ideological reasons.

The issue has also caused concern within Islam's global religious leadership: in September 2016, a group of Muslim clerics referred to Wahhabi belief as 'a dangerous deformation' of Sunni Islam. The prelates included Egypt's Grand Imam, Ahmed el-Tayeb of the famous al-Azhar, the foremost centre of theological study in the Islamic world, who a year before had attacked 'corrupt interpretations' of religious texts and called for 'a return to the schools of great knowledge' outside Saudi Arabia. The meeting took place in Grozny and was minimally reported, with the *Independent* in the UK and *Le Monde* in France among the few newspapers that covered it.

It is easy to see why there is cause for concern. The Muslim World League has opened offices wherever there is a Muslim population in the world and distributed millions of copies of the Quran but always with Wahhabi religious texts by thinkers approved by the Saudi state. If we look at the scope of the expansion since 1964 when King Faisal began to push the globalization of Wahhabism, by 2004 in non-Muslim countries alone, Saudi had built 1,359 mosques, 210 Islamic Centres, 202 colleges, 2000 schools or madrassas. Its funds also helped finance 16 American mosques, as well as 4 in Canada and others in London, Madrid, Brussels and Geneva, according to the official Saudi publication *Ain al-Yayeen*. The paper also reported that billions more in riyals were spent on training highly conservative Wahhabi scholars and imams.

US Senator Chris Murphy, member of the Foreign Relations Subcommittee on the Near East, South Asia, Central Asia and Counter-terrorism, has said he believes there is a causal link between the creation of Saudi-funded institutions such as madrassas and an increase in radicalization. Speaking at a conference in Washington, he used the example of Pakistan to make his point, explaining there were 24,000 madrassas funded by the Saudi kingdom in Pakistan that received a 'tsunami of money' to 'export intolerance'. He believes Pakistan is the best example to see how schools propagating an intolerant ideology can be a pathway to terror: 'In 1956, there were 244 madrassas in Pakistan. Today, there are 24,000. These schools are multiplying all over the globe. These schools, by and large, don't teach violence, they aren't the minor leagues for al Qaeda or ISIS. But they do teach a version of Islam that leads very nicely into an anti-Shia, anti-Western militancy.'

In 1954 the Pakistani population was 54 million compared to almost 190 million today—while the population has quadrupled over this period, the number of madrassas has risen a hundred-fold. Senator Murphy told the Council on Foreign Relations that many thousands of the 24,000 Pakistani madrassas were Saudi funded and Wahhabi. The pupils tended to be the children of poor families whose economic marginalization made them typical targets for radicalization. By the time of 9/11, it was widely acknowledged by security and intelligence experts that the Afghan-Pak region was the epicentre of global terrorism under the leadership of the Taliban and Al Qaeda, both of which were partly inspired by Wahhabi doctrine, as well as Deobandi Islam, emanating from India in the wake of the 1857 revolt against the British Empire. That epicentre of terrorism has now shifted under ISIS to Iraq/Syria and Northern Africa.

Extreme Islamist views were once confined to particular countries governed by those ideologies, but today they are the basis of belief for many millions globally, thanks to groups like MWL as well as the Internet. There is concern about how this is affecting the younger generation of Muslims, given the level of Saudi spending on such proselyting. In 2008, the documentary *The Qur'an* by British film-maker Antony Thomas put the total level of Saudi Wahhabi funding at over than $100 billion within a span of three decades. Dr Novikov wrote back in May 2005 that while not directly advocating terrorism, 'Wahhabi doctrine and institutions could serve as gateways to more violent organizations.'

With the rise of ISIS and Islamist extremism in Europe, this view has become more widespread. By September 2015, as Saudi's King Salman made his first visit to Washington after coming to the throne that January, the world was facing a new security paradigm, with old political realities turned upside down. Iran, long seen as an existential threat to Israel because of its past promise to wipe it from the map and as a supporter of terror groups like Hezbollah and Hamas, was no longer the primary American enemy in the region. Iran had agreed a nuclear deal with the US Obama administration and its partner nations, and there had been a rolling back of international sanctions in return for a commitment not to pursue a nuclear weapon. The threat in the Middle East now was ISIS, inspired by Wahhabi doctrine and whose army of jihadists were instructed with Saudi-published religious texts and books.

The US had become weary of Saudi Arabia even before this. Leaked Wikileaks cables indicated that in 2009, former Secretary of State Hillary Clinton believed Saudi was also a major funder of Islamist terrorist groups: Taliban, Al Qaeda and Lashkar-e-Taiba, the mastermind behind the 2008 Mumbai terror attack that killed 164 people in India.

'More needs to be done since Saudi Arabia remains a critical financial support base for al-Qaida, the Taliban, LeT and other terrorist groups,' said the leaked classified paper signed by the Secretary of State. 'Donors in Saudi Arabia constitute the most significant source of funding to Sunni terrorist groups worldwide,' she said. One cable details how the Pakistani terrorist group Lashkar-e-Taiba (LeT) used a Saudi-based front company to fund its activities in 2005. LeT's so-called charity wing, Jamaat-ud-Dawa, reportedly travelled to Saudi Arabia seeking donations for new schools at vastly inflated costs, then siphoned off the excess money to fund militant operations. Such was the scale of the problem, Saudi was described in the media as the cash dispenser of Islamist terrorism ('Wikileaks Cables portray Saudi Arabia as cash machine for terrorists', *Guardian*, 5 December 2010).

The demand for the truth about Saudi's role in 9/11 through disclosure of classified documents has also been another feature of the mistrust that has arisen. Fifteen of the 19 hijackers on 9/11 were Saudi, including bin Laden. In 2016, the US Congress voted for a law that would open the door to the families of the 9/11 victims to sue Saudi Arabia for damages.

The move to examine Saudi Arabia's culpability in the rise of recruitment to global Islamist extremism came after many years of official denial in both the US and Riyadh. In 2002, months after the 9/11 attack, Laurent Murawiec, an analyst with the Rand Corporation, think tank and adviser to the US military on defence matters, told the Pentagon's Defense Policy Board: 'The Saudis are active at every level of the terror chain, from planners to financiers, from cadre to foot soldier, from ideologist to cheerleader. Saudi Arabia supports our enemies and attacks our allies. It is the kernel of evil, the prime mover, the most dangerous opponent in the Middle East.' His view was not endorsed by the government at the time. But by 2016, the critics of Saudi were becoming mainstream and vocal.

'Nothing has been more corrosive to the stability and modernization of the Arab world and the Muslim world at large than the billions and billions of dollars the Saudis have invested since the 1970s into wiping out the pluralism of Islam...imposing in its place the puritanical, anti-modern, anti-women, anti-Western, anti-pluralistic Wahhabi Salafist brand of Islam,' said *New York Times* columnist Thomas Friedman shortly before the Saudi royal visit began in 2015.

In 2016, Wikileaks dumped another email cache online between the then Presidential candidate Hillary Clinton and her campaign chief John Podesta. The cache dates back to 2014 when Mrs Clinton sent an eight-point plan to Mr Podesta who at the time was advising President Obama on how to defeat ISIS. The leaked documents quoted Mrs Clinton as saying: '...we need to bring pressure on the governments of Qatar and Saudi Arabia, which are providing clandestine financial and logistical support to ISIL and other radical Sunni groups in the region.'

Decades of globalization of the Wahhabi doctrine, central to both Saudi and Qatari regimes, has eroded the pluralism of Islam. It has deepened the rift between Shias and Sunnis in countries where such sectarian divides did not exist before, such as the United Kingdom that is reporting more instances of clashes between the two groups. For example, on the evening of the Christian holy day Good Friday in 2016, Glasgow shopkeeper Asad Shah posted a message wishing his Christian friends ahead of the Easter holiday: 'Good Friday and a very happy Easter, especially to my beloved Christian nation,' he said. Shah was an Ahmadiyya, a Muslim group known for its interfaith tolerance. The message was seen by Tanveer Ahmed, a hardline Sunni Muslim from Bradford, northern England, who proceeded to rage to his fellow Muslims about the message which he saw as an insult to the Prophet. He also claimed to have been enraged by other messages in which Shah spoke of himself as a prophet. Ahmed drove that same evening to Scotland to the shop where Shah worked and attacked him with a large knife, chasing him into the street, stabbing him in the head and face multiple times.

According to eye witnesses, after Shah collapsed, Ahmed stamped on his face repeatedly, then walked over to a bus shelter to wait for the police. Asad Shah succumbed to his injuries within a few hours.

Ahmed Tanveer had been inspired by Mumtaz Qadri, the man who had killed the Pakistani politician Salman Taseer in Islamabad in 2011 for suggesting changes in Pakistan's blasphemy law. Sentenced to life in prison, Ahmed showed no remorse. From prison, he posted videos on social media platforms, saying, 'I stood guard on the honour of Prophet Muhammad and I shall do it again if I shall get a chance…' and 'The penalty for those who insult the prophet: cut their heads from their bodies.' (BBC News, 31 January 2017.)

The Wahhabi doctrine propagated by hardline imams denounces moderate Muslims and non-Muslims as kaffirs, unbelievers, worthy of having jihad waged upon them. Yet the Prophet himself acknowledged what he termed people of the earlier revelations, namely Christians and Jews, and their prophets Jesus and Abraham. In place of such pluralism and the common humanity and goodness of the majority of Muslims like Asad Shah, Wahhabism has spread an intolerant, violent and exclusivist form of Islam and this has coincided with MWL's creation of thousands of institutions globally—from schools and colleges to mosques and Islamic cultural centres. A generation has grown up under their tutelage.

One of the most excoriating analyses comes from Algerian journalist and author Kamel Daoud who believes that the West is deluding itself about its ally and describes ISIS (or Daesh) and Saudi Arabia as two sides of the same coin, naming them Black and White Daesh:

> 'The former slits throats, kills, stones, cuts off hands, destroys humanity's common heritage and despises archaeology, women and non-Muslims. The latter is better dressed and neater but does the same things.

> 'The West's denial regarding Saudi Arabia is striking: it salutes the theocracy as its ally but pretends not to notice that it is the world's chief ideological sponsor of Islamist culture. The younger generations of radicals in the so-called Arab world were not born jihadists. They were suckled in the bosom of Fatwa Valley. A kind of Islamist Vatican with a vast industry that produces theologians, religious laws, books and aggressive editorial policies and media campaigns...
>
> '(ISIS) has a mother: the invasion of Iraq. But it also has a father: Saudi Arabia and its religious-industrial complex. Until that point is understood, battles may be won but the war will be lost.' (*New York Times*, op-ed November 2015.)

As the Saudis exported their message, so they have exported thousands of mujahideen over decades. Like the *Ikhwan* of old, twentieth-century 'holy warriors' fanned out across the region in the name of a purist vision of Islam. This began in the 1980s as an international band of mujahideen fought the Soviets in Afghanistan, the war where Osama bin Laden and many of his Saudi Al Qaeda followers became battle hardened against their first superpower enemy. Back then Saudi expansionism, through the spread of Wahhabism globally and via its ciphers on the Afghan battlefield, allied with the US against common enemies: Shia revivalism and Communism. And they were aided by neighbouring Sunni dominated Pakistan.

But by 1989, when the war in Afghanistan was won, these jihadis did not retire quietly into the night to settle with families in the mountains of the Hindu Kush. The spirit of the *Ikhwan* of old had awakened from slumber: their inheritors fought on and formed terrorist groups that waged jihad in fresh theatres. Insurgencies flared around the world: Kashmir, Chechnya, Bosnia, wherever Muslim grievances burned. Into the 1990s they trained in terrorist camps alongside Al Qaeda, that rose from the ashes of the Afghan war of the eighties. Once the fires of radicalism were lit, they were difficult to extinguish, and it was a contagion of fires that spread with a ferocity the West found difficult to measure and contain. The events of 9/11 set in motion the ill-fated War on Terror that led to the invasion of Iraq in 2003, and the terrible fall-out from that war, as we have seen, sowed the seeds of ISIS, which was fuelled further by the collapse of old political powers across the Middle East as the Arab Spring began in 2011. And today's global league of jihadis has extended its fight beyond the Middle East into cities across the world. This time round, Saudi has seen 2,500 of its own citizens recruited by ISIS—more than any country other than Tunisia.

Wahhabism is ISIS's guiding light. Like the *Ikhwan* that went before them, they believe they are fighting the filth of the tide of modernity, beating back the seas of history to the seventh century. Like their forebears, they brandish swords, mask their faces in black, administer justice by beheading and ride across the East not on camels but Toyota Land Cruisers, Humvees and stolen tanks. While decrying modernity, they enshrine technology into their cause: the internet, smart phones, WhatsApp and modern warfare weaponry funded by donors.

Saudi Arabia denounces critics who claim it is the ideological father of Wahhabi inspired ISIS and modern Islamist terrorism. It rightly says that it is a victim of terrorism—attacks on the cities of Medina and Mecca by ISIS show that the House of Saud is firmly in the sightlines of the terrorists. Since the founding of Wahhabism in Arabia three centuries before, the tension between the sacred and the state has always been evident. Once Saudi Arabia discovered oil it signed a pact to become part of a wider geopolitical alliance; America became its ally. But there were those in the kingdom who believed the House of Saud must fall for that.

First, Al Qaeda and now ISIS vow to destroy the kingdom for the friends it keeps.

Thus Saudi Arabia is the victim of Wahhabi inspired terrorism and ally of the West in the war on terrorism *at the same time* as it is the exporter of Wahabbi doctrine that inspires the terrorists. And thus the world is caught in a cycle of terror. Saudi Arabia is like the man who hurls a Molotov cocktail at a building and watches it explode, then rushes in to douse the flames.

There is increased pressure on Saudi now to stem the flow of funds from its borders to ISIS and others. Much progress has been made and in December 2015, Saudi Arabia announced its part in a global anti-ISIS coalition. It is also one of the pioneers in the rehabilitation of Islamist terrorists under its de-radicalization programme that has been emulated in the west. And yet that is only half the story.

More deadly than the bullet is the idea. The recruitment role global Wahhabism has played in the rise of Islamist extremism and terrorism is a topic that remains taboo within the kingdom at a time when it is fighting to maintain the status quo so carefully constructed. The hardline religious ideology lies at the core of the foundation of the modern Saudi kingdom. The conjoined throne of the sacred and the state endures almost three hundred years after Ibn Abd al-Wahhab made his deal in the desert. As the world focuses on the effect that deal is now having on the rest of us, Saudi Arabia's challenge comes at a time of rising economic uncertainty at home—the oil price that once funded the global ideological expansionism and was used to placate domestic discontent within the kingdom in the past, has now collapsed to under $50 per barrel from a peak of more than $100 in 2014 for a number of reasons. The hydrocarbon age is coming to a close.

Saudi is at a most dangerous juncture in its history, facing a future where the oil economy is in decline, where a resurgent enemy in Iran is liberated from sanctions and seeks to return to the global economic fold. As in a coalescing of forces before the storm, all this coincides with Saudi's strained relations with the US and its allies over 9/11 amid accusations that it has been the financial and ideological puppet-master behind ISIS all along.

The costs of its role in the war in Yemen, as well as seeking to topple the regime of Assad in Syria, is burdensome to the Kingdom's purse at a time when it faces the daunting prospect of reforming a domestic economy which for so long has been oil dependant. Now it has to diversify its economy and do it fast to prevent rising unemployment and discontent among its large young population from bubbling over into increased militancy at home. Failing economics, political disenchantment and the rage of youth is the modern-day crucible of Islamic terrorism. If Saudi fails, could it face its own Arab Spring moment?

Saudi Arabia is a source of the problem, but it also is part of the solution. Which is why the US has been at pains to protect its relationship with the kingdom. Saudi offers the West vital intelligence in foiling terrorism plots in their own backyard. It is crucial in the fight to contain the Frankenstein monster that is ISIS. Western efforts to stanch the flow of cash from donors in the country to terrorist causes has made progress in recent years. As US-led military offensives have drilled down to loose ISIS's hold on Iraq and Syria, Saudi remains the key military ally in the Arab world. Yet the most difficult challenge of killing the idea behind violent Sunni radicalism remains.

Bankrolled for decades by Saudi to the tune of $100 billion, MWL—through the Wahhabi network it has spawned—continues to be the most powerful, globalized and influential organization in the world when it comes to shaping modern Islam. Few understand the scale of its dominion, built quietly and to devastating effect in our midst.

WORLD WAHHABI WEB

'The modern jihadi is a Wahhabi on steroids.'

—*Financial Times*, 7 August 2014

London, 2 November 2016

In an unremarkable glass fronted building tucked behind Goodge Street station in central London, bearded Arab men patrol the streets outside the entrance to the London office of the Muslim World League. There are CCTV cameras tracking every movement on the pavements outside. As I'm buzzed in for my meeting with Dr Makhdoom, the London Director, I'm aware of being filmed every step of the way to his office, from lobby to elevator, from corridor to waiting room.

The lobby outside his office is dominated by a vast flat screen television screening live footage of the Kaaba that lies at the heart of the complex housing Islam's most sacred mosque, Al-Masjid al-Haram in Mecca, with crowds of white robed pilgrims turning in ever decreasing concentric circles about the black cuboid building. A symphony of prayer permeates, a powerful evocation of the *ummah* speaking as one wherever they be, in London, New York, Baghdad or Mecca.

Dr Makhdoom's spacious office overlooks a skyline of

London stained grey and red as the sun prepares to set. Mounted on the wall to the left of his expansive desk is a bank of TV monitors portraying a kaleidoscope of images outside and within. Like *Big Brother*, it's impossible to move inside or out without being seen. Dr Makhdoom greets me with warmth, offering mint tea as is the custom and a silver platter piled with plump dates.

He is a large man with a mobile and friendly face yet inscrutable eyes and our meeting begins rather like that of professor and student. For that is what he once was. In his previous incarnation, the doctor was responsible for mentoring PhD and Masters students in Britain. And before that he was at the King Fahd Academy in Acton, West London, an Islamic school for children aged 3 to18, offering an education combining Islamic and Western teaching. His office retains the air of the don's lair, with a small library of Islamic books around him and his desk stacked with literature. He sits calmly amidst his forest of paperwork, his expression inquisitive and palms placed flat on the desk. His role comes at a challenging time: after years of close co-operation and trust with the Saudi regime, questions are now being raised in the arena of public opinion about the true nature of the work of the League here in London and elsewhere. Was it purely royal munificence that saw the kingdom plough billions into Muslim communities overseas or was there an ulterior agenda that only now is reaping its bitter harvest?

I begin by asking what the role of the League is in the modern world.

'Our purpose and vision is to be like a global incubator for the Muslim people to raise awareness of good practice and help the Muslims with the feeling of co-habitation and living in peace in their country. We wish to educate people about what Islam is—both believers and non-believers.'

'Do you teach Sunni Islam?' I ask.

'There is Sunni Islam and this is the *right* Islam. Shia Islam is something else,' he replies, gently dismissing the beliefs of the world's 350 million Shia Muslims in one answer as if brushing lint from his jacket sleeve.

'So are all Muslims welcome here, Shia and others?'

'The World Muslim League accepts everyone here. I was born and raised in Mecca and there we welcome all. But we wish to help Muslims follow and practice the *correct* Islamic faith. We do this by opening mosques, schools, helping the needy, disaster relief and these kind of works.'

'And through the building of madrassas here, you are educating the next generation of young Muslims?'

'You know, the term madrassa is school in Arabic. But the name has been demonized in the media. We as the League have no schools ourselves, but we fund schools. We pay for building, expansion, facilities, books, furniture and so on. We support and sponsor the students who wish to study, whether here or in Saudi Arabia. '

Here and around the world the Saudis have been responsible for the education of millions of children, including those from poorer backgrounds. It has served as much as a social enterprise as religious one. The schools take the children from as young as three until they are on the threshold of adulthood and this way the League is shaping the minds of the next generation of Muslims, from London to Bradford, from Brussels to Berlin, from Islamabad to Kabul.

'Why was the League set up in London,' I ask him.

'It was established in 1982 and since then we've done a lot. Mostly we clarify misconceptions about the faith. For example, before there was no halal food in this country because people weren't educated about this. We gave out information through our mosques, in Islamic classes and Quran classes. Now it's a very different story. Today, Muslims can eat halal safely.'

It is indeed a remarkable transformation. Within a few years, halal food has evolved from being available with a few Muslim-run butchers and wholesalers into a nationwide food supply chain, including major retailers and restaurants. The country's biggest supermarket chains now have aisles devoted to halal meat. There are apps to tell Muslims where they can eat halal in restaurants and it is a word that is part of the British lexicon.

The ritually acceptable method of slaughter for animals is something the Muslim shares with the Jewish people, explains Dr Makhdoom. He tells me the spread of halal was the first achievement attributable to the League's London office. The second is the spread of a better understanding of Islamic finance in Britain.

This too has made vast strides. Islamic financial products comply with Islamic religious rulings under sharia to pool risk and ban traditional interest payments. Britain has six Islamic banks and twenty more lenders offer Islamic financial products, more than any other Western country. In 2015, the UK Foreign Office announced that Britain had ambitions to become a world leader in Islamic finance, alongside Doha. Indeed, it is a religious practice embedded into the very ground of the capital, with London's tallest and latest iconic skyscraper, The Shard, built with Islamic finance.

While keen to explain the work on sharia finance and halal, Dr Makhdoom was more reticent about the most profound legacy of the League's decades in Britain: a network of Saudi financed or supported mosques, madrassas and Islamic centres across the country, as well as efforts to ingrain the need for Muslims in Britain to follow sharia law in all areas of life. The London office does not provide a country breakdown of how many schools, mosques or Islamic centres are financed by its coffers or influenced by its founding doctrine. Yet it is clear their work has altered the religious landscape for many British Muslims, from vastly different cultures.

In December 2004, an Arabic document entitled 'al-Alam al-Islami' (The Islamic World) was published by the League on its website talking about the leading role of Saudi Arabia in preaching Islam's heritage in the west. They believed that given the diversity of Europe's Muslims—from Turkish and North African Muslims in Germany and France to Balkan Muslim in Austria to South Asian Muslims in Britain—the mosque was the best place to disseminate the Wahhabi message of the true path, using Saudi trained imams. It was a unifying doctrine.

The Muslim World League is a leading global proponent of the adherence to sharia by Muslims worldwide—in matters of food, finance and other areas as well. Yet sharia as espoused by Wahhabis is opposed to certain basic democratic freedoms and values that have been built over centuries in matters of women's equality, gay rights and divorce. I ask Dr Makhdoom, what takes precedence: the law of the country or the law of Allah?

'A Muslim living in a country,' he replies, 'chooses to be a citizen and he signs up for a visa or passport, he has to go with the law of the land. It is an oath—if a Muslim comes and lives here he should fulfil the law and if he wishes to change the law he should do so within the framework of the law.'

'What about the views spread in some British mosques that are opposed to the law of our country, on gay rights, for example? In Saudi Arabia it is a crime punishable by death.'

'The idea of gay is not within Islam,' he demurs softly. 'If people drink alcohol, eat pork or practise actions that aren't permissible in Islam, they are not Muslim. If you're a Muslim, *do* as Islam asks. In this country, nobody forces you to eat pork, nobody forces you to be gay. If you don't like this way of doing things in Britain, you must go to another country. Nobody forces you to stay.'

Dr Makhdoom believes that the League's job is to show

the true path to God and over decades its work has focused on preaching the message of tolerance. Yet a paradox remains. Why does there appear to be a correlation between the global expansion of the League and the rise of Wahhabi-based extremism and violent jihadi sentiment? It is a question that rankles immensely.

'This is a very wrong judgement,' he admonishes. 'This is what the black media is doing. It is ignorant. These media groups, they demonize different colours, religions, to earn viewers, to sell papers. Some media do this on purpose to pursue political goals.

'You ask of Wahhabi Islam—there's no such thing. It's a label. I follow the Hanbali school of thought and so do millions of Saudis like me. If you ask them, "What is Wahhabi?" they will say, "What is that?" I am Muslim. The enemies of Islam are misleading the world. These people—Daesh—and others like Al Qaeda are criminals. They're not true Muslims if they hurt Islam. It's against Islam to wage war against civilians, to kill women and children, to kill old people.'

And yet the link between ISIS and Wahhabi belief is there, I point out, with some Muslims joining from institutions run or funded by the League, with ISIS using Saudi printed Wahhabi literature to educate their fighters on Islam. Dr Makhdoom has an alternative explanation for the global rise of Wahhabi inspired violence.

'It is ignorance,' he insists. 'They're misguided by their poverty, by their oppression, by injustice.'

Yet it is a problem that afflicts Saudi Arabia at home, as much as countries abroad that he accuses of being guilty of injustices against Muslims. The Saudi kingdom was the first country in the world to introduce a de-radicalization programme to tackle the threat to its internal security—recognition of the problem in its backyard.

'We've succeeded in helping many turn back from this path,' he admits. 'Given the right atmosphere and information, our success rate has been more than 80%.'

I ask him to explain why radicalism is so prevalent, here and even in Saudi, when the greatest global proponent of the faith is working so hard to deliver the true message. Is there something in the nature of Wahhabi belief that is to blame? Dr Makhdoom believes not, offering the answer that it is the human condition for some to follow evil.

'This is the nature of society, you see. Can you clean all of the community of criminals, drugs, thieves and assault? Can *you* do it? Is there anywhere in the world clear of all criminals?'

His question isw not rhetorical and waits for my answer before continuing to assert that the League has no power to lessen the lure of radicalism.

'Our organization and community has specific duties: schools, volunteer groups, charitable work. The mosque has the job of educating and teaching. We don't have the authority to stop those committing criminal acts. It is the job of all of us to keep the community safe: mosques, schools, families, government. Some unwise and lazy people want the teachers, the imams, to catch the criminal in the street. Can we do that? No. Throw the blame on us, Islam and you are not doing your work, I tell you.'

'So what's the answer?'

'Cooperation,' he says. 'A doctor cures millions of people over many years with his learning. Is he to be blamed if a few patients die? You ask the doctor, "You were working three or four decades and nothing happened. Now why are people dying despite all your work?" I cannot blame the teachers in our mosques for those who didn't succeed, who took the wrong road. I cannot force people to follow us and our way. We don't have the tools to direct people to do as we say.'

He insists there is no link between Salafist or Wahhabi doctrine, between the Saudi teachings, and the rise of radicalism here and elsewhere in the world. The root causes of terror lie elsewhere, he believes. They lie in the West's oppression of Muslims, in poverty, in inequality, in injustices against the *ummah*.

'People use their learning in their own way. They have their own goals. If they resort to terror it's retaliation against oppression or running away from their poverty or suffering. Our duty is to give people the right information. Our religion is urging us to communicate, co-operate, we're created to make the earth beautiful. We believe as Muslims we come from Adam and Eve and we are all brothers. Some people in our faith hide this. But it will not be hidden, for our Prophet Muhammad, peace be upon Him, was dealing with Jews, with Christians, with all in the community.'

'What do you say to those who believe the Saudis have a hand in the rise of radicalism, of ISIS itself?'

'There are theories that it is *we* who created Daesh. Those in Iran, Israel or the West say it. But Daesh is hurting Islam. It's not benefiting Muslims. So we're working now to change this view. On Ramadan, we now open our mosques, we invite the public in, we give out food, cakes, dates and leaflets.'

After more than a decade of media revelations of hate propaganda against Christians, Jews and other non-Sunni Muslims emanating from some hardline mosques and madrassas, the League is now on a mission to open its doors to all and spread a message of harmony. It would appear it has decided to lovebomb London.

On the December 2016, as in previous years, the MWL's London office handed out hundreds of red and white roses to members of the public. On International Women's Day it opened stalls on the streets to distribute scarves to passing ladies, offering to show them how to cover their heads, while explaining why this is done. The aim is to remove fear and end the stigma. Meanwhile back in Saudi, women are second-class citizens and daily live under the control of their male relatives. Until September 2017, Saudi women were banned from driving and many do not work. If they are beaten by their husbands, they have no easy right of redress.

Five times each year, the London office runs courses for British public sector workers, doctors, nurses, teachers and fire-fighters, to attend sessions explaining an edited version of their faith to non-Muslims in order to facilitate better community relations. They recognize that a closed culture has bred fear and mistrust, so they must let the light in. Doors to mosques are flung open across Britain during Ramadan and on the breaking of fast at close of the day, non-Muslims are invited to partake in the *iftar* meal. It is indicative of how Saudi Arabia is responding to the global perception that the cradle of Wahhabi belief is also the jihad incubator.

In 2007, there were 1528 mosques in the UK, of which 68 were Wahhabi or Salafist. That figure rose to 110 within eight years and the total number of mosques is now more than 1700. Almost 40% of those mosques adhere to another branch of Islam, Deobandism, which is similar in belief to Wahhabism and originates from India. Like the Wahhabis, the Deobandis also wish to revert to the Islam of the seventh century and see a world governed by sharia. It was the Deobandis that spiritually guided the Taliban, as Wahhabis guided ISIS.

Innes Bowen (author of *Medina in Birmingham, Najaf in Brent: Inside British Islam*) studied the make-up of Britain's mosaic of Muslim communities and wrote in June 2014 that only a handful of Britain's mosques follow a modern interpretation, unlike the US, where home-grown radicalization is less prevalent: 'As the Muslim population became more established, one might have assumed that a

Westernized form of Islam would have come to dominate Britain's mosques. According to a database of British Islam, however, only two out of 1,700 mosques in Britain follow modernist interpretations of the Koran. It's not the same elsewhere in the West. In a 2011 survey of Islam in the United States, 56 per cent of mosques described themselves as following an interpretation of Islam adapted to modern circumstances. This has not happened in Britain.'

Abdal Hakim Murad, the student chaplain at Cambridge University, told a British documentary maker that he believed the failure to teach a moderate and tolerant form of Islam in our mosques would be a grave error: 'I regard what the Saudis are doing in the ghettoes of British Islam as potentially lethal for the future of the community.'

In the last couple of years, after media investigations into the Wahhabi, Deobandi and Salafist literature being made available through such institutions, the government has begun to question whether it should allow foreign and particularly Saudi or Qatari funding of religious or educational institutions in Britain. Are they beneficent efforts to serve the religious needs of Muslims overseas or attempts to indoctrinate Western Muslims with a radical Islamist ideology at the expense of tolerant versions of the faith?

In 2015, Austria's foreign minister Sebastian Kurz said his government was right to ban foreign funding on a continuous basis in Islamic institutions like mosques. In Austria's case, its concern lay with Turkish-trained imams coming into the country, usurping the demand for moderate Austrian-trained preachers. Kurz is no right-wing xenophobe; he has instituted progressive policies for immigrants in matters such as education and the path to citizenship and insists Austria remains open to the world. Yet on the matter of imams, he had this to say: 'In our opinion, imams should be role models for young Muslims and must show that it is possible to be a proud Austrian and a believing Muslim.'

Kurz believes that this could be the model for all European countries. By 2016, France and Germany were also looking at following Austria's example. In January 2016, German Chancellor Angela Merkel's deputy told the *Bild am Sonntag* newspaper: 'We have to make clear to the Saudis that the time of looking away is over. Wahhabi mosques all over the world are financed by Saudi Arabia.' In Britain, the government authorized an investigation into foreign funding and support of UK jihadi and extremist groups—a matter some believe could foster tension with Saudi Arabia.

Fears are consolidating that funding of institutions of faith by Saudi Arabia, as well as Qatar, could be dividing communities in Europe and elsewhere. The line of inheritance between Salafist ideologies and global jihad can be seen in mosques, madrassas, sharia courts in the East and West, as well as in the virtual world online. It is a line that travels into the laptop, cellphone and mind of young people everywhere, a global network that wittingly or unwittingly fuels militant jihad.

THE ETON OF ISLAM

> 'This is a time bomb that under the guise of education is igniting under the world. It is funded by Saudi and Qatari money and that must stop. The question then is, "Does bombing people over there really tackle that?" I don't think so.'
>
> —General Jonathan Shaw, retired British Assistant Chief of Defence Staff, 2012, *Telegraph*)

Darul Uloom Madrassa, Chislehurst, England June 2010

The clock strikes 11a.m. and boys spill out of classrooms into the corridor to move on to their next lesson. There is no noise or jostling, instead the children walk in an orderly manner, heads bowed respectfully and eyes downcast to avoid my gaze. The boys, all aged between 13 and 19, are dressed in a school uniform of ankle-length white *salwar kameez* and white skullcaps and their feet are bare.

This is Darul Uloom, a madrassa set in the pretty and prosperous Kent village of Chislehurst, tucked away behind a wire fence and fringe of trees in the very heart of English surburbia. A madrassa education is becoming an increasingly popular choice among Muslim parents in Britain. Whereas elsewhere in the world the madrassa was often for children from poor and disadvantaged communities, here it is the norm among the middle classes. According to the Association of Muslim Schools in the UK, which represents 80 Islamic schools, 3% of Muslims schoolchildren attend such schools full time.

'Our parents represent the cross-section of British Muslim society,' said a mufti at one leading school in northern England. These parents include teachers, doctors and shopkeepers, the middle-class backbone of the community in Britain.

And yet the schools operate somewhat in the shadows, secretive and protective, fearful of a rising climate of Islamophobia. Darul Uloom schools have been operating in Britain for almost three decades, but since 9/11 they have faced far closer scrutiny by police who fear they may be academies of radicalism—a charge the madrassas deny.

Most people in Britain have never heard of the Deobandis but their significance in the Islamic world is paramount, equal to the Wahhabis. Darul Uloom in the UK and South Asia has received funding from wealthy benefactors in the Gulf, particularly Saudi Arabia, for they share many of the same beliefs. Islamic experts regard the founding Darul Uloom in India as the second most important Islamic academic institution in the world after Cairo's Al Azhar university and the school aims to raise the next generation of leaders of the Islamic world, men shaped in a purist and uncompromising doctrine who will become eventual guardians of Islam in the coming decades.

In terms of its significance, Darul Uloom is no less than the Eton of Islam. As that leading public school of England that has produced generations of political leaders and British prime ministers, so Darul Uloom is creating an elite cadre of Islamic leaders who will rule the Muslim world. It is offering a classical education and its very name inspires awe among the community that it will one day lead.

The first Darul Uloom or 'House of Knowledge' was set up in Deoband, northern India, in 1866. Nine years after the Indian revolt of 1857, when Muslims and Hindus lost what some regard as the country's first battle for independence from British rulers, a group of Islamic leaders retreated to the Indian village of Deoband in Uttar Pradesh to build a school that would eventually become a global movement. In their mind, it was a fortress of Islamic conservatism and purity in a sea of corruption. Deoband was a place to raise young Muslim men unpolluted by other faiths and modern life. The founding of the school came in the aftermath of the fall of the Mughal Empire after centuries of dominance in south Asia. There was an urgency among Islamic leaders to protect their religious identity from the forces of change sweeping the country under British rule.

In time, Darul Uloom became more than a school. It was a school of thought that would evolve into a global movement based on Sunni Islam that espoused sharia, deplored modernity or Western influence and called for a return to the ways of the Prophet when the faith first began. What started in a small Indian village as a rejection of Western imperialist hegemony was more than 160 years later resonating across the Muslim world.

Darul Uloom's brand of Deobandi Islam has radiated from India's UP to thousands of madrassas across Pakistan and Afghanistan, the Middle East and Africa and into Britain's educational establishment. Its alumni are some of the most important and influential Muslim leaders in the world: imams and scholars who shape the opinion of the *ummah* through sermons and fatwas. Whereas the founding madrassa was seen as relatively moderate, its sister schools on the Af-Pak border had schooled the Taliban. In April 2001, a Deobandi conference was held in Peshawar, Pakistan. Half a million Muslims came from around the world to pay tribute—from

South Asia, Saudi, Libya, Britain, Libya and Taliban-ruled Afghanistan. One Pakistani cleric from Jamiat Ulema-I-Islam said the following to rapturous cheers: 'The ulema graduating from Deoband have served the cause of Islam by opening madrassas to enlighten Muslims and prepare them for jihad.'

The Taliban leader Mullah Omar was a onetime student who attended a Deobandi school on the Af-Pak border, known as the 'university of jihad'. At that same April 2001 conference, months before the seismic events of 9/11, Mullah Omar addressed thousands of followers and mujahideen where he paid tribute to the founding madrassa in India. The original madrassa's vice chancellor, however, spoke of the need for moderation and a pan-Islamist brotherhood. The voice of the alma mater, however, was an isolated one. Talibanized Afghanistan had taken Deobandi teaching and fused it with Islamic militancy to create a society that promised to fight the infidel head on.

After the attack on America later that year, Deobandi Islam found itself under the spotlight. Faced with a backlash, the venerable and secretive founding madrassa in India issued a fatwa condemning terrorism and violence. But by now, the pupil had outgrown the teacher. As these events were unfolding, other Darul Uloom schools were quietly educating children around the world, many funded by Saudi and Gulf state money. In the aftermath of 9/11, as world leaders wrung their hands in grief and searched for answers, the political hierarchy was blind to what was being taught in their own backyards.

Thus one can trace the arc of history from the independence revolt of 1857 in India, to the founding of the madrassa in Deoband in 1866, to the war cry of Mullah Omar in the wilds of Peshawar in 2001, to the tragedy of 9/11 on American soil, to a village in the green suburbs of England in 2010. And not just in England, but in similar villages around the world.

On entering the school in Chislehurst that morning in 2010, I was instructed to remove my shoes and cover my head with a scarf before being led to a bare room overlooking the playing fields.

The boys are allowed to play football and cricket in their spare time but such encouragement of sport is unusual—more orthodox schools frown upon games or any kind of play. The headmaster, Mufti Mustafa, in his 60s, with a grey beard and solemn eyes, greeted with a *salaam*. It was Mufti Mustafa who had the dream of setting up this school in London 20 years ago. He had bought his first premises in Forest Gate, East London, in 1990 before moving to the current site in 1993. His was the second Darul Uloom in Britain—the first was in Bury, Greater Manchester. The Chislehurst site used to be an Army barracks. When the Ministry of Defence decided to sell it, the Mufti struck a deal, buying the complex for £2.7 million.

'As I wrote the cheque and counted off the zero, zero, zero, zero, my friend said to me, "Where will the money come from to run our school?" I told him, "The money will come from Allah." And so it has been.'

The Muslim community raised the money and by 2010 155 boys board there, and the Mufti said there were plans to raise that number to 225. The school charged £2,400 a year, which covered tuition fees, books and meals. It was extraordinarily good value when compared with Farringtons School, a mixed-sex independent boarding school nearby, where annual fees was £17,000.

So where did the money come from, I asked.

'Everywhere. Britain, overseas,' the Mufti said. 'We have donations from around the world, just as our students come from around the world—Britain, America, Pakistan, India, Africa, Saudi.' One businessman in the Midlands even remortgaged his house to give the school £150,000. Unlike other schools in Britain, Darul Uloom offers a classical Islamic education in the mornings and British National Curriculum subjects in the afternoons. The choice of curriculum subjects available is tailored to comply with sharia obligations.

'Our aim to is educate our students in a sharia environment,' Mufti Mustafa told me. 'We teach in the same way as the Deoband madrassa in India, except here we teach the children for GCSEs and A-Levels as well. The English education system doesn't offer this combination.'

The aim of his private school, however, was not to groom students for British universities and then enter mainstream professions. It was for students to devote their lives to Islam by becoming scholars, imams and religious leaders. However, Saiyed Mahmood, an adviser to the school and community liaison officer who showed me around the building, conceded that a number of pupils were drawn to jobs in IT or engineering.

'More important than exams is the learning of the Quran, the Hadith and Islamic law,' said Mufti Mustafa. 'It is the obligation of every Muslim to live according to sharia. 'As Muslims, we're not interested in an education that is simply about getting a job. We're not on Earth for this reason. We live on this Earth merely with a view to the next life.'

Preparing the boys for the afterlife meant having a gruelling timetable in this one. What struck me on entering the school was the discipline. The boys worked long hours, abstained from trivial pleasures; they were polite and dedicated to their work. I met one young boy of about 13 who had already learned the entire Quran.

The day started at 3.45 a.m. when students attended the first of five daily prayer sessions. They returned to their dormitories at 4.30 a.m. to rest for a couple of hours. Breakfast was served at 7.30 a.m. and lessons began at 8.

Throughout the morning, the boys learned how to

read, write and speak Arabic. They also studied Islamic jurisprudence or Fiqh, Tafseer (the translation of the Quran), Hadith and memorized the Quran. Lunch at 12.30 was taken in the assembly hall. Pupils sat cross-legged on the floor, with food served on a white cloth on the ground. I was not permitted to join the students for lunch because women are not allowed.

Instead, I was served lunch in a room alone, with the door closed. The head and his teachers ate separately in the next room. But lunch was not frugal: chicken curry, chickpea rice and chips—an example of Muslim and British fusion.

After prayers, lessons in National Curriculum (NC) subjects began at 1.30 and lasted until 4.30 pm. The subjects deemed acceptable included English, science, IT, history, geography and art. Music, drama and modern foreign languages were banned and deemed un-Islamic. Shakespeare was generally seen as a source of evil because his plays dealt with issues such as love, revenge, adultery, murder and betrayal. However, the school vigorously encouraged IT skills and study of sciences, and it planned to raise millions to build a new science block in the future.

Recreation time lasted until 7 pm but this was a group of boys for whom the iPod, Facebook, mobile phones and Harry Potter novels were banned, along with surfing internet sites other than those approved by imams.

Adviser Saiyed Mahmood explained: 'Music is *haram* for the children. There are things in it that can cause children to go haywire. It is not permitted. As for Facebook, there one can find the good, the bad and the filthy. Our job is to teach the boys morality.'

After more prayers, students revised and did homework until 9 pm when dinner was served. Final prayers were at 10.30 pm and bedtime was 11 pm. The boys' day has lasted almost 20 hours.

I was given a guided tour of the school. There were classrooms on either side of the main corridor, while a larger room was used as a mosque. It was painted green, and light poured in through huge windows to create a feeling of serenity. The classrooms on one side of the corridor contained desks, chairs, computers, whiteboards and overhead projectors.

This was where the students studied National Curriculum subjects in the afternoon. Those on the other side of the corridor contained low-level reading lecterns. These classrooms are used for Islamic studies. The school literally had the two sides of learning—British and Islamic—segregated. Walls in the corridor were lined with posters telling students how to behave by listing the *adab*, or etiquette, for various situations. For example, the *adab* for treatment of parents, leaders and elders said: 'Never show disrespect. Obey all lawful things, be humble, polite and do not raise the voice.' Another circular outlined a three-strikes policy for children who disobeyed.

If any child got three 'bad lives' over the course of a fortnight, he faced detention at the weekend. If a boy's room was unclean, or he was absent from lessons or prayers, that was three lives.

Scrutiny of madrassas intensified after the 9/11 attacks. Mufti Mustafa said the British media portrayed Islam as a religion of violence and terror and stressed that his school's message offered the truth about Islam—a message of tolerance and peace. Indeed his school instilled the kind of old-fashioned discipline and respect for elders of which many British headteachers would be proud.

The code of behaviour was exemplary. Unlike some other Darul Uloom schools, the Mufti at Chislehurst had worked hard to connect with the local community, inviting locals to tea and setting up competitions where non-Muslim children from other schools were invited to send in projects on Islam.

The winners were awarded prizes at a special ceremony

held once a year. He showed me some of the competition entries—beautiful pieces of work, lovingly created and showing a genuine interest in the faith and its people.

None of the winning entries discussed issues such as sharia's rulings on capital punishment or women's rights. 'Our Quran teaches us to respect the earlier prophets and the earlier revelations of the Bible and Torah,' the Mufti told me. 'If you do not believe in Jesus or Moses, you cannot be a true Muslim.'

Indeed, posters depicted the 25 prophets, including both Christian and Jewish names, as well as Mohammed.

Darul Uloom in India also emphasizes the importance of religious tolerance, a message of Islam that has been lost along the line for some. When I visited the founding madrassa for global Deobandism in India in the early 2000s I was told that respect for the people of the earlier books, the Jews and the Christians, was something that the Prophet himself had spoken of. I was shown the library at the founding madrassa, a hushed temple of learning filled with books on Islam, as expected, but also a glass-topped cabinet containing their prized copies of the Torah, the Bible, the Ramayana, holy books of the other world faiths. It reinforced the message that had been given to me throughout my five-day stay there: 'There is one God, but many paths.'

That message was lost and corrupted as Deobandi Islam travelled to the more hardline madrassas along the Afghanistan and Pakistan border, where Mullah Omar and his Taliban learned a very different variant of the faith.

And in Chislehurst, again, I found limits to the founding message of tolerance. While children from local state schools were invited to come inside and learn about Islam, Darul Uloom pupils were not permitted to enter a church or synagogue, as it would be seen as *haram*. I asked the Mufti why many thought these schools were linked to fundamentalism among some young British Muslims. He said while Deobandi Muslims believed in the sharia way, they also understood it could not be adopted by a country that was not an Islamic state. As for extremism, he replied: 'We're not here for that reason. Jihad. We don't get involved in politics. Two officers from the Metropolitan Police came here to find out my views on Iraq and I said to them, 'Look. This is a school. We have no interest in politics. We're interested in education. What goes on outside, we don't know.'

'What did they say?'

'They said to me, "What about student politics?" I told them the same answer I'm telling you. My boys aren't interested in Afghanistan or Iraq. We live here surrounded by non-Muslims. Our duty is to explain our way of life. That's our mission.'

After the Mufti left the room, I met a number of hand-picked interviewees.

One pupil, Hasan, 16, was careful to give formulaic replies. 'We're here to acquire knowledge of our religion, to teach Islam to the community and benefit the world,' he told me several times.

But Muhammad Hussain, who taught GCSE Arabic at the school, was more illuminating. He explained why he came to the school: 'I wanted to be a better Muslim. I can do that here rather than in a state school.'

What about fears of radicalism? He admitted young Muslims were politically aware and the subject came up regularly: 'Students are not blind to what some of these radicals are preaching. They claim this is true Islam. We have to counter that view.'

Saiyed Mahmood claimed that Muslims were now all viewed as terrorists or fanatics. The only way to change minds was through engagement. 'I was walking through Chislehurst the other day and two boys shouted, "Oi! Are you Bin Laden?" I said, 'Yes.' Then they laughed, came over and started to chat. In society, everyone's different. Some are doctors, some are geniuses and a tiny minority are fanatics. It's the same with our community.'

The school in Chislehurst is one of the more benign in the Darul Uloom family. But there is evidence that others are less so. In 2009, think-tank Civitas conducted the first major analysis of Islamic schools in Britain. Report author Dr Denis MacEoin said that younger British Muslims were more hardline than their elders, partly because such schools encouraged a separatist mentality.

'These schools are about producing more imams, more muftis. Their teaching is based on a 7th century system. Very few secular subjects are taught and the aim is to prepare them not for life in the wider world, but to give them an existence inside the Muslim world.'

His research showed many of the Darul Uloom schools in Britain resisted cultural integration. Instead, sharia values on issues such as women's rights, segregation of men and women, and capital punishment were being inculcated in children from a young age.

'It means no child attending a Muslim school of this kind will ever visit a gallery, attend a concert of classical or non-classical music, pass an evening mesmerized by *Romeo and Juliet* performed by the National Ballet. No Muslim girl will ever become a ballerina,' wrote Dr MacEoin.

(Actually, he was wrong about that one. In 2016 news reports and photos were published of the world's first hijab-wearing ballerina, a 14-year-old Muslim girl from Australia. Stephanie Kurlow is a convert and looked fierce and elegant in her petrol blue hijab and long draped tutu. She hoped to become the first professional hijab-wearing ballet dancer in the world. It was an example of a mindset among some younger Muslims who are rooted in multi-culturalism and proud of their faith.)

It is a question of attitude. I looked up a couple of the Darul Uloom alumni to see where they have ended up. One of their finest now runs a website called MuftiSays.com, which he describes as 'one of the fruits of Darul Uloom'. The advice given is far from the tolerant ethos espoused by Mufti Mustafa. One Muslim asked if it would be acceptable to attend a wedding in a church, synagogue or temple. 'Such places are the gathering places of devils,' was the answer. In another exchange, a student of aeronautical engineering asked if it would be OK to work for a Western defence company to 'gain knowledge that would be useful for the defence needs of the Ummah'. The answer from MuftiSays was: 'This is permissible.'

These are not the most extreme views given by Deobandi alumni. The leading voice in Britain is Riyadh ul Haq, a graduate of the Darul Uloom school in Bury. Aged 36, he is seen as the dominant influence on Deobandi mosques in Britain, which account for 600 of Britain's 1,400 mosques. His sermons are often inflammatory. On Jews, he has said: 'They're all the same. They've monopolized everything: the Holocaust, God, money, interest, usury, the world economy, the media, political institutions...they monopolized tyranny and oppression as well. And injustice.' And on integrating in Britain he has said: 'We are in a very dangerous position here. We live among the kuffar [unbelievers]...And anyone who thinks that they can work with the kuffar, associate with them, mix with them, stand and sit with them, move among them and not be affected, is in denial and is a liar to himself.'

Ul Haq is not only the leading voice of the Deobandis in Britain, he is invited around the world to speak, where he openly attacks British culture, Jews, Christians and homosexuals. He is an example of the most extreme face of the Darul Uloom culture, his voice louder than the clerics in India who have issued a fatwa against terrorism and a plea for tolerance.

Critics of Darul Uloom schools in Britain warn that it is time for the government to wake up to the reality of what goes on in the world of the madrassas, where the democratic, liberal way of life is deemed incompatible with that of the orthodox Muslim. Dr MacEoin, himself an Arabic scholar, argues that the British schools watchdog Ofsted often visits such schools and gives them glowing reports, focusing merely on their academic results and not the ethos of separatism.

'Again and again we are finding youngsters are becoming more hardline than their parents,' he said. 'It's the opposite of what we expect as these boys are British-born and bred... Part of the answer lies with these schools. Deobandi is geared up to shape the Muslim leadership of tomorrow. That's why this matters.'

When I visited Chislehurst's Darul Uloom I found it was interacting with the local community and working hard to build bridges. Its reputation with locals was exemplary, said Bromley police, while Ofsted ranked it as a 'good school with some aspects outstanding'.

These religious schools are now part of the fabric of Britain's education system, and there is much to admire in the more moderate examples: the instilling of respect, hard work, discipline and dedication to scholarship. There is also the central tenet of the Quran: a duty to one another, the *ummah*.

Those are values that are cherished within wider society and are much needed beyond the walls of the school. Yet such schools are focused less on integration and more on isolationism. The risk lies in allowing such schools to become islands of orthodox Islam within Britain. To avoid tomorrow's generation of Muslims retreating into a separate world, greater integration and a respect for core British values is key. Some of these values chime with the values taught within these schools, as we have seen and surely this is room for hope.

When I spent a week at the founding madrassa in India in 2005, it was the first time they had allowed a woman to stay onsite. Ironically, I found it more open and more tolerant than some of the sister schools in Britain. While staying at the campus in India, I was given a gift: a rare copy of the two-volume history of Darul Uloom or the House of Knowledge. Inside was a quote dating from 1866, from the founder of the Darul Uloom movement, Qasim al-Ulum, who received a vision from Allah in a dream to set up a school where Muslims could learn, untainted by other faiths. Much like the mufti in Chislehurst, all those centuries on, Qasim al-Ulum described the dream that would start a journey, a school and a movement: 'I am standing on the roof of the Noble House of Allah and canals are flowing from the fingers of my hands and feet and are expanding in all directions of the world.'

That 150-year-old dream is now a reality in Britain and around the world, the waters of knowledge of Deobandi Islam flow into the hearts and minds of children everywhere. Darul Uloom is controlling the way many British Muslim children think and it will inform the way they view the world and other people of faith as adults. It is shaping their future relations with the rest of society.

Seven years after my visit to Chislehurst's Darul Uloom, such schools have grown in number and there is a greater understanding of the influence madrassas hold in Britain's Muslim community. The government has shifted towards demanding registration of *all* Islamic schools in the country, closer monitoring of what is taught and whether it is consistent with British values. Before Prime Minister David Cameron resigned after the Brexit vote in June 2016, he addressed the issue of madrassas head on in a speech to the Tory Party Conference in which he said such schools should be open to inspectors, just like any other in Britain. He feared in a few cases children were 'having their heads filled with poison and their hearts filled with hate'. Teachers who taught religious intolerance should be removed, he said. The move sparked anger in some Muslim quarters and was branded an attempt by the state to interfere in matters of religion. The Northern Council of Mosques, which represents 400 places of worship, said this 'encroached' on religious freedom itself.

Britain is a good example to examine a democracy that has a widespread base of Islamic schools. Here, the government woke up late to the risks of turning a blind eye to what happens inside madrassas and now, in its newfound zeal to address the issue of radicalization in schools, it risks going too far. In 2015, the government launched an initiative aimed at empowering *all* schools and other educational institutions to prevent the radicalization of children. It placed a legal duty, under Section 26 of the Counter Terrorism and Security Act of 2015, on all education professionals to protect young minds. This is known as the 'prevent duty'. The law states that they must have 'due regard to the need to prevent people from being drawn into terrorism'.

Schools comply by offering training to staff on the 'prevent strategy'. Many Muslims fear it has led to a culture of fear, of spying—people being reported to the police for their political views. Public sector teachers, workers as well as those in independent schools and other establishments dealing with children are now being asked to act as informants. They are given several hours of training on how to spot the potential signs of radicalization, and if a child is suspected, he or she must be referred to the government's de-radicalization programme called Channel.

Both Prevent and Channel are rapidly losing the faith of the Muslim community. There is concern that the strategy may be stoking fear and stigmatisation of Muslims. There is also the worry that such targeting could make young Muslims feel alienated and *more* likely to be radicalized. The number of referrals has jumped exponentially. In 2015, almost 4,000 people were reported to Channel, triple the number of 2014. That is 11 people a day, according to figures published by the National Police Chief Council under the Freedom of Information Act.

Newspaper reports in national newspapers say the net of suspicion has been cast wide, even over nursery children. One case is cited of a 4-year-old boy who was threatened with being reported by his teachers because they thought he said the words 'cooker bomb'. The child was trying to say 'cucumber'. In another incident, a 14-year-old was quizzed over his answers in a French lesson where he spoke of eco-terrorism. His name was given to Channel. His story is not a rarity.

Some MPs in Britain fear that the programme has become counter productive. Two teachers a day now call the government radicalization hotline and such is the concern that teaching unions are asking for the government to think again. The training of teachers under the Prevent programme sometimes veers close to scaremongering. In one exercise, 20 teachers are sat around a video screen in a music room in a Bristol school, as a DVD intones, 'If I hadn't intervened [ominous music playing], this might have ended very differently.' It presents the story of a teacher who has reported his student for writing an essay he is not comfortable with, but the exact content is not specified. He tells the camera that the girl was 'struggling to fit in and not sure, culturally, where she belonged...I am not suggesting she was going to support terrorism, but the opportunity was there if someone wanted to push her down that path'.

The quote could apply to any angst-ridden teenager and yet some Muslim children are being subjected to horrendous assumptions.

When the clip is over, a woman comes forward and tells the group: 'We're not asking you to spy but to look out for troubling behaviour.' She is Kalsoor Bashir, co-director of Inspire, which works with the government on counter terrorism under the Prevent strategy.

Prevent is in danger of becoming Provoke. It has the whiff of Communist East Germany's Stasi or the informant culture of Mao's China. How long before children will be asked to inform on one another or their families or submit self-criticisms? Prevent is supposed to be about winning the war for hearts and minds and yet it is becoming part of a culture of suspicion that stalks the Muslim community at a time of rising Islamophobia. In July 2016, 280 British academics, lawyers and public figures signed a letter that warned this policy would divide communities, silence legitimate dissent and free speech.

The fear of radicalization and terrorism is real. However, fuelling fear and alienating yet more young Muslims is not the answer. We must separate the poisonous ideology from the individual and it is a delicate line to tread. Other countries have shown where there is persecution, alienation and abuse of rights of religious groups, there is fertile breeding ground for radicalism. So countries like Britain must stamp out intolerant beliefs while defending tolerance towards its citizens, regardless of faith.

One place to begin is to monitor foreign funding of schools to ensure they comply 100% with the laws of democracies and the rights of all therein. Any foreign funding must be declared and registered. Such institutions must be subject to monitoring to ensure that they comply with democratic values and encouraged to use imams and scholars who are tolerant of liberal values. The protection of freedom, equality and opportunity is enshrined in democracies. In a world undergoing seismic change, these values remain the best defence.

SHARIA UK

> 'If what we want socially is a pattern of relations in which a plurality of diverse and overlapping affiliations work for a common good, and in which groups of serious and profound conviction are not systematically faced with the stark alternatives of cultural loyalty or state loyalty, [sharia] seems unavoidable.'
>
> —Archbishop of Canterbury Rowan Williams, advocating sharia law in Britain in 2008 in a speech at the Royal Courts of Justice

In 2008, the Archbishop of Canterbury, the head of the Church of England and a man universally respected for his liberalism and judgement, provoked uncharacteristic outrage across the country when he told an audience of 1000 people at the Royal Courts of Justice that Britain must accept some form of sharia as many Muslims did not relate to the British system of law. Muslims could not be expected to choose between nation and faith. His speech was a landmark lecture on civil and religious law in which he said a move towards sharia was inevitable. The Prime Minister's Number 10 rebuttal unit went into overdrive to insist that British law was based on British values and there would be one law for all. When the fury subsided, one thing quickly became clear: the Archbishop was right about inevitability. Sharia was happening already; it was part of the lives of millions of ordinary Muslims across Britain.

Leyton, East London, July 2009

In a nondescript converted sweetshop in East London, a group of burka-clad women sit in a waiting room, for an appointment with Dr Suhaib Hasan at his twice-weekly surgery.

The women look worried. There's no talking in the airless reception area, the only sound is a fan purring in the corner as temperatures outside exceed 80F. Inside, the atmosphere is just as stifling, with no magazines, television or other diversions. The beige walls are bare except for a flow-chart depicting the process of securing a Muslim divorce, and a picture of Mecca.

It might look like a doctor's surgery but within these walls lies the nerve centre of sharia law in Britain: the headquarters of the Islamic Sharia Council, which oversees the growing number of Muslim courts operating in Britain. For the first time, the Council has granted access to an outsider to observe the entire sharia legal process in Britain. Over several weeks, I was allowed to witness the filing of complaints, individual testimony hearings and the monthly meeting of imams, or judges, where rulings are handed down. It is a window into a world unknown to most Britons.

Sharia has been operating here in parallel to the British legal system since 1982. Work includes issuing fatwas—religious rulings on matters ranging from why Islam considers homosexuality a sin to why two women are equivalent to one male witness in an Islamic court. The Islamic Sharia Council also rules on individual cases, primarily in matters of Muslim personal or civil law: divorce, marriage, inheritance and settlement of dowry payments are the most common.

However, in the course of my investigation, I discovered how sharia is being used informally within the Muslim community to tackle crime such as gang fights or stabbings, bypassing police and the British court system.

A few hardline leaders would like it to be taken even further. One told me that Britain should adopt sharia punishments such as stoning and the chopping off of hands to reduce violent crime. There are 12 councils or courts operating in Britain under Dr Hasan's group, based in London, Birmingham, Manchester, Rotherham and Bradford. Scores more imams dispense justice through their own mosques.

A study in 2009 by the thinktank Civitas claimed that there could be as many as 85 sharia courts in Britain, although Dr Hasan says most of these are not formal courts. But undoubtedly it is a growing network. In his courts, support staff interview plaintiffs and compile a case study. Judgments are delivered by senior imams at closed monthly meetings and are sent in writing to the concerned parties. Up to 7,000 cases have been handled till 2009, when I meet Dr Hasan.

The Islamic Sharia Council is listed as a charity but people seeking a divorce, or *talaq*, must fill in a form and pay a fee. For a man it is £100; for women, it is £250 because the imams say it takes more work to process a woman's application as her word has to be corroborated. How this sits with Britain's sex discrimination laws, no one says.

The literal meaning of sharia is 'source of water in the desert', meaning the source of all spiritual life for Muslims. This is not just a code of law, but a way of life and like water it must permeate everything, washing away impurities. In sharia-based countries, such as Saudi Arabia or the old Taliban-ruled Afghanistan, crimes against society are punished by beheadings, stoning to death and amputations. Women are kept in purdah and mostly limited to child-rearing and caring for the home. Alcohol, music, dance, television and movies are forbidden. Anything that deviates from the rigid prescription for Islamic life from the days of the Prophet in the 7th century is considered to be *haram*.

In Britain, sharia courts are permitted to rule only in civil cases, such as divorce and financial disputes. Until last year, these rulings depended on voluntary compliance among Muslims. But now, due to a clause in the Arbitration Act 1996, they are enforceable by county and high courts. Sharia courts are classified in the same way as arbitration tribunals—with rulings binding in law, provided both parties in the dispute agree to give these courts the power to rule on their case.

However, a Muslim couple must still be divorced in the British courts for it to be recognized under British law. The same provision in the Arbitration Act applies to Jewish Beth Din courts, which resolve similar civil cases.

Dr Hasan is the man who introduced sharia courts to Britain almost 30 years ago. The softly spoken, grey-bearded scholar was born in Pakistan, studied in Saudi Arabia and worked in East Africa before moving to Britain in the 1960s. He is the Secretary of the Islamic Sharia Council of Britain and a member of the senior panel of imams who sit once a month at the grandly beautiful Regent's Park Mosque in central London. We are worlds apart and I find little to agree with in what he says and yet there is a gentleness in him that I take to despite our differences. He is no doubt sincere in his belief that his message will bring people closer to God, and his industrious schedule is arduous for an old man.

In the rather basic conditions of the Leyton office, Dr Hasan calls the women into his office to begin a private session to gather evidence. It is similar to a closed court setting and while the setting is modest, its proceedings have all the gravity of a British courtroom. Most cases are conducted in English. Under Muslim law, a man can divorce his wife simply by uttering the word '*talaq*' thrice, but a woman cannot be granted a divorce without the consent of her husband or winning a dissolution of the marriage from the imam. Even if the couple is divorced under British law, they remain married in Islam until divorced under the religious law, too.

Dr Hasan believes that far from trampling on women's rights, the Islamic Sharia Council is empowering Muslim women in Britain, giving them a way out of abusive and violent marriage. Sitting behind a plywood desk, flanked by shelves of books on Islamic law and copies of the Quran, Dr Hasan hears evidence from an Afghan woman called Ameena (her name has been changed for her protection). She claims her husband is violent towards her and their five children, and she wants a divorce. Ameena, 35, is backed by the testimony of two social workers, one of whom is Muslim, from a women's refuge.

'He beats me and the children, he doesn't give us our rights, he doesn't love me or the children and he is not interested in me and the children,' she says, also citing her husband's 'mental behaviour'. The couple had entered an arranged marriage in the sand-blown city of Kandahar and came to Britain as refugees from war. Some years later the marriage faltered.

Dr Hasan's sparely written notes set out the extent of the marital misery: 'He beat her. Then he asked her to massage his shoulders and legs. When she said no, he beat her.

'One time her nose was broken and an operation was carried out. Another day, because of the beating, there was a miscarriage.'

Ameena's evidence is corroborated by statements from one of her daughters: the teenager has said that as well as hitting her mother and the children, the father, who is in his 40s, forced her into an arranged marriage in Pakistan. She wants her marriage dissolved, too.

So far Ameena's husband has refused to grant her a divorce, accusing her and his daughter of being 'not mentally fit'. Dr Hasan decides the case, which has been going on since 2008, is sufficiently serious to merit the consideration of the monthly meeting of senior judges at Regent's Park Mosque. Now Ameena's future lies in their hands.

Later that week, seven imams gather in a bare committee room in the shadows of the mosque's magnificent golden dome. Seated around a rectangular table set with mineral water, a bowl of fruit and a box of Fox's luxury biscuits, they go through the various cases. I am permitted to watch from a distance. To the casual observer, it may appear like a rather dry council planning committee meeting. But these men are in effect running a legal system that critics fear could fragment the legal framework in Britain. Laws that once ruled supreme in Kabul under the Taliban are now being enforced in cities across Britain.

It becomes clear that Ameena's story of violence, abandonment and difficulty in securing an Islamic divorce is not isolated. Several other cases during the meeting detail claims of 'terrifying abuse', including one where a gun was placed against a woman's head, and another where a man tried to strangle his wife and children.

If the husband has disputed his wife's word, the court demands that her account be corroborated by other witnesses, preferably male as more credence is given to their testimony. If the wife refuses to agree to give the husband access to their children, even in cases of possible child abuse, the divorce is stalled until that issue is resolved.

In another case, the imams agree a husband has treated the wife badly, beating her and their children and leaving them without support once he had been granted legal status to remain in Britain. 'He ran away and left the family, and the children began to hate the father,' says one of the imams.

The man signed a petition for a civil divorce but had so far refused to allow a divorce under Islam. The imams discuss the division of assets between the couple, including any dowry jewelry. They also decide to contact the husband one last time—if he fails to respond, he risks a dissolution.

Ameena's case is then raised and it is decided that her husband will be given another opportunity to respond. If all efforts to reconcile fail, then the marriage might be dissolved, but it remains unclear who will care for the children. Under Islamic law, a child over seven usually goes to the father unless he, the father, agrees otherwise. Thus Ameena's fate remains in limbo and her suffering and that of the children continues.

The following week I accompany Dr Hasan into enemy territory: he has been asked to speak to a group of female students in East London about sharia. The audience is made up of educated, articulate feminists, both Muslim and non-Muslim, and I fear for him.

He begins simply enough and tells the women his organization is concerned with implementing sharia law in Muslim personal legal cases and that 90% of the clients are women seeking a divorce. The women nod appreciatively. Then he explains that sharia is about preserving the dignity, health and honour of the individuals. The nodding continues. Confident, Dr Hasan tells them that in every part of the world, there can be only one authority.

'In Britain, the ultimate authority is the Prime Minister. In an army, it is the commander-in-chief. On the bus, it is the bus driver. And in the house, the smallest unit of society, sharia says authority must be with the man to maintain the house. The woman's duties are much harsher. Biologically, she differs,' he says. Her duties, according to him, lie with cleaning and childcare.

The mood turns black as Dr Hasan continues that under Islam, the woman is seen as someone who needs the protection of a man. In matters of divorce, the right of ending a marriage lies with the man because 'women have emotions, whereas a man thinks first before he speaks'.

At this, one white woman berates Dr Hasan. 'If you had said these things about a Jew or a black person, it would be totally unacceptable. Yet you think it is OK to say women are inferior. I cannot listen to this without making a stand.'

Another woman, an African Muslim professor, adds: 'In my house, my husband and I look after each other. It is an equal partnership. I don't need anyone to protect me.' Applause ripples through the audience.

Dr Hasan tries again to make them understand and decides that a cooking metaphor might help: 'The law is like curry—the different elements help improve the flavour,' he ventures.

An hour later, after receiving a tongue lashing from London's feminist finest, Dr Hasan emerges from the meeting exhausted and in shock. He has been attacked verbally but physically he is unscathed and for that he is grateful. As we walk together back to the tube, he tells me that virtually all the imams in the UK are trained either in madrassas or religious schools in India and Pakistan, or are graduates of Islamic universities, such as Al-Azhar in Egypt. And he insists their work is not an attempt to bypass the British legal system; the Islamic Sharia Council does not seek to extend its powers beyond divorce, marriage, dowry and inheritance cases.

'Muslim personal law can be accommodated within the British legal system. In the divorce process, if the British courts recognize Muslim divorce, then there would be no need for us to apply for a divorce through the UK system.'

He refuses to accept that there is an inherent conflict between sharia and British law in areas such as equality for women and human rights.

'The problem with the feminist movement is they don't

listen to the other side,' he observes gravely, stroking his beard. I am not sure he is aware that a woman still stands beside him.

I ask if he believes sharia is the best code of law.

'We cannot ask for sharia in Britain for criminal cases,' he concludes. 'For that to take place, the State needs to support sharia and I recognize Britain does not. People say it is harsh, but we say it's a deterrent. In Saudi Arabia very few hands are cut. People will not commit the crime as they know the punishment is so horrible, unlike the UK system where people are jailed and the prison system does not work.' (I haven't had occasion to meet this gentle-eyed imam after that 2009 meeting, or we could have debated the deterrence value of beheadings and amputations: in 2015, advocacy groups like Amnesty International reported that the number of beheadings in Saudi Arabia was 157, the highest in two decades.)

Despite the feminists' fury, Dr Hasan is a relative moderate on the subject. Some hardliners want Islamic law to be extended to all criminal cases, ranging from knife crime and robbery to rape and under-age sex. One such figure is Sarfraz Sarwar, leader of the Basildon Islamic Centre in Essex. His views have attracted controversy—his mosque was torched three times and eventually destroyed, and his home has also been attacked. He tells me the windows of his living room are smashed every six months but the police have never caught the perpetrators. He now leaves the windows permanently broken in defiance.

Mr Sarwar insists sharia should be adopted to address rising crime in Britain. 'The British legal system is fair, but it's also very sweet for criminals,' he tells me. 'Sharia is the ultimate deterrent. If you commit a crime and you're punished by sharia, you won't commit it again. But if we praise anything from Islam, people jump down our throat.'

When I suggest that many people in Britain would find some of sharia's provisions extreme and difficult to accept, he agrees. 'We need to adapt sharia for British law. We could use some of the more moderate measures.'

Such as?

'Child abuse, under-age sex, teenage pregnancy, for example.'

I ask what the penalty would be for under-age sex.

'You won't like it. But sharia says if they're caught doing it, you stone the woman.'

Mr Sarwar's other suggestion is to adapt the 'three strikes' policy on crime. Instead of being jailed on the third conviction, a criminal could face having a hand chopped off.

'That would fit in with the way of life here,' he says brightly. 'I'm not being extreme. This has to be used in *moderation*, for serious crimes, not petty robbery. In this country, people get away with murder.'

He refuses to accept the notion that values of human rights are enshrined in the British way of life and demurs that history says otherwise.

'In Victorian days they applied sharia. They held people in stocks—there were public floggings, hangings. Why not go back to it? What's the big beef now? Too many goody-two-shoes talking about human rights.'

Mr Sarwar adds that the violence and intimidation he has faced will not silence him. 'I am not a sheep. I am a British Muslim. I pay my taxes, I obey the law. People break my windows but I say to you, why can't we mix and match? Take the best from both worlds. The law is like a curry. Different elements improve the flavour. Why not help improve the law of this country with elements of sharia?'

I imagine in some past Grand Conference of imams and muftis, there must have been a decision taken to use the 'curry' analogy to sell sharia to sceptics.

The effort to push sharia into new realms is already happening with certain Muslim communities, regardless of whether the mainstream likes it. The Somali community in Britain has long relied on the sharia principle of mediation and arbitration in criminal cases. Saynab Muhamad, leader of the Somali Family Support Centre and one of the few prominent females in the Somali community, tells me how sharia law was used to resolve the case of knife attacks among teenagers a few years ago. The family of one victim and the attacker came together under Somali elders and an informal hearing decided that the victim should be compensated by the attacker, who in turn would be forgiven for the crime. The police were not involved and the matter was settled amicably. In Somali Muslim culture, after a conflict or crime is committed, a hearing is held. The judge, or *quadi*, will act as arbitrator, rectify the crime and reconcile the two sides.

'In Somalia, the victim would forgive and then be compensated with camels, say 100 camels,' says Saynab. 'Here it would be with money. Sharia is embedded in our society and it has worked well to tackle problems here, too.'

She believes this way of getting community elders involved and taking direct control is more effective than simply relying on the courts, and if the British police wished to attend the hearings, they would be welcome. For her, this is an example of how the sharia way has been adapted successfully to the British way of life. But critics remain unconvinced and see it as the route to a two-tier legal system, pointing out that under sharia, the law is heavily rigged against women.

Early in 2009, Keith Porteous Wood, director of campaign group One Law for All and the National Secular Society, raised the issue with European Commission President Jose Manuel Barroso, in Brussels. Hitting out at the use of Muslim arbitration tribunals, he said: 'Women are particularly vulnerable as they're forced to submit to these tribunals and Islamic law treats women less favourably than men. It's essential that it is one law for all in every country and that the law is democratically established and human rights compliant. Sharia fails that test.'

The subject of sharia is personal and capable of arousing deep passions in the community—inextricably linked as it is with Muslim identity and sense of honour. And on the subject of honour, there has been a growing call from women of all faiths to protect Muslim girls and women from forced marriages and so-called 'honour killings' if they fail to comply with the family wishes. The tenets of the sharia legal framework are in these ways superseding the rights of the individual at the most basic level: the right to love, the right to live. Partial acceptance of some laws of sharia makes the fight on issues such as 'honour killings' much harder.

However, it is clear that despite criticism, many conservative British Muslim women rely on sharia courts as a way out of an unhappy marriage that is consistent with their faith. Without these courts they would remain trapped in abusive or violent marriages as they would not turn to the British court system for relief. For these practicing Muslim women, sharia is their only path to freedom.

The women I met were unwilling to talk directly about their cases. Apart from divorce being deeply personal, a failed marriage is often seen as a source of shame in their communities and the very idea of bypassing sharia and seeking a divorce solely in the British courts would bring far more disgrace to a family's social standing.

But while sharia gives Muslim women a chance to escape unhappy marriages, it fails to grant them equal status—they are considered inferior to men as witnesses, they have unequal status in divorce and the dividing of marital assets and custody of the children. Abuse or violence by the husband is not tackled by the British courts but informally through these hearings and it is all too easy to sweep under the prayer rug the sorrows of a thousand women.

Back at the office in Leyton, I prepare to meet another of the senior Islamic judges. The office staff are cheering on Andy Murray at Wimbledon, a scene being played out across the country and I watch as veiled heads and beards swivel back and forth, tracking play. In a back room, Sheik Haitham Al-Haddad, one of the most senior imams in Britain, sits in a large chair, looking every inch the harsh executor of judgement. Tennis is far from his mind as he contemplates the fundamental split between religion and state. He believes it is inevitable that a dual system will prevail, even in Western democracies despite an inherent tension between two ways of life.

'There is a conflict between these two sets of values,' he concedes. 'Muslims believe our values are best. The non-Islamic British believe theirs are better. But at the end of the day, understand this: Muslims are never going to give up certain principles, even if they are in conflict. That is a fact.'

Sharia law in Britain is here to stay and may even spread. But it's a perilous tightrope we tread—the line between multicultural tolerance and the sanctity of one law for all and for the rights of the individual.

Equality before the law for all, regardless of sex, race or religion, is one of Britain's enduring principles. It is now firmly enshrined in our legal code that has evolved over centuries to reflect the pluralist democracy Britain has become. Similar, and even more progressive, laws are central to other modern, liberal democracies across the globe. But sharia sees modernity as the weed-ridden pathway to an immoral society. And yet, we must all co-exist. That is one of the greatest challenges our world faces today.

Within hours of my story on sharia in Britain being published in 2009 in the *Mail on Sunday* newspaper, I received a phone call on my mobile from a prominent radical imam who shall remain nameless. I took the call upstairs, away from my family making lunch, as he began to unload a volley of abuse down the line, followed by threats. The article was not to his satisfaction. I asked him if any fact or quote was wrong and he conceded it was factually accurate and yet he was enraged. As we argued back and forth, he told me he would issue a fatwa on the internet against me. I told him that if in true conscience as a devout Muslim he wished to do that and be judged by God, I could not stop him. He paused, furious no doubt at having to argue with a woman and a kaffir at that. And then, as the threats subsided and his rage dimmed, he became quiet, almost peaceful and said something that struck me at the time with greater force. He meant every softly uttered word; for him it was no longer a threat, but a promise:

'You people think you can stop us? You kaffirs think articles like this will stop us getting what we want? We will not rest. We will not rest until sharia is spread across the world. I tell you solemnly, there'll come a time when the flag of Islam will fly above Downing Street itself.'

He never did issue the fatwa. But radical would not rest, that much was true. In 2015 as Europe was convulsed by terrorist attacks on its home soil, I heard that last phrase again when ISIS issued a statement that one day the black flag of the Islamic State would fly over Rome. It took me back to that phone call on a Sunday morning in 2009.

Today the spread of sharia is a topic of national debate in Britain, Europe and Asia for Muslims and non-Muslims alike. The debate is out in the open and in some cases combative. In March 2011, Haitham Al Haddad wrote an open letter to the then Prime Minister David Cameron in which he made it disrespectfully clear that sharia would never come second to the law of the land. British laws and values may change, but sharia was eternal: 'Muslims will not be bullied by "muscular liberalism" into compromising on their teachings and the principles of their faith as Christiandom and others may have done, nor will we be forced to embrace values that oppose the faith of millions of Muslims in Britain, Europe and the world over. Interpretations of British values change as governments do, and what may be in keeping with liberal values may be completely unacceptable to our belief...'

What is the immutable sharia and where does it come from? It is a law that derives mainly from the Quran, the *hadith* or sayings and ways of the Prophet, and fatwas, which are rulings of Islamic scholars on any number of subjects affecting a Muslim's life. For the Muslim, sharia is a code of laws that protects their faith and the *ummah* and for them its strictures are not emasculating of freedoms, but the path of the divine. For some conservative Muslim converts, the literalism of sharia liberates them from personal responsibility, telling them how to behave down to the most prosaic detail.

It is believed by those who follow sharia that life sets out many paths and yet only one is clear and true and that is the path of sharia. Its meaning is redolent with water: purity, clarity; and just as water is vital for human survival, so sharia is essential for the soul and mind. Under sharia, there are five categories of human actions: obligatory, recommended, permitted, disliked and forbidden or *haram*.

When one reads the requirements of sharia, away from the penal punishments and inequalities first set out 1300 years ago, there are things that resonate with our own values and these are the things that Archbishop Williams spoke of in his 2008 lecture. Yet in the unyielding doctrines of Wahhabism and Deobandism, these are often underplayed, overshadowed or totally ignored:

* To ensure the preservation of human life
* To promote sound intellect and knowledge and abhor that which weakens it, for intellect is the source of morality.
* To support oneself and one's dependents
* To ensure fair dealing and justice in commerce and transactions with others.
* To forbid the taking of life.

These are great values for all humanity. The difficulty arises in sharia's pre-medieval punishments such as death by stoning, hanging, amputations, lashes and beheadings', its views on women being lesser persons to men, its refusal to acknowledge the existence of homosexuality except as a sinful deviance, and other such laws and prescriptions. A sharia pick-and-mix approach to law is not an intellectually and morally satisfactory solution for many. Yet there is division among Islamic scholars about the above punishments and only the most hardline Islamic societies enforce these 7th century methods.

Clearly, there is scope for greater understanding and dialogue, as Archbishop Rowan Williams and many others ask for. However, the hardline Wahabbi and Deobandi forms of Islam found in Britain are espousing the kind of sharia found in few other countries outside places like Saudi Arabia. In 2016, Professor Elham Manea of Zurich University published a study of the sharia courts of Britain and found that the rulings, typically rooted in Wahhabi and Deobandi doctrine, were more extreme here than in Islamic nations like Pakistan.

After four years of investigation of 80 Muslim arbitration councils in Britain, she discovered clerics who ignored marital rape, condoned wife beatings and believed girls of 12 and 13 were old enough to marry. Professor Manea's conclusion was that sharia was being used to 'legitimize systematic discrimination against women and children'.

As a human rights specialist her views carried weight. In December 2015, Theresa May, the then Home Secretary and now Prime Minister of Britain, ordered an independent review into the application of sharia law in the UK, as part of a wider counter extremism strategy. When May was Home Secretary she was aware of the impact of sharia on women who were 'divorced', left in penury or denied rights. She saw cases of women forced to return to abusive husbands. It moved her to action. 'There is one rule of law in our country,' she declared, 'which provides rights and security for every citizen.'

Yet she was mindful that in the multicultural mix that is Britain, people of different faiths and practices followed their own religious codes and society needed to find a way to ensure that the best of these codes and practices could benefit all. The hope is that the inquiry she has commissioned is the first step to achieving this.

In the summer of 2016, as ISIS waged its worst war on capitals around the world, the American Pew Research Center published a major study on Muslims and Islam around the world. It reported that Islam is now the second largest religion in the world after Christianity, with 1.6 billion followers. By the close of this century it will be the most dominant religion on the planet, based on current demographic trends. Most Muslims live in Asia and the Middle East, 10% live in Europe and less than 1% in the US (a revelaing statistic, given Trump's scaremongering about a Muslim 'invasion'). On the issue of sharia, this comprehensive study found there was a lack of unity on the topic.

In the 39 countries surveyed, Pew asked Muslims whether they wanted to live under sharia and for it to be made the official law of the land in the country where they lived. Nearly all Muslims in Afghanistan (99%) said yes. In Iraq, 91% said yes; in Malaysia, 86%; in Pakistan, 84%; in Morocco, 83%; in Bangladesh, 82%, in Egypt, 74% and in Nigeria, 71%.

And yet, in central Asia and Eastern Europe, the picture was radically different. For example, in Turkey, gateway between east and west, just 12% said yes. In Azerbaijan, 8%t said yes.

The Pew survey did not specify European Muslims' views on sharia. However, a separate European study by the German research house, the Berlin Social Science Center, said: 'Two thirds of Muslims interviewed say that religious rules are more important to them than the laws of the country in which they live. Three quarters of respondents hold the opinion that there is only one legitimate interpretation of the Koran.'

This study said it looked at data from 9,000 telephone interviews in Germany, France, Netherlands, Austria, Belgium and Sweden. It also sampled Christians as a balance. 'These numbers [of the Muslims who favoured religious rules] are significantly higher than those from local Christians,' it said. 'Only 13 percent of this group put religious rules above national law; just under 20 percent refuse to accept differing interpretations of the Bible.'

The author of the study concluded: 'Religious fundamentalism is not a marginal phenomenon in Western Europe...Fundamentalism is not an innocent form of strict religiosity. We find a strong correlation between religious fundamentalism (in either faith) and hostility toward...groups like homosexuals or Jews.' (WZB Berlin Social Science Centre website.)

This last inference is evidenced surely by the rise of the neo-Nazi far right in many Western countries, whose poison is directed at Muslims, Jews and gays alike. And similar attitudes prevail amongst hardline Muslims. Almost 60% of the Muslim respondents reject homosexuals as friends; 45% think that Jews cannot be trusted; and an equally large group believes that the West is out to destroy Islam.

Yet the most powerful voices countering the fundamentalists are not the academics, the politicians or the media commentators. The best counter arguments are coming from liberal Muslim groups, particularly women who are increasingly using blogs, activist groups and other public forums to liberate themselves from the male-dominated debate about sharia law, radicalization and women's place within Islam.

Here are just a few examples of grassroots initiatives emerging where Muslim women are seeking to take ownership of their faith: In the US, a group has been set up called Women Against Shariah, which comprises American Muslim women resisting the attempt to impose draconian and age-old Islamic laws on their lives. It calls on Muslim women worldwide to resist sharia.

In India in 2016, a Muslim women's group called Muslim Women's Quest for Equality, petitioned the Supreme Court against arbitrary triple *talaq* (which grants a man divorce). The group called for a ban on sharia courts saying they should not operate as a parallel judiciary under the guise of mediation and conciliation, thereby usurping national justice.

Then in May 2017, something remarkable and rather wonderful happened, again in India. An ordinary Muslim woman had had enough of her violent husband and the Islamic legal balance being skewed in favour of men. One day, Amreen Begum's husband unceremoniously took her and their two small children in his rickshaw and dumped them beside some fields in Meerut, 70 km from Delhi. He would never see them again. She knew what was coming—it was only a matter of time before she heard the words or read a mobile text declaring '*talaq, talaq, talaq*' which would divorce her and ruin her life and that of her family.

This 25-year-old mother, enraged at her treatment and the planned disposal of her and her children like so much garbage, decided to take control. She travelled to a police station in Uttar Pradesh (the same Indian state that was the birthplace of the Deobandi Islam movement); there she reported her husband for domestic violence and shouted out the words '*talaq, talaq, talaq*' alongside her husband's name. Breaking with centuries of tradition of Islamic law that only allowed a man to divorce his wife, *she* divorced him.

The rickshaw-wallah's wife is believed to be the first woman in India to use the triple *talaq* to divorce her husband, reported the *Guardian* newspaper ('If a man can do it, why can't I?' *Guardian*, 11 May 2017). Thus with one bold stroke, Amreen Begum reclaimed not just her dignity as a Muslim woman, but her faith.

She was the trailblazer as change was coming anyway. By August 2017 the Indian Supreme Court made a momentous ruling: it declared the practice of men using triple *talaq* to divorce their wives as unconstitutional. Delhi's Supreme Court issued the verdict after examining a petition from seven victims and women's groups and the majority of the bench declared that triple *talaq* was 'not integral to religious practice and violates constitutional morality'. The decision was hailed as a victory for India's 90 million Muslim women. And all their future daughters. Triple *talaq* is already banned in many Muslim countries including Pakistan and Bangladesh and only survived in India because its Muslim, Hindu and Christian communities are permitted to follow religious law in personal matters such as marriage, divorce, inheritance and adoption.

In this respect, India has outpaced the UK by being unafraid to take on certain aspects of sharia law to ensure that religious law is consistent with the constitution and law of the land.

In Saudi Arabia in 2017, a group of women staged a silent protest walk to demand their right to walk alone in public.

The women also wished to protest against the ban on female drivers, which had been in place in the country since 1957 and was a serious restriction on women's personal freedom. Posting footage under the hashtag #resistancebywalking on social media, Saudi organizer Mariam Alhubail, said on Twitter: 'We want to encourage women to go out alone for a walk or to do their daily tasks and reject the idea men take care of these tasks. I walk alone. Until we have the streets again.'

In September 2017, these women could count themselves as winning a landmark victory when Saudi Arabia said it would allow women to drive. It is a small step but an important one for Saudi Muslim women's equality.

Thus religious evolution begins with such ordinary acts of resistance. Muslim women like Amreen and Mariam are provoking change in India and even Saudi and showing that acceptance of hardline sharia is no longer inevitable or desirable for all Muslims. And while these struggles are waged in the East, hardline imams and clerics in the West are seeking to enshrine sharia law in its secular democracies.

MINDCRAFT

'Put the chicken wings down 'n come to jihad bro.'

—Tweet from the ISIS frontline

In 2002, as shockwaves emanated from 9/11 and Osama bin Laden was the world's most hunted man, the Al Qaeda leader secretly dispatched a letter to the Taliban's Mullah Omar. The terrorist attack on America had shown how the media could project their message onto a global stage and even in his moment of triumph, while hiding from the wrath of American bombs, bin Laden's mind was on the next offensive. He believed theirs was a war that would be shaped by the media still further in the years ahead: 'It is obvious the media war in this century is one of the strongest methods; in fact, its ratio may reach 90% of the total preparation for the battles.' (Document located in the Combating Terrorism Centre at the US Military Academy, West Point.)

The jihadi terrorists' ideology is rooted in the 7th century but uses 21st century technology. In Wahhabi and the more hardline Deobandi madrassas across the world, alongside the Quran, *hadith* and *fiqh*, many Muslim children from the age of four have been taught that the ways of the West and modernity are *haram*, while simultaneously being given lessons on the Internet, the media and cutting-edge computer technology.

In 2004, when Al Qaeda was still the premier global terrorist brand, ISIS's first incarnation, AQI, began releasing brutal beheading videos including that of Nick Berg, a telecom engineer from Pennsylvania. The aggressive tactics roused deputy to bin Laden, Ayman al-Zawahiri, who wrote to the AQI leader Abu Musa al-Zarqawi and told him such graphic violence risked damaging the cause: 'I say to you that we are in battle and that more than half of this battle is taking place in the battlefield of the media. And that we are in a...race for the hearts and minds of our Umma.'

Abu Musa al-Zarqawi was in no mood for compromise. He was not interested in consensus building; in US military parlance, he was playing to the base. AQI videos won a cult following online amongst the fanatical fringe, the dispossessed, the enraged and disturbed of society energized by the blood lust displayed. The AQI leader believed success lay in recruiting the most violent, craven people to his cause in order to fulfil his ambition of creating an Islamic state.

As the ISIS manual *Management of Savagery* had said, the aim was to debunk the idea that their enemies were unassailable. They had to destroy the 'media halo' of invincibility of America and its allies. In order to do this, they needed their own media operation and it was modelled on the West. It copied Western media's modus operandi to constantly feed the news cycle with a stream of startling and terrifying news footage. Their own shock and awe campaign began.

By the time Abu Musa al-Zarqawi was killed by a US air strike in 2006 and AQI had reincarnated into ISIS, the seeds had been sown to create a propaganda machine that would serve the group well in the coming years and recruit tens of thousands of jihadis online from around the world.

This formidable machine, which combined old media platforms such as documentary footage, the ISIS *Dabiq* magazine and press releases with new social media outlets, enabled ISIS to expand at dizzying speed in 2013/14, taking advantage of the collapse of governance in parts of Syria and Iraq.

One propaganda film, *Clanging of Swords*, made during the ISIS's Iraqi offensive in May 2014, showed embedded filmmakers carrying handheld cameras filming ISIS death squads as they hunted down and executed Iraqi security personnel who pleaded for their lives in vain.

These propagandists were well paid. In a November 2015 interview with the *Washington Post*, a former ISIS cameraman said he was paid $700 a month—five times what a fighter was paid then. For a young man from Morocco this was lucrative work at a time when four out of five people in his country aged 15 to 34 were unemployed.

ISIS created provincial media offices that distributed their literature not only to conquered communities but across the world, mainly through the Internet. Foreign recruits were particularly valuable for this type of work, rather than pure cannon fodder. Ahmad Abousamra, a former American computer science student, for instance, became a leader in non-Arabic content (there are rumours he is now dead). Such people brought advanced technology and sharpness to the jihadis' propaganda campaign, which was once the preserve of tired, bearded ageing men filming themselves in caves against a black-flag backdrop.

Now GoPro cameras were attached to AK47s and rifles, capturing the action of young jihadis in cinematic detail. It played like a Hollywood blockbuster trailer or a video-game. The virtual worlds of Call of Duty, Assassin's Creed, Minecraft were made real. Why play, when you can live it, ISIS seemed to exhort excitable and disturbed youths from around the world. It was using its message to control minds and bring them to the cause.

The personal narratives of the individual fighters became

important—they had *noms de guerre*, monikers that in a social media world would become jihadi mini-brands. They had online profiles of their exploits, built up fan bases from around the world including young women as well as aspirant fighters and communicated via message platforms, thus becoming recruiters as well as fighters for the cause.

MailOnline, the largest English-language news website in the world, ran an ISIS section every day, charting the latest atrocities from the frontlines as well as colour stories. Their reporters trawled the online space for gossipy stories about these fighters—whether boasting of 'Five Star Jihad' or cuddling kittens with machine guns slung on their backs. I remember one online editor telling me she had reason to believe that these people monitored how the media and public was responding to their coverage. The ISIS media machine fed the West's media machine and in some cases, the West's media machine fuelled the cult of the jihadis. It was a cycle of reciprocity—they got coverage, the media got clicks.

Whereas Al Qaeda had been elitist, professional, secretive, controlled, highly centralized, ISIS is truly open to all, amateur or professional, publicity hungry and decentralized. Once terrorists communicated via encrypted Arabic-language chat rooms and forums, now they did so quite openly on media platforms owned by Western companies and in the public domain. In that sense, they traded secrecy for publicity, elitism for populist power.

I had seen first-hand the beginnings of the phenomenon of how social media could be used for mass change in the Arab Spring movement in Tunisia when the revolution was in its infancy and before it had turned to repression in much of the region. In Tunis in 2011, the people organizing the mass protest that toppled the establishment and unleashed the forces of change were kids with smart phones. In a few swipes on their phones they were mobilizing protestors in tens of thousands via Facebook. I called them 'the Facebook Generals'.

ISIS has perfected this idea of using the language of the internet generation to communicate, recruit, engage and direct. The social media has proved to be the perfect conduit into the hearts and minds of the base. Charles Kurzman, a sociology professor at the University of North Carolina who studies Islamic terrorism, believes that ISIS's command of the medium that all of us are now enslaved by has meant it is given an almost disproportionate status. Yet there is no doubt that the online campaign is connecting with those looking for a cause: 'There are people who, for whatever reason, have some sort of personal difficulty, some sort of break in their lives and are attuned to engaging in violence,' he said. 'And so they will [latch] on to whatever the biggest, baddest revolutionary ideology of the moment is.' ('Cultivate the Brand', Wired, April 2016)

The Al Bayan Center for Planning and Studies in Iraq examined the propaganda machine of ISIS in its 2015 paper 'Fighting Media with Media'. The Center, a non-profit independent think tank based in Baghdad, warned there can be no defeat of ISIS without a counter communications strategy to defeat the ideology itself. 'IS employs its sophisticated media apparatus to circulate propaganda which has proved effective to recruit fighters, inspire attacks and wage psychological warfare on enemies, both decision makers and civilians, whether near or far,' said the report. 'Military engagement in the conquered territories can help contain but not permanently annihilate IS, as radicalized followers from around the globe come to share and spread its timeless ambitions and continue to join its ranks. Defeating the Islamic State is unlikely without a communications campaign to challenge its ideology and offer an alternative narrative that can disrupt its recruitment and intimidation tactics.'

The fusion of terrorism and technology spawned Terrorism 2.0. Just as there was Web 2.0, in which citizens engaged in creating content and linking with others via digital platforms, so terrorism has made a quantum leap in its evolution. Media warfare has been digitized. The IT-led media machine of ISIS has been central to its composite strategy of propaganda, recruitment, fund raising and psychological warfare

The internet has allowed the Islamic State to go from being a small group of disaffected jihadis in the Middle East nursing localized grievances to a unified voice with a global platform and reach. Information and Communication Technology lies at the heart of its strategy. It offers the terrorist group ease of access to the base, puts it beyond the control of governments, and facilitates fast-moving responses. Al Hayat Media Centre, a kind of command and control centre for all the media units across territories where ISIS has allegiance, is used to disseminate material through its online magazine *Dabiq*, videos, documentaries, press statements and recordings of messages and edicts.

Platforms used include: Twitter, Facebook, Soundcloud, Instagram and askFM, with the first two most instrumental because of their sheer scale. Twitter is effective because it can be used for visual, audio, text and is good for places with intermittent web access, according to Jytte Klausen in the report 'Tweeting the Jihad' (2015). According to a British House of Commons Defence Committee report, by 2015 ISIS and its sympathizers were sending out 90,000 tweets a day.

Other mainstream platforms for messaging are also useful to recruit those who may be vulnerable to extremist propaganda, enabling a real-time dialogue across borders and time zones: Whatsapp, Kik, Wickr, Zello, Telegram.

The Al Bayan Center produced a graphic taken from ISIS itself, originally circulated in January 2015. That graphic was used in ISIS tech training tutorials to help the terrorists/recruiters/followers hide their communication from government surveillance. The graphic ranks the encryption safety of chat apps from 'Safest' to 'Unsafe': 'Safest' are Silent Circle, Redphone and ChatSecure, among others; 'Safe' are Telegram, Wickr, Threema and Surespot; and among the 'Moderately Safe' and 'Unsafe' are Whatsapp, Tango, WeChat, Kik and Viber. It is a chilling demonstration of how organized the terrorist group is in utilizing technology for its ends.

This is how it uses new media, but old media is valuable still. Execution videos, pioneered by previous terrorist groups, have been enhanced by ISIS as it targets civilians and governments. These have provided the group with blanket coverage in mainstream media outlets as well as on their websites, providing a double strike for the terrorist propagandists. It amounts to nothing less than using the media to distribute terrorist porn, creating an appetite for such material online, lowering the thresholds of tolerance of the viewing public with each film, until we are numbed by it, motivating ISIS to come up with ever more inventive ways of invoking terror. By watching this carefully constructed footage in which a life is no more than a propaganda prop, we are somehow complicit. Watching the deaths of victims like James Foley and countless others of many nationalities did not give them dignity in death, it stripped them of it and made media stars of their executioners; it fuelled the cult of terror and invincibility.

Such was the power of the starring executioners we gave them names like 'Jihadi John' (the now dead British Arab Muhammed Emwazi, believed to be the person seen beheading hostages in several ISIS videos). Overnight, they became terrorist celebrities and it mattered not if they were 'liked' or 'unliked', they dominated the online space. Those terrorist propagandists behind the videos that Western outlets released without hesitation were given an even greater status within ISIS as a consequence, moving up the ranks into the upper echelons of the terrorist group's hierarchy. 'These senior media operatives are treated like emirs and enjoy a reputation not dissimilar from that of military leaders,' said the Al-Bayan Center.

The videos were disseminated by the established media as well as bots programmed to release content. The illusion of 'success' was fuelled by ISIS buying fake followers to lure real people to follow the trail of propaganda breadcrumbs laid out online. ('ISIS is not a terrorist group', Foreign Affairs, 2015,).

ISIS propagandists hijacked hashtags for major events such as the 2014 World Cup to win audiences of millions. They wanted the young, urban, internet generation brought up on a diet of Western culture, video gaming and films to join them. Slick editing, short snappy messaging, gore, guns, the thrill of martyrdom on the frontline were all designed to entice and recruit a certain demographic. Control of the debate was seen as key to successful recruiting, fund raising and military enlargement. By documenting their victories, the destruction of their opponents and their identity, by creating the illusion of a functioning state through air brushed reality, they believed they could draw more people in.

Building the mythology of success and creating their own 'media halo' is key to persuading potential recruits it is not madness to leave everything behind and join the Islamic State. What they were offering was a chance to step into the revolutionary elevator on the ground floor. CIA analyst, Emile Nakhleh noted 'the perception of quick victories and territory and weapons and bases means ISIS does not need to try hard to recruit…Young people look at their footage of fighters riding on big tanks and say, "By gosh, they're doing it."' ('ISIS Displaying Deft Command of Varied Media', Nytimes.com).

It is an astonishing reality: a terrorist group with a medieval mindset using Western social media companies to radicalize and recruit young people at a time when the world faces great economic divide, anger and uncertainty. They have succeeded in turning the West's principle of freedom of speech into a weapon, using it as an instrument of hate speech, hate crime and religious persecution. Until recently, they did so pretty much uninhibited. In 2016, Twitter suspended 350,000 accounts for violating its ban on promoting terrorism and violence. At the time, Salaam Bhatti, a spokesman for True Islam which partnered with Twitter to identify extremist content, told the *Guardian* newspaper: 'This is a great step in the right direction. Twitter [has become] a digital social media battlefield... which is also a way of recruiting people. As we can see that the extremist groups are losing on the territorial front, so they're going to social media again and again to recruit the youth.'

Yet American law enforcement agencies noted that just as quickly as accounts were shut down, new ones were opened. In January 2016, Silicon Valley's finest met with US Homeland Security to discuss how technology could be harnessed to defeat the spread of extremist ideology online. By the close of the year, Google, Facebook, Twitter and Microsoft announced a plan to work together to identify and remove extremist content on all platforms through a new information-sharing initiative. This involved setting up a shared database where images, video and other content promoting terrorism would be identified and once banned by one party, it would be banned by all. The same system used to target paedophiles was now being applied to terrorists and their sympathizers. Hany Farid, a computer scientist who helped work on the PhotoDNA project on silencing extremist content, said at the time: 'It's long overdue...If it is removed from one site it is removed everywhere. That's incredibly powerful. What we want is to eliminate this global megaphone that social media gives to groups like ISIS.' ('Facebook, Twitter, Google and Microsoft team up to tackle extremist content', Guardian, 6 December 2016).

And yet this is not the end of the battle of the online space. Cockroach-like, ISIS finds new ways to survive and subvert the ban and censorship efforts and throughout it has remained active on the dark web. The joint action by Silicon Valley was one step forward. The other part of the solution lies in more effective counter narratives flooding the internet to drown out the voice of the extremist Islamist. It is already happening, although some believe these first attempts are crude and ineffective.

The US State Department's counter narrative Twitter account Think Again, Turn Away, has been called 'embarrassing and counterproductive' (Al Bayan Center). *Time* magazine also called it 'an embarrassment', providing a platform for terrorists to argue their cause rather than the US successfully debunking their ideas. The English-language version began in 2013, following an Arabic and Urdu version that rolled out earlier. The account sent out six to seven tweets a day and is deemed to have failed. *Time* called it a 'gaffe machine' which not only doled out foolish lines of argument that sometimes descended into pettiness, but also skirted moral danger: in some instances the State Department tweets communicated directly with known terrorist leaders, thereby giving them a legitimacy of being recognized online by the US government. ('The State Department's twitter War with ISIS is Embarrassing', *Time*, 16 September 2014)

Who was the State Department employing to press the button on these tweets? Are they even Muslim or experts in radical Islamist ideology? If there is to be a rebuttal online, it must be intellectually and theologically credible to the *ummah*, engage in the language of the target audience of the terrorist, endeavour to 'groom' people to the path of moderation in the same way that people are groomed to become jihadis.

The aim is to convince such targets that joining ISIS would be a violation of the Quran and Islamic law, while underscoring the message of tolerance and peace in the faith. It must expose Wahhabist and Deobandi doctrine as a relatively recent phenomenon in the history of Islam and one that destroys the unity of the *ummah* that is a family of overwhelmingly moderate and peaceful Shia *and* Sunni faithful.

In Iraq in 2015, religious leaders from various denominations gathered in Karbala to discuss how to rebut ISIS's controversial position on *takfiri* thought, whereby one Muslim accuses another of apostasy. It was a first step where Iraqi Muslims and other minorities came together to defeat a poisonous ideology; here was the many opposing the few. It is through respected, moderate leadership both online and in the real world, that extreme and violent Islamist ideas must be challenged.

The *MIT Technology Review* published a report in September 2015 called 'Fighting ISIS Online', which said the greatest impact can be felt through personal contact. Just as many jihadis are recruited through one-to-one contact either in person or online, so people must be drawn away in the same way. Studies such as one by the London Institute for Strategic Dialogue have found that peer-to-peer efforts to steer people away from radicalization are effective.

Technological innovation is delivering solutions all the time, such as the use of a Facebook feature by a group of former extremists (both far right and jihadists) who work as an intervention force online. The Facebook feature Graph Search can zero in on people whose interests, likes, pages and memberships show they may be moving towards extremism.

This list of targets is honed down and the intervention force can send a message to them and start a conversation. Experiments have shown that if the conversation is open, non-judgemental and empathetic, it can be effective in reorienting people from the path of extremism.

Another effective way of rebutting the online falsehoods about Islam is being pioneered by a social tech company called Affinis Labs in Arlington, Virginia, which has developed an app called 'QuickFiqh' in which Muslims can ask 60-second questions about Islamic law and get answers from mainstream and moderate Islamic scholars. These can then be shared online, and thus moderate viewpoints are disseminated.

Changing the narrative is another way to deconstruct the media message of ISIS by destroying *its* media halo and proving that beyond its savagery there is a void: ISIS has no basis in Islamic law, it has no functioning Caliphate, its territories are being burned beneath its feet, a large number of its fighters have been killed and many are on the run, captive populations in ISIS-run territories choose escape or death rather than life in a violent dystopia run by terrorists. A single powerful public testimony that exposes the hypocrisy of this terrorist state is more valuable than a thousand poorly conceived US State Department tweets. Muslims will not take advice on their faith from the same people that gave them the Iraqi invasion, Guantanamo and Abu Ghraib.

By the close of 2017, the biggest victory in overturning ISIS's propaganda of invincibility was the fact that it had lost almost all its territory in Iraq and Syria thanks to the anti-ISIS Coalition. News began to flood out daily about what life was really like under the Islamic State: a brutal tyranny of millions rather than an Islamic utopia. In the case of the oppression of the Yazidi population in Iraq, many girls and women have come forward to share their stories of sexual slavery, rape and degradation. They have issued their stories through respected NGOs or through the auspices of the UN. Their first-hand accounts of life in the Caliphate and the savagery of the jihadis is just one example of how truth is destroying the mirage of the so-called caliphate.

Some bloggers are taking it upon themselves to fight ISIS propaganda, by resorting to mockery—for when the horror becomes too much, all that is left is parody. Bloggers have taken to re-editing ISIS videos, super-imposing kittens on the faces of jihadis brandishing weapons and riding atop tanks. Videos of the ineptitude of some of the fighters are also increasing. When ISIS threatened that it was on the verge of taking Rome in the summer of 2016, jocular Italians tweeted that they should be sure to avoid the ring-road as traffic tailbacks could be a nightmare.

An ISIS hashtag has been set up called ISISClaims where wags mock the terrorists for claiming a hand in everything from Cadbury's chocolate Freddo frogs shrinking in size to the Great British Bake-Off television programme being poached from the BBC by Channel 4.

These jokes may seem petty next to the magnitude of ISIS's crimes, and yet by turning ISIS into the butt of jokes online, they destroy its mystique one punchline and LOL at a time. They all contribute to larger efforts to shatter the myth-building online that this is the army of the global Caliphate, the harbinger of the End of Times: instead, the tweets portray ISIS fighters as desperate losers.

Equally, the message of solidarity and tolerance is emerging in the wake of each new terrorist incident that ISIS mounts in cities around the world. In the aftermath of attacks in London, Manchester, Barcelona, Paris, Orlando, people of every background, religion, age and ethnicity unified on the streets to host vigils and this was mirrored online with message boards calling for solidarity and tolerance. Priests walked alongside imams and rabbis to reinforce this message at the highest levels.

Most of the online responses—shared by video or tweets—are uplifting while others are more robust in their message, such as the Manchester United football bans who downloaded a video online of themselves chanting at a match just after the Ariana Granda concert bomb attack: 'ISIS stick it up your a***'

But even as the terror threat has led to many ordinary citizens fiercely and publicly expressing their solidarity, there is no doubt that the rise of ISIS as a threat in Western cities now and the fear of terrorism coupled with economic uncertainty has spawned another uglier response: the Islamophobe in our midst. Xenophobia in our multicultural cities is evidenced by the emergence of a new form of politics. Call it anti-immigrant, alt-right or fascist, here too the media message plays its part. There is a terrible hypocrisy at play in some sections of the Western media: decrying the rise of ISIS while fulfilling its narrative by fuelling division and fear of 'the other'.

The European Commission Against Racism and Intolerance (ECRI) published a report in 2015 that said some reporting on immigration, terrorism and the refugee crisis was 'contributing to creating an atmosphere of hostility and rejection'. The worst example was where a British female columnist for the rightwing tabloid *The Sun* referred to refugees from Syria and other countries in the grip of civil war as 'cockroaches'—this at a time when refugees, including children, were drowning in their attempt to flee warzones and come to Europe for a chance at life itself. The columnist's words evoked Nazi propaganda against the Jews.

The media has helped stoke a dangerous new political climate of demonizing refugees and immigrants—Muslims, in particular—in Europe and America. But also in Asia: Muslim

Rohingya refugees fleeing horrific ethnic and state violence in Myanmar are being denied refuge in India, for instance; both the BJP central government and the mainstream media justify this citing security concerns, thus branding thousands of penniless and often starving persecuted women, men and children as potential terrorists.

In the wake of Britain's Brexit vote in June 2016 and with the rise of far right politics in Europe, police statistics have shown a dramatic rise in Islamaphobic, anti-Semitic and xenophobic assaults. Religious buildings and Muslim migrants have been targeted. 'It is no coincidence that racist violence is on the rise in the UK at the same time as we see worrying examples of intolerance and hate speech in the newspapers, online and even among politicians,' said ECRI chair Christian Ahlund.

Anti-Muslim, anti-migrant political rhetoric has stepped from the shadows into the political spotlight and mainstream. In Slovakia, an EU member, the prime minister, Robert Fico, has called for the 'restriction of the freedom of Muslims in Europe', and said Islam has no place in his country. The far right Hungarian prime minister Viktor Orbán is another vocal leader on Islamaphobic and anti-refugee views, talking about a planned invasion by Muslims. He has referred to the migrants as 'poison'.

It is not just a European phenomenon. One of the first major global democracies to elect a muscular nationalist and populist leader was India—it put Narendra Modi in office as prime minister in 2014. Modi and his BJP Hindu nationalist party has risen to national prominence on the back, mainly, of two issues: economic liberalization Islamophobia. This strongman populism was drawn from the same poisoned well of politics that Donald Trump would use to propel himself to victory in 2016. Both men were initially deemed as dangerous mavericks and political outsiders, both depicted the Muslim as the enemy within, both clothed their dangerous nationalism in the garb of protecting the common man and the domestic economy. One was Hindu Christian America First.

In the US, *Newsweek* reported in the summer of 2017 that FBI data showed that in 2015 there were 257 hate crimes against Muslims—the highest level since 2001 and a surge of 67% over the previous year. Anti-Muslim hate crime in America accounted for 4% of total cases reported, even though Muslims represent 1% of the population.

In India, according to reports in June 2017 by two human rights groups—the Mumbai-based Centre for Study of Society and Secularism (CSSS) and the UK-based Minority Rights Group International (MRG)—there had been a spike in communal violence, particularly against Muslims, since 2014 when Modi and his BJP party came to power. According to official statistics alone, India witnessed more than 700 incidents of communal violence in 2016 that killed 86 and injured 2,321 people. Muslims—who form just under 15% of the country's population—again bore the brunt of these hate crimes, such as lynching, shooting, stabbing, threats, attacks on places of worship and forced conversion.

In the autumn of 2017, the beacon of European tolerance, Germany, held elections in which the anti-immigrant and far right Alternative for Germany party won its highest ever share of the vote and entered parliament for the first time in 60 years. Chancellor Angela Merkel clung on to power but her sympathetic stance towards refugees had cost her a heavy political price.

It was not all bad news in 2017: France, Austria and the Netherlands all rejected the far right populist candidate in elections. But even as it was defeated the far right spoke louder than ever in all these countries.

When political leaders and the front pages of respectable global newspapers become the home of hatred and populism, when Islamophobia is part of everyday public discourse, ISIS's propaganda efforts are helped. It is what the *Management of Savagery*, the blueprint for modern-day Islamist terrorism had recommended as strategy: stoke the fires of hate against the majority of peaceful Muslims living around the world, fan the flames of division until moderate Muslims are fearful in their adopted lands and forced to choose between a world of co-existence and the so-called Caliphate, between values of a common humanity and those of ISIS.

In 2002 Osama bin Laden had the dark foresight to see the importance of the Internet and the media, but not even he could have predicted the dawn of a new social media age which would instantly connect people around the world: back then, Facebook, Twitter, YouTube and Whatsapp had not taken the world by storm. The invention and proliferation of the smart phone democratized the medium for the masses and has placed unprecedented power in the hands of young people across the globe. Most young people in their early 20s and younger, of all faiths, including Islam, have never known a world without the Internet, and the battle for their hearts and minds is now being waged through the smart phone. It is this same demographic that has been worst hit by the fallout from the 2008 global economic crisis. These young people, especially if they feel persecuted or denied economic opportunities, are particularly vulnerable to extreme ideologies.

We live in a political era where the globalized power of the message can transcend everything, even truth. The citadels of establishment are no longer trusted—whether they are media scions or government elites—and the world is witnessing a turbulent age of political iconoclasm. By 2017's close, ISIS has pretty much lost its terrorist kingdom after coming under debilitating military assault from the West and its coalition of allies. Faced with territorial losses, now the online media sphere is set to become a priority battleground for ISIS. For those recruits it has lost, it will target fresh blood online.

The media war has only just begun.

3

ECONOMY

ANATOMY OF A TERRORIST ECONOMY

> '[ISIS is] the best funded terrorist organization we have ever confronted.'
>
> —Daniel Cohen, US Under Secretary for Terrorism and Financial Intelligence, October 2014

Clothed by night, in the early hours of 16 May 2015, American Delta Force commandos landed 20 miles southeast of Deir al-Zour in Syria for a mission that was to be one of the first ground raids since aerial bombardment began by the anti-ISIS Coalition in September 2014. Spilling like scorpions from the belly of Black Hawk helicopters and V-22 Osprey aircraft, the special forces fanned out to surround a multi-storey residence which fast became engulfed in lightning bursts of fire-fighting. Every step of the covert mission was recorded in the grainy green glow of night-vision cameras.

The target was Fathi Ben Awn Ben Jildi Murad al-Tunisi, a senior ISIS commander from Tunisia known by his Arabic *nom de guerre* Abu Sayyaf, or 'Father of the Swordsman'. Abu Sayyaf was the Islamic State's emir of oil and gas and more, for he was also the money man who orchestrated a complex web of financial operations which reportedly had assets worth an estimated $2 trillion (Thomson Reuters Risk report 'The Economy Based Terrorist Funding', October 2014). Its annual revenues were estimated to be between $2 billion and

£2.9 billion per annum in 2014 (US Treasury, Thomson Reuters' report, 2014 and author interviews).

Abu Sayyaf presided over a financial empire of terror, with money raised not just from oil and gas, but human trafficking, extortion, kidnappings and executions. Its fund-raising capability was unlike that of any terrorist organization before, relying not just on the shadowy nexus of rich Gulf donors that bankrolled Al Qaeda, but a policy of self-sufficiency, raising revenues from captured territory by squeezing every last pound or dinar from its hostage civilian population.

It operated along the lines of a business, with accounting systems and databases of 'customers': individuals and companies who were extorted and who paid their dues directly to the self-proclaimed Caliphate. It opened its own revenue collection ministry, Al Hisba. Manned by black-garbed men behind desks stacked with officious files, the tax offices looked like ones in any other Eastern nation, except here their inspectors would send their spies to patrol local shops and offices, challenging locals at gunpoint about whether they had indeed paid the correct amount.

In the Caliphate, death and taxes were not only certain but central to survival, for theirs was a kingdom founded on the executioner's sword and financial tyranny. Abu Sayyaf was the orchestrator of all of this. If ISIS was to be stopped, then the sources of money had to be identified and the flow of funding staunched, and its financial emir was the key.

That night in May 2015, US forces backed by British counterparts embarked on a mission that was a crucial first step in achieving that objective. Special ops closed in and swiftly found themselves engaged in hand-to-hand combat as they penetrated the building. Abu Sayyaf used women and children as human shields until he and his wife Umm Sayyaf were cornered in a room alone. The US soldiers wrenched her apart from her husband before killing him with shots to the chest.

His wife was taken into custody and would become a valuable source of information on the group's global fund-raising machine. Intelligence showed her to be just as culpable as her husband, being instrumental in the trafficking of human beings and a modern-day sex-slave trade that dealt in women and children, some just infants. Together with the gathered intelligence from the site, Umm Sayyaf was boarded onto the waiting American aircraft and amidst clouds of red dust, it rose into the velvet night sky until the shattered complex below was no more than a speck and then a memory. Umm Sayyaf was no longer Islamic State's powerful sheikha, the emir's wife reigning over a kingdom of misery, but a terrorist and prisoner of America, bound for an unnamed Iraqi jail where she would face her interrogators.

The Obama administration, keen for news of a triumph, trumpeted the audacious mission but not everyone was convinced of its value, with some demurring that few had heard of Abu Sayyaf beforehand and that he was not a crucial piece in the game as his name was absent from the most wanted list of ISIS leaders. Searches online yield little information ahead of the 2015 raid that killed him. But his low profile may well have been deliberate and the US believed there was evidence of regular and sustained contact with the elusive ISIS leader, Abu Bakr al-Baghdadi. At the time, White House National Security Council spokeswoman Bernadette Meehan pointedly noted that it was Abu Sayyaf's direction of financial operations 'that enables the terrorist organization to carry out their brutal tactics and oppress thousands.'

The mission did not take the emir alive, which meant that the potential fruits of interrogation of a live captive were lost. But his wife's insider knowledge as well as the cache of intelligence retrieved from the building in Amr—laptops, computers, cell-phones and other materials—marked a breakthrough in the fightback. It helped the Americans and their allies decipher the anatomy of a modern terrorist economy: how ISIS's blood money is raised, spent and flows into operations at home and abroad. It was the best insight thus far into the terrorist body's financial circulatory system.

When the cavalcade of terror swept through swathes of territory in Iraq and Syria in 2014/15, ISIS portrayed itself as liberator, there to return the country and elevate Muslims to a 'pure' Sunni-based Islam rooted in Wahhabism and their interpretation of sharia law. Their territorial advances were punctuated at every step of their journey by crucifixion, decapitation and execution, designed to terrorize civilians into obedience. One of the earliest examples of ISIS carrying out crucifixions came in May 2014 when the UK-based Syrian Observatory for Human Rights reported on photographs showing two men's bodies crucified on a cross in Raqqa. The photos showed civilians, including children, looking upon the bodies tied to the wood with green rope and underneath the bloodied corpses was a banner that read: 'This man fought against Muslims and set off an explosive device here.' Wherever ISIS held sway, such atrocities would follow. On the Christian holiday of Good Friday in 2016, the day Christians around the world mark the day of Jesus's crucifixion, ISIS kidnapped an Indian priest in Yemen and crucified him. Father Thomas Uzhunnalil's crucifixion resonated around the world and was announced by the Archbishop of Vienna, Christoph Schonborn.

Such terrors have become the hallmarks of ISIS's reign that secured the fealty of its captive subjects, for the grand mission was always to consolidate and keep conquering. And for that ISIS required submission and cash flow.

At its apex, ISIS ruled over more than 8 million souls in a landmass across northern Iraq and Syria the size of the UK. It had an army of jihadis tens of thousands strong that needed to be paid, fed and equipped as well as their families taken care of. And it had an expensive multi-fronted war to fund against a coalition of enemies, including the most powerful nation on earth. ISIS had distinguished itself from predecessors like Al Qaeda by establishing a so-called Caliphate in the present, rather than a distant utopian future. An aspirant state needed a functioning economy to finance the war machine and infrastructure, with sustainable, multiple revenue streams that could fund the grand project to fruition: a *global* Caliphate based on an apocalyptic vision and an extreme interpretation of sharia law.

Whereas the Taliban and Al Qaeda had relied heavily on donations, the emerging narrative in Iraq and Syria showed ISIS was a different beast. It had learned early on that self-sufficiency was crucial if it was to retain independence from interfering foreign paymasters—such as rich sympathetic donors from countries like Saudi or Qatar—and be ruthlessly focused on the final objective. ISIS documents showed its strategists believed external patrons could exert control by threatening to withhold funding, or as one ISIS insider wrote: 'Make your dog hungry and he will follow you.'

Thus ISIS evolved into an autonomous money-making machine, run with the accountability and diversity of a conglomerate, leading the international media to call it 'ISIS Inc'. As its financial emir surveyed an empire of oil fields and other natural resources, at his fingertips were records of revenues and outgoings as well as a database of pricing structures and customers for its various business divisions. If ISIS needed staff, it advertised, headhunting for its oil operations using WhatsApp and Kick messaging platforms. Applicants were either locals or expatriates who already worked and lived in territories now under the Caliphate or those sympathizers who were recruited online to come and join the terrorist kingdom. From the beginning, ISIS wanted not just fighters but engineers, administrators, oil workers—every kind of Muslim who could help them make this a lasting enterprise.

Despite facing international sanctions, airstrikes and the full opprobrium of the West, it strove to maintain its business, and well into 2015 it was managing to do so. In the early months of 2015, a religious leader in Mosul revealed to a Qatari newspaper a copy of ISIS's first ever annual budget which detailed up to $2 billion in expenditure and a $250 million surplus which it said would be diverted to the war effort. The scale of funding was staggering. The religious leader, Naji Abdullah, a tribal elder in the city of Mosul, told *Al-Araby al-Jadeed* in early 2015 that the budget was part of the terrorist group's development programme for the Caliphate. It contained details of the monthly wages for fighters and their families, and for the widows of those fighters killed in coalition airstrikes.

The 'leaking' of the budget came days after the establishment of an Islamic Bank in Mosul. But the ledger, meticulously detailed, was more than just a dry list of debits and credits. It was a financial statement of intent. Here was the terrorist pariah that posed as the nation state, funded by diversified revenue streams that would make it hard for the Coalition allies to go after it and shut it down. Its diversified range of business interests spanned oil and gas, taxation—or rather extortion of residents in ISIS territories—trafficking of people and stolen antiquities, slave trade, agriculture and bank raids.

If we take all this evidence together from multiple sources ranging from the above leaked report, news stories and my own interviews, in 2015, before the collapse in oil prices and air strikes had their full impact on ISIS's energy interests, total revenues looked like they were well in excess of $2 billion.

The $2 billion figure mooted in leaked documents was confirmed in 2016 in an interview with a senior US government source who spoke on condition of anonymity. This source put

ISIS's oil revenues alone at around $500 million per annum at its peak in 2015, without even looking at other income streams from things such as extortion, taxation, kidnapping and so forth. Oil revenue was the primary Coalition financial target. Efforts to destroy as much of ISIS's oil income stream as possible began to pay off and by early 2016, that figure had been degraded by up to one third due to three factors: Coalition air strikes, the collapse in the global oil price from a peak of $114 a barrel in 2014 to below $30 a barrel at the start of 2016, and, lastly, greater efforts by the Turkish government to clamp down on cross border smuggling of oil.

Apart from oil, raids on bank vaults in ISIS-held territory in Iraq and Syria had yielded at least $750 million, with some estimates being as high as $1 billion. Here, the terrorists broke into state banks and local banks, plundering national reserves as well as individual accounts, according to intelligence that emerged from the ground. 'There was $750 million worth of dinar in those banks. It was a huge score, but once they've burned through that, it's not renewable,' noted the senior US Obama administration source early in 2016 as the air strikes were stepped up. 'We've got Coalition airstrikes targeting those funds. They are bombing those vaults.'

How much of those funds were destroyed or spent is impossible to know. ISIS was also taxing all salaries paid by the Iraqi government in Baghdad to employees under its control—they could do so because they had access to the national and international banking account network. Those who now lived under ISIS control found their accounts plundered by terrorists who controlled the local bank branch network. Also, because ISIS had control of the banking network there was a fear that it could get access to *all* accounts, even those outside its territory.

The anti-ISIS coalition became aware of the scale of ISIS's financial activities back in 2014. In a speech in the autumn of that year, the then US Treasury under-secretary David Cohen said there were scores of banks located in Syrian and Iraqi ISIS-controlled areas, including international banks. In Iraq alone, 90 such branches continued to operate in contested areas such as Kirkuk, Anbar, Ninawa and Salah al-Din. The US and Iraqi governments had to work with the international financial community to shut down this network which allowed free flow of funding even after ISIS took control of these areas. The Central Bank of Iraq had to stop wire transfers of money into ISIS-held areas—one, because it was in danger of becoming a source of terror funding, and two, such accounts could result in wider access by the terrorist network.

By early 2015, preventing ISIS from using the global financial network to move and access funds became one of the main priorities of the Coalition in defeating the terrorist group. In March 2015, the US, Saudi Arabia and Italy co-chaired the first meeting of the Counter ISIL Finance Group in Rome to do just that. The Group said ISIS had used a backdoor to enter the system and that route now had to be closed off. The worry was that national and international financial institutions continued to be used in ISIS controlled areas. If ISIS had links through them into the global financial system, it could move money unchallenged.

One case study cited in the Financial Action Task Force—a multi-lateral international group aimed at countering illicit financial activity—said in a report in early 2015 that it had evidence of monies being transferred electronically from international accounts to accounts in areas close to ISIS territory and then accessed via local ATMs. The Netherlands reportedly found indications that foreign terrorist fighters were using debit cards 'linked to their national bank accounts when withdrawing money from ATMs in those areas near where ISIS operates'. The US Treasury identified all of these as potential sources of funding that could grow in the future and so it led efforts to turn this tap off.

The taxing of civil servants' salaries ended in August 2015 when the US Treasury worked with the Iraqi administration to arrange for all civil service payments in ISIS-held areas to be paid into secure escrow accounts, ring-fencing it from terrorists' hands. An escrow account is controlled by a third party, so that the funds can only be used for a particular purpose, thereby protecting the money from being hijacked for illicit purposes.

Other means of funding ISIS had developed were harder to target. ISIS's revenue from kidnapping and ransom was put at around $40 million per annum by US intelligence, although some independent analysts estimated it could be as high as $10 million a month or $120 million per annum. Kidnappings had served a dual purpose of raising cash and also global awareness of the ISIS brand. Every time ISIS conducted a kidnapping it made videos of their captives in orange jumpsuits and played their demands to the outside world, demanding huge ransom amounts from foreign governments to free their nationals. It traded on the media extravaganza that ensued and in some cases it also got paid the ransom—monies that went into furthering the terrorist cause.

Most governments refused on principle to bow to the terrorists' financial demands. On 20 January 2015, ISIS posted a video of a black-garbed masked militant standing over two kneeling Japanese hostages, journalist Kenji Goto and security consultant Haruna Yukawa. The voice intoned that unless a ransom of $200 million was paid they would be executed. Japan's government refused and by the end of the month ISIS claimed it had beheaded both Goto and Yukawa.

But the biggest pay day was one that cannot be fully quantified and targeted by sanctions or airstrikes and it was estimated by the US and other reports, including my own interviews with US Treasury officials, to be around $1 billion at its peak in 2015. This was the extortion of money from the civilian population living under ISIS rule.

Secret benefactors were seen to be a less pivotal part of the picture, according to most analysts. Of the estimated peak total revenues of between $2 billion and $2.9 billion, most analysts and the US government said no more than 5% came from Gulf donors. The US remained sceptical about assertions from some regional analysts that ISIS was a creature funded to the tune of tens of billions by Sunni paymasters such as the Saudis and the Qataris. Although it is clear that the Saudis have been directly instrumental in the spread of an ideology shared by ISIS, whether this translated into direct and major government funding remains uncertain. As one senior US State Department official noted in early 2016: 'I'm open minded. If there's billions coming from the Gulf, show me the evidence. US intelligence has not found that evidence.'

What is undeniable is that diversification has allowed ISIS to insulate itself from the vagaries of international oil prices as well as punishing US air strikes targeting its oil industry infrastructure. As the US stepped up strikes on oil fields, refineries and the distribution networks, so ISIS expanded the one revenue stream that could not be entirely destroyed by bombs: the brutal and relentless extortion of the civilian population in and around the territories it controlled. For every success the Coalition had in attacking ISIS's funding, the terrorist group squeezed its enslaved civilians yet further. Destroying ISIS Inc was akin to killing a hydra: strike at one head and another rears in response.

How did one defeat such an enemy, an enemy that places no limits on the sorrow that shall be reaped by the people? How could ISIS be broken without crushing the innocent? Faced with such an adversary, the answer of one senior Western coalition member was single minded: 'We have to defeat them,' he said quietly. 'We have to deny them the resources to operate. The best thing we can do for the innocent is to finish what we started. As soon as possible.'

BLACK AND GOLD

Qurrayah, Iraq, 23 October 2016. A barefoot boy on a bicycle paused from his play, a look of bemusement on his face as he gazed into the newsman's camera. His skin was stained with soot and behind him unfolded a tableau of biblical-like devastation: the Iraqi desert was transformed into blackened moonscape. Fires raged across the horizon, turning morning to night. Sulphurous gases and smoke hung in the air.

The boy in the photograph was one of the 20,000 inhabitants of Qurrayah, a desert town of oil fields that ISIS had set ablaze before retreating from US-led Coalition forces in October 2016.

Mirroring the scorched earth tactics of Saddam Hussein during his withdrawal from Kuwait in the 1991 Gulf War, ISIS burned the house down before being expelled by a US-backed military offensive led on the ground by Iraqi and Kurdish forces, reinforced by the Russians. The Coalition offensive to destroy the Islamic State's oil revenue stream had began a year earlier, in October 2015, with attacks on refineries, followed by a targeting of extraction capabilities, from pumping facilities to the transportation network that had been built across the so-called Caliphate. By December 2016, the anti-ISIS Coalition had delivered a massive military and financial blow to the terrorist state's funding and the future viability of the Caliphate. But the toll on civilians in these areas was immeasurable.

In Qurrayah in October 2016, as it retreated, ISIS torched more than a dozen oil fields in the region, releasing a cloud of toxic smoke as large as the city of Los Angeles that blotted out the sun and left thousands in 'a smoke-filled hell', according to local reports. It set fire to a sulphur plant, unleashing a form of chemical warfare: NASA said the move had emitted 'tremendous quantities of sulfur dioxide', causing breathing problems for those left behind, including babies and children.

In the aftermath, the people of Qurrayah endeavoured to piece together the remnants of their life now that the tyranny of ISIS had been lifted. And yet there was weariness in their liberation and a realization that nothing would be the same. On the outskirts of town a shepherd tended his flock of sheep black from soot, fearing their fleeces had been rendered worthless. Shaka Ibrahim Khalifa, a butcher, hung blackened carcases outside his shop knowing even this polluted meat would be purchased and consumed by those who had little else to eat. All food and water supplies in the region were contaminated and would remain so as long as the fires burned. A local militiaman in uniform approached the butcher shop, carrying his young child whose breathing came in rattling gasps because of the sulphur in the atmosphere. The butcher shared his concern and told him his family washed and went to bed every night and when they rose in the morning their faces were black once more. Oily soot permeated everything: livestock, water, the food supply. And each day the sun rose and set against an unchanging horizon, darkly visible behind the veil of smoke and dust.

This is what victory looks like to those battling the Islamic State. If it could not deliver the End of Times, ISIS would turn defeat into a seeming apocalypse.

At its apogee, ISIS was earning as much as $500 million to $600 million a year from seized oil assets in northern Iraq and Syria, the biggest source of self-financing for the terrorist group. By February 2016, the US State Department told me, that figure had been cut by one third, with hopes of further reductions as the air and ground attacks unfolded. By the close of 2016, the Iraqi oil ministry reported that ISIS had lost control of all oil fields in its territory in Iraq. Its Syrian oil assets had been cut by almost half. 'The air campaign has been quite effective on ISIL's ability to raise revenues here,' the senior State Department source involved in disrupting terrorist financing under the Obama administration said in an interview. 'We are targeting [everything from] extraction to the transportation chain. Those trades are disrupted now. Together we've made it more difficult for ISIL to profit from oil.'

And by the end of 2017, ISIS lost its Syrian capital Raqqa and also its largest oil field, in Deir Ezzor; the US-led Coalition said it had cut ISIS's oil revenues from a peak of $50 million a month to less than $4 million a month.

As noted earlier, three things conspired to deliver a debilitating blow to the Islamic State's fledgling oil empire: US-led air strikes allied to ground assaults, tighter Turkish border control to curb illegal trade and a collapse in world oil prices. Global oil prices fell from a 2014 peak of $114 a barrel to below $30 a barrel by the opening of 2016, due to overcapacity of supply. As growth in pivotal economies like China slowed in 2015/16, global demand for oil fell and supply increased as Iranian oil came on stream in 2016 due to the lifting of international sanctions following the implementation of the Iran Nuclear Deal with the US and its partners.

Before the conflict began, Syrian oil production capacity was 385,000 to 400,000 barrels a day. When ISIS seized up to 60% of Syria's oil assets, it had potential capacity of 200,000 barrels a day—though it was producing nowhere near that amount, with oil experts such as Luay al Khateeb, director of the Iraq Energy Institute and a Brookings Institute fellow, estimating production of around 50,000 barrels at the most. (Interview with the author, February 2016.) Similarly, its peak Iraqi output of between 20,000 and 40,000 b/p/d did not match its potential oil producing capacity of 80,000 b/p/d.

Despite this, the revenues ISIS earned from oil were vast. The oil fields in both territories were manned by not just ISIS operatives and supporters but other insurgents or local players facilitating the terrorist state. It was a large network. The price at which ISIS and its associates sold oil, according to al Khateeb and other analysts, was within a range of $20 to $60 a barrel—vastly cheaper than the international market rate, which in 2014/15 was averaging at around $100. As a consequence, it had many buyers.

The global glut and resultant price collapse effectively undermined ISIS's profit margins and profits—with cheap, guaranteed and *legal* oil available to many of its illicit customers, they had less of a reason to turn to the black market being operated by ISIS across the Iraqi and Syrian borders. Global economics did as much to hamper terrorist oil revenue as coalition air strikes.

The buyers of ISIS oil and thereby direct funders of its terrorist activities were three-fold: internal, local and regional. Of these three, the internal customers were the most important in terms of revenues. Despite the collapse in the oil price and reduction in capacity due to coalition strikes, ISIS' internal demand remained largely intact as long as it held onto its territory. As an aspirant terrorist state, ISIS had at one point as many as eight million people living under its control in Iraq and Syria. These people had no access to international oil markets and were economic as well as physical hostages of the terrorist regime. In a war zone, they paid what the black market dictated.

The other customers of ISIS oil were local and regional

players. They included Turkish-backed rebels who held territories in northern Syria, Syrian Kurdish militia in control of eastern territories, as well as the Syrian Assad regime itself. In December 2015, US Treasury official Adam Szubin, former acting Under Secretary for Terrorism and Financial Intelligence, told the Chatham House think tank in London that significant volumes were being sold to the government of President Bashar al-Assad, the enemy of ISIS. 'ISIL is selling a great deal of oil to the Assad regime,' he said. 'The two are trying to slaughter each other and they are still engaged in millions and millions of dollars of trade.' (Reuters report, December 2015). Both stood to gain from the continued regional instability, with Assad claiming to stand against terrorism while terrorizing his own people in order to remain in power and ISIS vowing to fight the Shia Assad regime while its only interest was in propagating Sunni Islamist terror. Theirs was mutually beneficial war and trade.

In August 2016, reports emerged that Israel was another beneficiary of black-market ISIS oil. The Middle Eastern business press said Kurdish and Turkish smugglers were transporting oil from the Caliphate territories across the border and they found many surprising buyers. 'The oil is extracted from Dir A-Zur in Syria and two fields in Iraq and transported to the Kurdish city of Zakhu in a triangle of land near the borders of Syria, Iraq and Turkey. Israeli and Turkish mediators come to the city and when prices are agreed, the oil is smuggled to the Turkish city of Silop marked as originating from Kurdish regions of Iraq and sold for $15-18 per barrel (WTI and Brent Crude currently sell for $41 and $45 per barrel) to the Israeli mediator,' summarized a special investigation by al *Araby al Jadeed*, a Qatari funded news organization based in London, on 26 November 2015. The go-between then transported the oil via several Turkish ports, with Israel among the main destinations, said the report.

But the Israeli government vigorously denied these reports, with a foreign ministry spokesman describing it as 'groundless science fiction'. In turn, Israel accused Turkey of profiting from ISIS cheap oil in a diplomatic merry-go-round of blame. On 28 January 2016, the Global Research website quoted Israeli Defense Minister Moshe Ya'alon as saying in Athens: 'As you know, Daesh enjoyed Turkish money for oil for a very, very long period of time. I hope that it will be ended. It's up to Turkey, the Turkish government, the Turkish leadership, to decide whether they want to be part of any kind of cooperation to fight terrorism. This is not the case so far.' Ankara denied the allegations.

How did ISIS succeed in leveraging its control of crude oil, turning black gold into greenbacks that financed terror to the tune of hundreds of millions?

The Islamic State's oil business hinged on two oil producing regions: the main Iraqi one was in Qurrayah, south of Mosul in northern Iraq, which produced 8,000 barrels per day before it was retaken in October 2016, two years after ISIS took control. This was a heavier grade product mostly used to make asphalt. But the main source of output was Syria's eastern Deir Ezzor province which has production of 35,000 to 40,000 b/p/d. Deir Ezzor is a critical crossroads junction, with roads connecting to Iraq and areas ISIS controlled in Homs province, including Palmyra. It is also surrounded by some of ISIS's most valuable oil fields, which have been targeted by both US and Russian air power. These attacks have been focused on disabling the extraction and distribution process rather than destroying the oil wells themselves.

The majority of refining takes place in ISIS controlled Syria, producing petrol and *mazout*, is a type of diesel used in generators common in the many areas where there is limited or no access to electricity. Effectively, this is the economic lifeblood of the community within ISIS controlled areas.

Prior to the air campaign, ISIS relied on large fixed refineries in its territories, but as the Coalition and Russian bombing increased, a lot of the refining increasingly became dependent on small mobile units which were more difficult to target but also less efficient. The local mobile units were operated by residents who signed purchase agreements with ISIS. ISIS supplied the oil and in turn their partners produced *mazout* and split the profits. Analysts say ISIS operated its own transportation of crude to these refinery units, for maximum control and maximum profit.

The refined product was dispatched into ISIS controlled territory to specialized fuel markets where locals could buy and sell. It was an organized system whereby traders would present documentation showing they had pre-paid the *zakat,* religious tax, to ISIS or they would pay on the spot. Fuel was then sold at small makeshift pumps or mini petrol stations embedded in civilian areas and difficult to target from the air.

The customer would buy oil from the traders in jerry cans and transport it onwards to other towns or over the border on foot, by donkey or on horseback. When taking fuel to markets with a higher price threshold, larger amounts were transported in several jerry cans, which were then loaded onto small boats and shipped out.

Necessity proved to be the mother of invention: as the airstrikes forced ISIS to come up with alternatives to convoys of tankers and trucks transporting fuel, collaborators invented new ways to keep the revenues flowing. Some towns on the Syrian and Turkish border buried rubber pipelines under the border at places such as Besalan, forcing the Turkish authorities to step up controls at the border to disrupt this new distribution channel. But with hundreds of miles of border it was difficult to police this smuggling of ISIS oil and its by-products.

All this is illustrative of the inventiveness of an organization and its cohorts who are under heavy attack, but also indicative of the amateur nature of the oil operations that have been the subject of so much fascination in the global media. While the Islamic State has employed and co-opted (forcibly or otherwise) some of the existing oil industry professionals who were working the region prior to the war, it has also relied upon non-professionals or civilians to keep the oil flowing.

Who were, and are, the civilians helping ISIS? Locals with their own historic grievances against the powers-that-be—in Syria and Iraq—set up businesses to refine or transport fuel, feeling little allegiance to the status quo, while seeking to survive and make a living under their new regional overlords. In the earlier stages of the Syrian conflict, these local people set up basic refineries by procuring equipment from steel works across the border in Turkey. Grain silos and other facilities were also cannibalized for materials and parts. It was enterprise of the desperate and of opportunists: the Islamic State's Caliphate, portrayed in its propaganda as a land of the pure and free, was in truth a haven where the aggrieved, the poor and the criminal could operate as smugglers in order to survive.

In August 2016, the Dutch NGO PAX released a report called 'Scorched Earth and Charred Lives' which examined the health and environmental impact of these mobile refineries. After analyzing satellite images of ISIS's Syrian controlled areas, including Deir Ezzor, it found that 5,791 backyard oil refineries operated in the region. They were visible on satellite imagery as thousands of tiny black smudges and each smudge pumped out noxious gases including benzene, benzopyrene, carbon dioxide, carbon monoxide, ethyl benzene, methyl tert-butyl ether, sulfuric acid, toluene and xylenes.

These refineries poisoned communities but that was not the worst of the findings. The report's author Wim Zwijnenburg said the satellites indicated that tens of thousands of civilians, including thousands of children, were involved in the Islamic State's oil industry. With adult men either dead or away fighting, children were being deployed to run these mobile refineries. At one site a local doctor claimed 2000 children were working in 300 refineries. 'Considering that in our analysis we found (almost) 5,800 refineries...[it is] safe to say that thousands of children are likely working at these sites spread over all of northern and eastern Syria,' said Zwijnenburg in his report.

Apart from facing the risks of explosions that could kill or injure, these child workers were—and many still are—exposed on a daily basis to toxins that can poison the liver, kidneys, nervous system and blood over time. During its investigation, PAX also saw 'children covered by second- and third-degree burns, with oil still in the wounds'.

The long-term effects of this terrorist oil economy were already being seen: UN observers noted in 2013 that even before Deir Ezzor fell to ISIS in January 2016, the growth in makeshift oil refineries was causing cancer, respiratory disease, crop failure and birth defects. The report said it believed the 'rapid increase of these vast makeshift oil sites are likely to be a direct result of the increased targeting of the ISIS-controlled professional static oil refineries by the US-led Coalition forces and the Russian Air Force.'

Children were also used to sell product on the streets for the traders, as an investigation by Save the Children and UNICEF found in late 2016. Their report quoted Khalid, a 12-year-old boy, who sold diesel at market every day: 'When the man selling the diesel gives it to the customer, I stand next to him and soak up the diesel that has spilled on the ground with a sponge. I hate the diesel market and the clothes that I wear there, all of it makes me sick. One day some red spots appeared on my body and when I went to the doctor he said it was because of the diesel.'

The health of Iraq's and Syria's children is one price being paid and its effects will resonate for years to come in the environment that has been poisoned. Rivers and streams are contaminated, soot from oil fires is making the land infertile and in turn that has affected the health of livestock and crops and the wider populace.

The Islamic State's oil industry has earned the group hundreds of millions and it has been portrayed globally as a terrifyingly impressive example of how the group has created the illusion of a functioning economy with the potential to build a lasting Caliphate, a 'land of the pure' ruled, they say, by the laws of Allah. The PAX and UNICEF reports expose the reality: the exploitation and poisoning of thousands of young children and civilians to keep oil revenues flowing into the coffers of Islamist terrorism. It was a business empire as rapacious as it was amateur, draining the region and with no ability or interest in developing, protecting or investing in the long-term interests of the people or the country. Beyond the shimmer of propaganda, the Islamic State is a hollow kingdom, stripped and barren; a wasteland.

DEATH AND TAXES

Until the fall of Mosul in the summer of 2017, there was almost no way of gauging day-to-day life under ISIS rule as the region was deemed too dangerous for journalists and aid agencies to travel to. One powerful insight was the BBC's 'Mosul Diaries' series, comprising anonymous emailed accounts by civilians living in the heart of the terrorist state. These diaries gave a silenced people a voice again. In November 2014, a series of entries unveiled ISIS's latest hubris-laden ambition as part of the masterplan for nationhood: its own currency. The following section is reconstructed from those entries:

Mosul, 24 November 2014

It was almost time for Friday prayers and Faisal was washing and getting dressed to go to the mosque. To be properly prepared and on time was more important than ever since ISIS took control of this part of Iraq and imposed sharia on its people. The Hisbah or morality police were patrolling the streets to ensure that shops were closed and that men and women were observing Friday prayers. Failure to comply could result in fines or taxes being levied, or worse.

Today the sermon was about the value of the gold dinar in the era of ancient Islam, an epoch described to those assembled as one of flourishing trade and economic wealth. But this was no mere history lesson. It proved to be a momentous announcement for all those living under the terrorist group's control. Faisal and others heard the imam speak of how ISIS had made a decision to mint a new gold coin, evoking that bygone golden era.

Some 1300 years ago, in the 690s CE, under the rule of Caliph Abd al-Malik the first gold Ummayad Islamic coinage was introduced, replacing the Sassanian silver coins in Iran and Iraq and the Byzantine gold coins in Syria and Egypt. The move was politically motivated to provide unity in the Muslim-ruled territory. In an era of conquest, coinage was a symbol of the permanency of power. The new coins proclaimed the omnipotence of the nascent religion of Islam in these lands. In the case of the gold Byzantine coins, the cross was replaced by a column placed on three steps topped with a sphere and in the margin surrounding the design was the Arabic inscription 'In the name of God, there is no deity but God. He is One; Muhammed is the messenger of God.' These lines were taken from a verse in the Quran.

In reference to this past association and in a bid to consolidate its power over its fledgling territories, ISIS announced that under its new coinage there would be coins of silver and copper as well as paper notes and this would be the new national currency of the 'Caliphate'. This Islamic currency would one day, said the imam in Mosul that November day, be a force to be reckoned with and would take on the currency of the infidel itself, the US dollar.

The imam's sermon was a compulsory message to be conveyed in every mosque, in every ISIS-held territory that Friday. For ISIS, it was another landmark on the road to nationhood: the Caliphate would transform itself into an economic power. The Islamic dinar would usurp the old Iraqi dinar in the marketplace and on global currency exchanges. In the Islamic State itself, the world's reserve currency, the US dollar, would be banned.

Faisal and others in the mosque went home that day not fired by the promise of a new muscular Islamist nationalism but plagued with worry that ate into their hearts. With those few words from the imam, what little security that was left was about to be swept away. Later, in the safety and privacy of their homes, away from the hateful, ever-watchful eyes of the Hisbah, Faisal and his friends dissected the day's revelations. They agreed to change their dinars for hard currency and gold in the morning.

'I have business and bank accounts and bank dealings with other countries. How can I use this new currency which is only recognized in IS territory?' he said in his Mosul diary entry. 'We agreed that the IS plan was not religious or ideological but merely a scheme to rob us of our money and savings. The next morning a state of chaos gripped the market as everybody was trying to get rid of the Iraqi dinar and buy dollars or gold.'

So it was in Mosul that Saturday the voice of the free market spoke, and not even the tyranny of the terrorist state could silence it. In those brisk morning deals in the money-changers and bazaars, the people of Mosul gave their verdict as deftly as any currency trader in New York: the Islamic dinar was not going to be the dawning of a golden age. It was cold robbery, pure and simple. And it was just the latest example of how ISIS was determined to extract every drop to finance a vainglorious ambition that had nothing to do with Allah.

Every asset, trade or financial transaction, every salary cheque, every perceived transgression against Islamic law was taxed under the Islamic State. If you were a person selling fruit or stolen tankers of oil, a shopkeeper or an arms dealer, a baker or an antiquities smuggler, a tailor or a trafficker, you faced the Islamic State tax. Reports on the ground put the tax at anything from a few dollars to 50% of earnings. US government sources said (in an interview to the author) that the average level of tax on civilians in ISIS territory was 15-20% and they saw that figure rising as revenues from other sources such as oil were squeezed.

As ISIS progressed in seeking to establish administrative control of its territory, so taxes increased. In Mosul, just one district which was under its control, ISIS raised $8 million in taxes in a month, according to a *Forbes* report in August 2014 which showed levies ranging from a 5% tax for social welfare services on all salaries in the region, to a $800 custom tax per truck entering ISIS-controlled Iraq through Jordanian and Syrian checkpoints, to a 50% tax on looting of antiquities from archaeological sites in Raqqa. Non-Muslims had their own special protection tax known as *jizya*. The choice made available to the residents was threefold: pay the tax and live; convert to Islam and join us; or die.

The evolved 21st century terrorist mindset was exposed in a leaked 24-page strategy document from ISIS in December 2015, which outlined exactly how the terrorist group aimed to put itself on a sustainable financial footing. It did not seek to be an outlaw group operating out of the caves and slums of failed states. Instead, the Islamic State was about building a country, an economy, a base from which to export its ideology and thereby extend the Caliphate around the world until its currency was universal and the black flag fluttered over the fallen capitals of its enemies. To enact this ambition, it required an economic strategy.

The ISIS Papers, translated by a young British researcher and self-styled 'jihadi hunter' Aymann Jawad al Tamimi, were leaked to him by a disaffected businessman within ISIS territory. Al Tamimi in turn released the documents to the world's media. The manual entitled 'Principles in the administration of the Islamic State' showed exactly why

ISIS is the richest terrorist group in modern history. When it seized land, it was appropriating not just territory but assets that would be continuously exploited in the name of its global jihad:

'There is no doubt,' said the manual, 'that among the assets of the ummah are: its wealth, the nature of its land, its inhabitants and its water...It is the principal component and source of financing for all internal and external operations and the existence of secure financial resources whose value does not change...it is a must.'

The 'wealth' was the physical land, the mountains and all the minerals and natural resources therein. It was the rivers, the sea, topography lying at the heart of ancient trade routes that could be used to conduct illicit trade in oil, gas, slaves, antiquities and arms.

Last, it was the captive civilian population themselves, whether they were to be taxed, trafficked, used as sex slaves or executed for gruesome propaganda purposes; each person had a monetary value to the cause. Human beings along with all other 'assets' were carefully logged in ISIS's profit and loss columns, their revenue generation being their only value.

Yet the strategy document was overblown with the grandiose language of liberation, of these same captive people throwing off the chains of exploitation and tyranny of previous regimes or foreign colonial powers to become their own masters. The truth was they were more completely enslaved now than they ever feared possible.

The manual recognized that for the Islamic State's plan to continue into the long term, it was not just a question of pillaging but managing assets under its control: it spoke of 'preserving capabilities' by having the right staff and infrastructure in place to run those assets, whether that be an oil facility or cement plant. Accountants were depicted almost as elevated beings in the ISIS hierarchy, placed at the heart of every revenue generating area for the group. For a terrorist entity focused on cash generation, the bean counters were second only to the fighters in terms of their usefulness to the grand plan—sometimes even more important than the fighters. The manual extolled the virtues of controlling expenses in a centralized and uniform fashion across provinces, just as a government would, and it spoke of self-sufficiency of production, particularly with regard to food and arms.

Lastly, it alluded to trading within the region by opening up old routes to traffic goods and slaves. It aimed to integrate itself into the wider black economy, a strategy aimed at bypassing international sanctions and air strikes on its fixed assets. It no longer wanted to do business through middle-men but a 'direct exchange' that could deliver a principal source of income. This has already taken place as these are the conduits for crude and refined oil extracted and processed and sold on across the border, into Turkey and Syria.

There was one over-riding caveat for those who wanted to do business on behalf of the Islamic State: they must first pledge allegiance to and thus legitimize the fledgling state. Those who wished to invest in oil or gas fields must have 'the pledge of allegiance round his neck to the Caliph'. Those who wished to excavate for gold or antiquities must obtain permission from the Resource Department. Those who wished to build an arms factory to produce weapons must get a permit. And so it went on, even for the production and distribution of the very staples of life such as livestock, wheat and water.

From land to sea, from the wheat-fields to goats on the hillside, from the oil in the ground to the rivers and reservoirs that gave life to all around, from munitions warehouses to bakeries, bullets to loaves of bread, ISIS wanted its cut.

From the summer of 2015, as it faced pressure from the

US and its allies who were succeeding in choking off some of its revenue sources, ISIS pronounced it would levy a new religious tax known as *zakat*. It invoked the time of the Prophet, when Muslims were ordered to pay alms of 2.5% of their wealth as part of their religious obligation and in turn those funds would be used to help the poor. ISIS seized on the idea of a tax founded in the principle of showing compassion to the needy and twisted it, using it to compel its captive people to fund a violent 'holy' war. It was a far cry from the propaganda on YouTube of a state of religious purity and plenty.

'While inviting people to come and live a pure life in their Caliphate, what is not shown in the glossy brochure-like videos is how Islamic State ripped the necklaces and earrings off the women of territories conquered. [It] stole livestock, furniture, cars,' says Sayed Jiyad, an Iraqi analyst at Integrity, a London-based think tank.

The gap between the reality of a brutal and predatory movement and the Photo-shopped myth was becoming increasingly evident. ISIS enlisted a network of spies and informants as well as tax collectors who would speed about its territories in Iraq and Syria on bikes and trucks, gathering information on every businessman, every shopkeeper, every farmer earning a livelihood. Even those earning foreign remittances would find their bank accounts raided in the name of the Caliphate. The US Rand Corporation estimated in a report that before its capture of Mosul in the summer of 2014, ISIS had already amassed $875m in extorted money or *zakat*. That figure rose in the following years to $1 billion or more, fuelled by desperation as the terrorist group's territorial grip was loosened by relentless airstrikes and by Coalition successes in closing off routes of funding.

Under this broad revenue stream of *zakat*/tax/extortion/ looting, ISIS fighters and aides raided bank accounts, homes, offices, military compounds and took their booty to the 'war spoils' office where everything was valued. The looters were paid a share and civilians' goods sold at official markets with members of the Islamic State given a half-price discount, a kind of terrorists' supermarket loyalty card.

A report in the *Financial Times* showed the kind of bargains on offer at the ISIS marketplace:

> 'A fairly new Kia car costing $4,700 can be had with the IS loyalty card for $2,350.
>
> A motorbike costing $186 is a bargain at $93.
>
> A generator large enough to supply a family costs $714 but can be purchased for $357.
>
> Table and chairs for the lady at the back? In the shops it would cost $34 but to the shopper with the IS loyalty card, a bargain at $17.'

Goods were stolen, valued and sold on. Some looters did have their hands chopped off, as stated under ISIS sharia law, but were rewarded with a 20% share of the profit on sale.

Another way to extort the captive population was to impose ever more ingenious forms of taxation. In spring 2016, as the global media was filled with stories on the Panama Papers and tax avoidance on a grand larceny scale by the world's rich and powerful, the Islamic State was turning taxation into another form of torture, taxing ordinary people to the point of penury and starvation. As US air strikes stepped up against ISIS's oil facilities and transportation networks, the terrorist group invented new ways to financially bleed its population. The taxes came in the form of 'permits'. This could be simply protection money to ensure nobody stole from you or a share of your monthly profits. Or in the case of doctors in eastern Syria, free shifts at ISIS hospitals in lieu of tax. Medicine and aid was also subject to the same tax. Farmers paid in livestock or crops, with spies and tax collectors arriving at premises armed with guns and calculators to ensure the Caliphate was not cheated. Under the IS caliphate, larceny was institutionalized.

In the June 2014 Thomson Reuters report 'Islamic State: The Economy Based Terrorist Funding', the authors quoted the UN Food and Agriculture Organisation (FAO) as saying that the Iraqi provinces under ISIS control were the most fertile in the country, accounting for 30% of national wheat production. Taken together, ISIS-controlled areas accounted for 40% of wheat production and 53% of barley production.

At one point ISIS controlled government wheat silos in Iraq with 1.1 million tonnes of wheat or the equivalent of 20% of total annual consumption. It was not enough for the terrorists to tax the bakers and the consumers, it wanted to own the entire supply chain, like the oil industry it had taken control of.

ISIS's illegal transportation network shipped some of the wheat and barley output into Syria to be turned into flour where it was sold, said the Thomson Reuters report. The ambition of ISIS was such that it even tried to sell cereal to the Iraqi government through middlemen. Black-market trade in wheat and barley globally was worth a potential $200 million. From the field, to the silos, to the convoy of trucks that transported the goods to the bordering countries, to the processing facilities to the shops that sold the end product, ISIS received a percentage at every stage. It took the very food from its people's mouths and sold it on to fund an expansionist war. And how could it enemies defeat it on this front? Blanket bomb the fields, the grain silos, the bakers that sold their loaves and paid the terrorist tithe? The terrorists knew this to be impossible for their enemies without driving yet more Muslims into their arms.

And yet, ISIS's strategy is one that cannot be effective

in the long term. Its survival depends on its ability to pay: pay its fighters, pay for services, maintain some semblance of a functioning society. But evidence is emerging daily of the group failing to live up to its own propaganda. US and coalition actions have led to a funding collapse that has resulted in the ISIS fighters' pay being slashed by 50% compared to the middle of 2015. At the group's peak back then, its fighters earned between $400 and $1,200 a month, plus a $50 stipend for their wives and $25 for each child, according to the US Congressional Research Service.

Pay is not the only measure of its failings. Electricity, water and telecommunications supplies have been intermittent and unreliable. Financial pressure has made ISIS more brutal than ever on its own hostage population. And history has shown that in the end terrorist movements crumble when the atrocities, exploitation and injustices visited on the civilian population become too much to bear.

That point is being reached and so ISIS must draw in fresh recruits from around the world, and it is here that its propaganda machine is most valuable. But it sells a false dream—for the truth of its so-called caliphate was a nightmare lived every hour of every day by ordinary people. ISIS's 24-page economic strategy document showed everything had its price—most of all the 'inhabitants' of its 'Caliphate'. They were, and are, assets to be stripped, taxed or killed for propaganda.

And yet such is ISIS's depravity, there are things worse than death: an inhuman trade that exploits the weak and the vulnerable and subverts every principle of man and God.

AN INHUMAN TRADE

> 'Girls are being sold for a packet of cigarettes. [A girl's] value is a pack of cigarettes. I am just heartbroken. I have seen a lot of conflict in the world. But the scale and the magnitude of this: putting girls in the open market, stripping them naked for people to come and examine them. This is what used to happen in the slave trade 400 years ago.'
>
> —Zainab Bangura, UN Special Representative of the Secretary General for Sexual Violence in Conflict, in 2015, after visiting Yazidi girls and women, former victims of ISIS's sex trafficking and slavery, in Middle East refugee camps.

In the aftermath of ISIS declaring its so-called caliphate in 2014, a list was put into circulation in the region. The pamphlet detailed captured children and their price tags alongside. The price for an Iraqi boy or girl aged between 1 and 9 was set in dinars at the equivalent of $165. Prices for adolescent girls fell to $124. The list was distributed to potential 'customers': the group's own jihadis and wealthy Middle Easterners. When Madame Zainab Bangura, the UN Special Representative of the Secretary General for sexual violence in conflict zones, first saw the document she questioned its authenticity. The trafficking of babies and children was so barbarous it could not be true in the modern age. It took almost a year for her team to verify it. The children featured in the price list were real. This was not a secret trade on the Dark Web, nor was it opportunistic and sporadic. This was an open, systematic and very public market in babies, children and women in the 21st century.

ISIS justified its inhumanity to the world by saying this was permitted under sharia, spreading a horrific fallacy. 'One should remember that enslaving the families of the kuffar—the infidels—and taking their women as concubines is a firmly established aspect of the sharia,' one of their online magazines pontificated. The Islamic State had crossed a moral boundary in modern conflict and terrorism. This was not just rape but profiting from the serial abuse and rape of women and children as young a year old.

As a Muslim woman and a former refugee from Sierra Leone, Madame Bangura had seen her share of war atrocities against women and children, but realized with ISIS the world was in uncharted territory and it was unclear how this trade could be defeated in a war where air strikes and sanctions are the main response. 'This is not an ordinary rebel group. When you dismiss them as such, then you are using the tools you are used to,' she said. 'This is different. They have the combination of a conventional military and a well-run organized state. They have a machinery, they have a program. They have a manual on how you treat these women [and children]...They have a price list.'

Within a year, after meticulous checking, Bangura revealed her findings to the world. The terrorists had a menu that set out the options for buyers who would be invited to slave markets held in the open market squares. The older the child or girl, the cheaper the price, from $165 for a one-year-old to $41 for a woman aged over 40. Video footage released on YouTube shows children and women lined up in front of a crowd of men. In Mosul, one such slave day showed an ISIS fighter declare to jeers and laughter: 'Today is Distribution Day. Each one shall take his share. We have women waiting for you, we have virgins waiting for you.' When ISIS recruitment videos promise foreign jihadis their virgin brides for joining their war, these are the 'virgins'.

In the distorted reality that is the 'caliphate', purity comes at a premium. When a women is resold and no longer a virgin, ISIS decrees she must be 'purified' and remade into a virgin to be fit for their fighters and to raise a higher price at market.

The most sought after by the buyers and fighters are the young, the virgins, those with unusual features such as green or blue eyes or great beauty. Yet everyone has a value, including the older women who are paraded alongside the others, wreathed in chains. Many of these women and children are Yazidis, people of a minority faith in Iraq and Syria, among other places, who are classed as infidels by the terrorist group. After capture, the children and women are paraded with price tags on their necks, they have endured beatings and sexual violence even before being sold on. And many are resold again and again, as many as 20 times. Each time, ISIS makes a cut out of their trade. If these 3,000 victims were each sold at an average of $100 that would make a profit for the Islamic State of $300,000. Times that by 10, as many of these captives are sold between five and 20 times each, then you have a conservative average revenue of $3 million a year. The numbers are nothing compared to the incalculable human suffering, the scarring of the body and mind of both victim and perpetrator. ISIS has taught a generation of young men in its thrall that this is acceptable under Islam.

In 2015, Madama Bangura travelled to the refugee camps of the Middle East and there she met a young Yazidi girl of 21 who laid bare the reality of the jihadi 'virgin brides' propaganda. Already, she had been married to fighters 22 times since her capture. Before each marriage, her captors would forcibly carry out an operation to 'rebuild' her virginity so that she would 'qualify' as a virgin again and therefore be suitable for a virgin marriage to a jihadi. With each operation and 'marriage' her price as a virgin was restored. With each operation and 'marriage' a little more of her spirit was diminished.

'She was remarried 22 times just so someone could make money from her,' said Madame Bangura. 'These stories are real and these people need our help.'

Madame Bangura's intention was not to provoke the tears and outrage of the good but to expose the truth to misguided young men and women around the world drawn by the siren call of jihadism. The price list of the slave market showed their caliphate is not a place where the dutiful Muslim can find a path to God. Nor is the Islamic State a valiant guardian of the poor and the weak. The self-ascribed caliphate portrayed itself as a refuge from the debauchery and moral decline of the West: see how our Muslims have allowed themselves to be defiled by the trappings of modernity for too long, they said. They said their fledgling state was a haven of purity where the *ummah* could reject the West and its moral decline and revert to the true meaning of Islam. Yet the price list showed the terrorist group's 'caliphate' is built on lies and has nothing to do with the faith. Just as it trades a stolen car, a barrel of oil, Syrian and Iraqi history, so ISIS sells the body of a child.

The story of one victim is a more powerful indictment of ISIS and its hypocrisy than a million analyst reports. Below is the raw testimony of Nadia, a young Yazidi woman who was an ISIS sex slave, sold on before eventually escaping the terrorist state. It is her evidence to AMAR, a British charity working in Iraq to provide support to refugees in the camps, including psychological help to Yazidi girls who have been victims of kidnapping, rape and torture by ISIS.

The Yazidis fled to the slopes of Iraq's Mount Sinjar to escape ISIS. They are an 800,000 strong Kurdish-speaking community and just one group of minorities that has found itself targeted by ISIS, alongside Christians, Shiites and Kurds. The Yazidis believe the world is created by God who entrusted its safety to seven angels, the first of whom was the Peacock Angel, also known as Melek Taus. Today they are a displaced people, whose womenfolk have been subjected to some of ISIS's worst crimes against humanity.

Today Nadia campaigns against ISIS's war crimes and its sexual exploitation of women to raise money for terrorism in the hope that one day the terrorists will be defeated, convicted and brought to justice at the International Criminal Court. Nadia's story, as reported by AMAR, shows the devastation caused by ISIS on one family out of millions:

> Nadia is 22, from Kojo. Her family consisted of her mother, two sisters and eight brothers and her father died before the IS crisis began. Nadia lived with her two sisters and two of her brothers in the IDP camp in Zahko. Her mother was living somewhere under IS control after being abducted along with Nadia and she had occasional contact with her via a mobile phone. There is no contact with her other six brothers whom she fears are all dead.
>
> Her story begins on 2 August 2013 when IS invaded Sinjar and came to her town, Kojo. The family wanted to run towards the mountains but IS surrounded the village. They told all the Yazidi residents to raise a white flag over their homes and they would be safe. IS fighters came and ordered the villagers to hand over their weapons. They told the people they had three days to convert to Islam or they would be killed.
>
> A man calling himself Abu Hamza arrived and ordered all the residents to be taken to a big two-storey school in

the village. Nadia noticed there were some heavy diggers being driven into the village by IS soldiers and asked one of her brothers about it. The brother said he didn't know what they were for, but thought it might be to help clear the roads locally. The reason was more sinister, but they did not know that then.

IS soldiers then ordered all the women and girls to go upstairs and the men were told to remain downstairs. This they did, and the girls were robbed of their identity cards, jewellery and any cash they had.

Sometime later, buses and pick-up trucks arrived and the IS soldiers herded the men onto them and they were driven away. Later the women heard sounds of repeated gunfire. After some time, the IS fighters came back to the school and said if the women still refused to become Muslims they would be taken to Sinjar Mountain and they could go to Kurdistan.

They then brought buses and cars and pushed the women inside. They were driven off, but at the first IS checkpoint some of the girls were dragged from the cars and taken off, they believed, to different towns.

Nadia said they realized they had been cheated and they were not going to the mountains to be released. Instead they were taken to another village where all the girls were put inside the teaching institute building. There was a guard outside the door and he snatched all the scarves off the girls as they were led inside.

They then asked the married women to go upstairs, and most of the women went that way. Nadia realized later that she should have said she was married but didn't think quickly enough because she was so frightened, so she stayed on the first floor. She remained there with two of her nieces, aged about 15. Nadia and the other girls were taken into the building's big yard where there were about 150 young girls. She recognized they were mostly from Kojo. There were four IS guards, one was reading the Koran.

The man then talked on his mobile phone and said 'four buses should be enough' so she knew they were going to be moved again. Later that night, they were ordered onto the buses and driven off, with a car in front and behind, full of IS fighters.

On board, one of the guards was taking photos of them and kept touching the girls and grabbing their breasts. Eventually they arrived in Mosul. The guard started herding the girls off the bus, and grabbed Nadia very roughly, badly bruising her.

It was around 2 a.m. by the time they reached Mosul, and they were taken to a big house that she was told belonged to a judge. When they got inside she found a woman there with a young boy and she asked her what was happening to the girls and women. The woman told her there were 400 girls living there and 'everyone from Daesh' comes there, chooses one of the girls and then leaves.

Nadia said after that she was too afraid to sleep and she stayed awake until morning. Then an IS man came into the room and said they needed 63 of the girls and the rest would be taken to Syria.

Nadia and some other girls were then taken from that house to another two-storey building where they were kept on the top floor while IS soldiers camped downstairs.

The windows were painted so they could not see out and there was no television or furniture. Each day IS gave them rice and tomato sauce to eat and a cup of tea between every three girls. They were on these rations for three days and they saw nobody except the guards.

On the fourth day, IS men came and asked them to go into two of the rooms and said a man was now coming to marry them.

Later another very tall and very fat, ugly man came. Nadia was wearing a black dress and orange jacket. He came up to Nadia and said, 'Hey you with the orange jacket. Come with me.'

Nadia didn't know what to do. She told him she wouldn't go with him and then another man appeared and wanted to take her two teenage nieces. He said they were so young and he wanted them and they were dragged away from Nadia.

She noticed that there was another man behind the huge man and she begged him to save her from the big guy. She said she was ready to go to Syria, or anywhere, but please don't let this man take me.

The other man was called Selman and he told the big guy that he had already selected Nadia and he would take her. Selman took her and her niece to another place that he said was temporary. When they got there, they saw approximately 200 men were praying. They told Nadia they were going to separate her from her niece and they would not see each other again. Nadia said her niece started crying but they forcefully took her away.

Selman took Nadia back to the judge's house. The only people now left there were Nadia, Selman and six guards. Selman took her to a room and locked the door. He then pulled out a letter which had the Daesh flag on it and he said ISIL are in Syria, Iraq, they have taken Mosul, Zumar, Tal Afar, and every member of ISIL will now have several Yazidi girls.

He then demanded that she take off her clothes. She said she had her period and he said she was lying. He said "If you are not going to take off your clothes, I am going to ask the guards to take off your clothes forcefully."

In the morning he said he was going to Zumar, but that night he would be back, he would rape her. Nadia was looking at the guards and they were staring back at her. They were so frightening, that she said she actually wished that Selman would not leave so that he would protect her from the guards.

She was kept locked in the room and during the day she found some contraceptive pills so she took two and then she took two more a couple of hours later because she feared they would not be effective.

At 11 pm, Selman came back and raped her. This happened every day. He would go out during the day and return at night. One of the guards told her that Selman had been in Badush Prison in Mosul for more than seven years before Daesh released all the inmates.

Later, Selman took her to a house where he said they could get married, but the official who would do this wasn't there, and they were told to return the next day.

He took her back to the room at the first house and ordered her to undress. She did and then Selman opened the door and allowed the six guards to come in. He switched on the video to show a sex film and then he allowed all six of the men to rape her all night.

The next day, she was taken to another building where a man gave the guard 200,000 Iraqi Dinar (Approx $167) in exchange for Nadia.

The driver was asked to take her to an empty house and he demanded she get a shower while he got her new clothes. He said he was to take her to Syria. He left and while he was gone she walked out and up the street. She knocked on door after door and eventually a young man opened his door to her and she begged for his help.

She told him she was a Yazidi and she had been attacked and raped and held prisoner for such a long period. She said if he couldn't help her could he at least show her the right road to get away.

At that moment the man's father came to the door and he took her inside the house. The older man asked her if she knew the Director of Sinjar District. Nadia said she didn't know him personally but if the man told the Director of the name of her father he would recognize him.

He asked Nadia to call the Sinjar Director. She used a mobile they gave her to ring her brother and he gave her the number for the Sinjar District office. Then the old man called the Director who did indeed know her name and confirmed she was a Yazidi from Kojo.

She spent two weeks at the house and they were very kind to her. They made an ID for her, pretending she was the wife of the young man. They bought her an abaya and niqab and they drove her to Kirkuk. This was at the end of September, 2014.

She was then taken to safety in Kurdistan. Today, Nadia says she wants to tell her story because she hopes there will be a court case one day that says very clearly genocide took place against the Yazidis.

She said she suffered very badly at the hands of Daesh. She is angry. She is in pain. She lost her family, including her mother. Before her abduction she had hardly spent a night away from her mum and was close to her. She was six months old when her father divorced her mother and she never saw him again. Her mum looked after all the children very well after that. They lived in a poor house in the village and her brothers worked on farms and raised sheep and goats.

After her escape from IS, she kept alive the hope of seeing her mother again. Then came the shocking news that her mother's body had been found in a mass grave in Sinjar. The wives of five of her dead brothers are still missing and believed to be held by Daesh. A young nephew was kidnapped and she believes he has been radicalized after he sent her photos of himself wearing military uniform and carrying a gun.

THE TWO-TRILLION-DOLLAR PROBLEM

'The sinews of war are infinite money.'

—Cicero

Chaos and economics is written into the Islamic State's DNA. One feeds the other, and for ISIS to endure, its leaders understand the cycle must keep turning, despite the reverses it has suffered in 2016-17.

ISIS always understood that to those Muslims who were poor, disempowered and caught in the crushing vacuum of history, it had to offer a job, a purpose and a homeland. The promise was a powerful one, even if it was a lie. To propagate the lie and draw disaffected and suggestible young men and women in, ISIS needed money to bankroll its jihad, pay its fighters and finance a nascent state. From the very outset it turned to criminal activities to raise funds.

By 2006 it was raising between $70 million and $200 million a year from oil smuggling, kidnapping and counterfeiting, among other crimes. ('US Finds Iraq Insurgency Has Funds to Sustain Itself', *New York Times*, 26 November 2006). Like an ambitious start-up it quickly diversified—into drug trafficking, artefacts smuggling—and reinvested and up-scaled to gain critical mass. Around this time, Al Qaeda in Iraq (AQI), as ISIS was known then, was already more financially secure than its progenitor Al Qaeda itself. In July 2005, Al Qaeda wrote a begging letter to AQI asking if it could lend 'a payment of approximately one hundred thousand [dollars]' because its own lines of cash had been severed under a very successful effort led by the US Treasury. (*Washington Post*).

The Islamic State's revenues continued to climb dramatically, and at its peak, as we have seen, it was raising $2 billion to $2.9 billion a year. But the more startling figure was the total potential value of its assets—over $2 *trillion* even by conservative estimates (according to the Thomson Reuters report 'Islamic State: The Economy Based Terrorist Funding').

Apart from the funds that came from bank raids, extorting civilians and taxing criminal activities, this 2-trillion-dollar figure was based mainly on a physical asset base that spanned oil and gas, minerals and agriculture. The land beneath the Islamic State's feet was its biggest source of power and money.

Oil was the largest commodity revenue generator. While the US and its allies could obliterate the oil infrastructure, they could not wipe out the oil in any ground held by ISIS. Iraq alone, by some estimates, may have a quarter of the world's total oil—it is the least explored of the world's oil-rich countries. ('How Much Oil Does Iraq Have?' Brookings report, 12 May 2003.) That is why taking back territory was so crucial for the US and the anti-ISIS Coalition: when ISIS lost those lands and oil fields, it would lose its asset base and future earnings power.

The oil fields in ISIS territory in Iraq had a total production capacity of 60,000 barrels a day, according to the International Energy Agency, via 13 oil fields in Nineveh, Al Anbar, Salah ad Din and Kirkuk. In Syria, it had control of seven oil fields in Deir ez Zor and Raqqah, including the country's largest oil field, Al Omar. As of May 2016 ISIS held three large refineries, two in Syria and one in Iraq, in addition to mobile refineries and pumping stations. It had a transportation network of tankers, as well as storage tanks.

Next on the asset list was natural gas. ISIS had control over gas fields in both Syria and Iraq, including Iraq's largest reserve at the Akkas field in the Al Anbar province. Natural gas plants under ISIS control had the capability to generate $979 million a year. (Thomson Reuters report.)

Natural minerals were the other assets ISIS controlled. It had cement plants, sulphuric and phosphoric acid plants, sulphur extraction plants and phosphate mining units in its seized lands. Together these were capable of generating hundreds of millions of dollars.

Then there was agriculture. As cited in an earlier chapter, the Food and Agriculture Organization at the UN said in an analysis that ISIS had captured some of the most fertile agricultural land in the region. At its peak, ISIS controlled land that produced 40% of the total wheat from the region and 53.3% of the total barley. Trade in such crops, too, would have yielded hundreds of millions of dollars per annum.

These were the riches—in the ground and from the extraction and sales infrastructure—that constituted ISIS's astonishing asset value. Unlike the Taliban in Afghanistan and Al Qaeda on the Af-Pak border, ISIS had placed itself in the position of controlling vast, diversified natural resources that could yield a huge income for years to come, provided they were fully exploited.

But this would happen only if ISIS held on to its territory.

As long as ISIS retained control over assets potentially worth $2 trillion, it had the ability to remain a self-financed terrorist state—extortion and taxation of its captive population, after all, could only be a feasible modus operandi for so long. At some point, the people would be too impoverished to tax and may well rise up in protest, just as they had done against their previous dictators in the Arab Spring.

Therefore, destroying the terrorist group's capability to extract and sell the natural resources in its territory, destroying its ability to move and spend funds from those sales and—most crucially—taking back territory that contained those resources was central to defeating the group. The longer any of those lands remained in ISIS control, the greater opportunity it had to exploit the natural assets, embed itself into regional markets and criminal networks, build up its war chest and establish a long-term economic framework to finance its dream of the caliphate. The asset base would enable ISIS to pay for fighters, weapons, a war on two fronts, as well as build a nation state: hospitals, roads, electricity, water, civil servants, schools—the building blocks of a functioning society to which ISIS aspired, and which it invited the *ummah* to join.

The Coalition had to act quickly to obliterate not just the possibility but also the perception that the Islamic State had the means to establish permanency.

Efforts to degrade its asset base began primarily with the oil industry in Iraq and Syria. Air Vice Marshal Edward Stringer, the senior UK civil servant in charge of destroying ISIS's finances, told a parliamentary hearing in London in April 2016 that the strategy had worked: 'They are running short of cash and they are looking for more imaginative ways to do things. It is early days, but only in the last week we have heard that the taxation system is becoming more arbitrary, more looking to fines and so less progressive and less easy to sell to the population. We are starting to see corruption and embezzlement among senior leaders, suggesting we're having success.'

The counter terrorism journal *CTC Sentinel* reported

that by early 2016 ISIS was struggling to pay its fighters in Iraq and Syria. The US Treasury confirmed fighter wages had been slashed by 50% as ISIS's oil infrastructure was being destroyed by airstrikes and falling oil prices were affecting profit margins. As fighters' pay was cut, recruitment began to fall—reports on CNN.com, in the *Washington Post* and other newspapers and sites quoted US military sources and leaked internal documents of ISIS that said foreign fighters were being offered salaries as low as $50 a month, and that the number of foreign fighters joining ISIS had dropped from 1500-2000 a month in 2014/15 to around 200 in 2016. In the end, jihad was not just a warped religious mission for many, but a job.

The US Treasury said the next step was to isolate the Islamic State's war chest and stop it from spending on arms and the apparatus of a functioning nation. Daniel Glaser, who was in charge of tracking the terrorists' money under the previous Obama administration and who was integral in choking off Al Qaeda funding, was a man focused on his task like a laser. The tough-talking burly lawyer noted in an interview with me, 'In 2014, the US Treasury said there would come a moment in a year or so where ISIL would reach a pinch point financially and that would prove to be the watershed moment when the US and its allies gain the upper hand in a fight back. Have we reached this point yet? I don't want to have a "mission accomplished" moment. But let's just say we're making substantial progress.'

Glaser wasn't going to be triumphalist, but he wasn't going to be affected by ISIS mythology, either. He had remained unfazed even in the early stages of the US and Coalition fightback by analysts who spoke of the scale of ISIS's success and the professionalism of its leadership. Like Al Qaeda before it, Glaser believed ISIS would be defeated and said the world must be careful not to allow terrorists to create their own mythology: 'A lot of people said to me when they took Mosul [that] they were professional and organized. I wonder...Let's just make sure we don't say these guys stand ten feet tall, you know.'

And yet, as coalition efforts succeed in reducing the Islamic State's footprint in Iraq and Syria, it has demonstrated yet again its ability to evolve in a quest for fresh expansion. As Libya has become the next country to be drawn into the vortex of political chaos following the deposing and execution of Gaddafi, so ISIS has spotted a new market. In 2016 it gathered momentum in the North African country—operating terrorist-training camps, building numbers and using it as a base to send jihadis into Europe, just across the Mediterranean Sea.

Political chaos and the desperate economic position of the Libyans and others in the region has created another opportunity for the terrorist group, and ISIS Inc has acted quickly to reap the rewards. Like Iraq and Syria, Libya is another hydrocarbon economy with mineral riches. In 2015, it was ranked 9th in the world for crude oil reserves. It also has substantial reserves of natural gas, gypsum, sulphur, nitrogen, lime and cement. As its territory in Syria and Iraq comes under pressure, Libya is the new expansion opportunity for ISIS. Already in February 2016 the UN was noting that 'the relative ease with which groups such as ISIL have expanded their spheres of control and influence over the past few months is a matter of grave concern.'

In early 2015, ISIS had established control of a stretch of coastline in Libya and the city of Sirte. It proclaimed its presence by videoing a mass execution of Christians on a beach. In September that year, its English propaganda magazine *Dabiq* carried an interview with Abu al-Mughirah al-Qahtani, the leader of the Islamic State's provinces in Libya, where he proclaimed the importance of this new terrain. He called for doctors, legal specialists, bureaucrats and fighters, encouraging them to make *hijrah*, or holy migration, to the North African state. While numbers of recruits in Iraq and Syria were falling in 2016, American intelligence reported that within just a year 6,500 recruits had joined ISIS in Libya: 'Libya has become a magnet for individuals not only inside of Libya, but from the African continent as well as from outside,' John O. Brennan, the director of the CIA, told a Senate panel in February 2016.

ISIS has also made forays into Yemen, another country submerged in chaos. Yemen's civil war began in 2015 and is a quagmire of conflict that pits tribes and religious and political factions against one other. The political chaos has meant that it is today one of the world's poorest countries, with 20-40% of its youth unemployed. But it also has large oil and natural gas reserves and agriculturally productive land. In short, ideal territory for the Islamic State. Already, the US has started bombing ISIS positions within Yemen to prevent them gaining further traction.

Faced with these multiple fronts of expansion, the anti-ISIS Coalition has doubled up the urgency of disrupting the Islamic State's money-making machine before it becomes a financially viable terrorist state capable of operating across multiple territories. Has it succeeded? That is a 2-trillion-dollar question.

To truly defeat ISIS, we must grasp that at the heart of its success lies a nexus of chaos, poverty and undemocratic economics. While the West and its anti-Coalition allies fight ISIS, it is worth remembering that these same countries have played a role over decades in creating the very conditions that made it possible for ISIS to capture territories in Iraq, Syria, Libya, Yemen and elsewhere.

CONCLUSION
The Hollow Kingdom

> 'For the survivor death is not the problem. Death was an everyday occurrence. We learned to live with Death. The problem is to adjust to life, to living. You must teach us about living.'
>
> —Elie Wiesel, Holocaust survivor, quoted on Holocaust Memorial Day, 27 January 2017

Across the world, the old order is overturned. We live in times of baffling, depressing change. A rise in global Islamist terrorism; millions of refugees displaced by wars in the East that the West helped create; the Trump Presidency; Brexit; the rise of nationalist populism, even xenophobia, and majoritarianism in every other country. All are seismic events on their own, but together they form a momentous sea-change that risks democratic values of tolerance, peaceful co-existence and compassion for those in need. The changes will resonate for years to come and their catalysts are two events in modern times that altered the political landscape for everyone: 9/11 and the global financial crisis of 2008.

It was the decade that changed our notions of security, both physical and financial. America's 9/11 in 2001 heralded an era of fear for our physical safety from the terrorist, as well as for our way of life. It triggered almost two decades of retaliatory wars in Afghanistan and Iraq, followed by a great unravelling in the Middle East and the creation of ISIS that has made our security weaker, not stronger.

The 2008 economic crisis precipitated a collapse in living standards for working and middle-class people across the world: jobs were lost, homes repossessed, savings wiped out; and the burden of debt crippled both the global economy as well as personal households. It made many believe that globalization had failed the weak and enriched the elite and this opened the door to protectionism. Out of the wreckage of that economic storm an anxiety emerged among some of those who lost out—that the *other* was to blame. By 2016, Trump in America and the Brexiteers in Britain spun these arguments into a single narrative of fear: beware the immigrant or refugee who takes our jobs and imperils our security.

This threat to security, both financial and physical, was blamed on the outsider, and in an echo of the 1930s, those fears have formed into a movement that has swept Trump to the White House, Britain out of the European Union and now afflicts the EU itself, the Union that has preserved continental peace and prosperity for decades.

The Arab Spring of 2011 was born of an explosion of anger against poverty and the venal corruption of the region's rulers. The revolution began as a call to arms for all who aspired to democracy and economic justice but swiftly turned into despair. What ensued was not liberation but fragmentation of old powers, and greater economic and political turbulence. It opened a vacuum for Islamist extremism to take hold and flourish in countries like Libya and Syria, with a large impoverished and marginalized youth. The prize on offer from the Islamist militants was not democracy but an uprising to create a 'Caliphate'.

After an era of globalization, mass migration and blurred identities, we have retreated into an age where the dividing lines are sharpened once more, where some of the emerging political forces are redrawing the world map into *them* and *us*. There are calls to seal borders; majority voices clamouring to deport 'outsiders'—most often Muslims, and not just refugees fleeing civil war or persecution (like the Syrians in Europe and America) but also centuries-old residents (like the Rohingyas of Myanmar or the Muslim Bengalis of Assam, India).

A polarized world threatens to *help* ISIS fulfil its vision of 'eliminating the grey zone'. Every Islamaphobic policy or comment makes it easier for it to recruit more young Muslims. The age of fear and the politics of rage have aided the rise of the Islamic State just as surely as they have fuelled protectionist nationalism at home.

Trump and ISIS are two sides of the same political coin.

On Holocaust Memorial Day in January 2017, without any sense of history or irony, Trump signed an executive order banning people from seven Muslim countries from entering the US: namely, Iraq, Syria, Iran, Libya, Yemen, Somalia and Sudan. It was the first step in realizing his promise to ban *all* Muslims entering America. He promised a Muslim register for those already in the country, something that evoked memories of the Nazi treatment of the Jews. He said the US Israeli embassy may move from Tel Aviv to Jerusalem, killing all hopes of a Jewish Palestinian peace deal and giving succour to fanatics on both sides who opposed peace. He also said he believed torture worked and that he would consider reopening the notorious 'black-op sites' responsible for the illegal detention, interrogation and torture of Muslim terror suspects in the darkest days of the post 9/11 Bush presidency. Within days, Trump's presidency had alienated Muslims around the world, reawakened a sense of Muslim grievance and emboldened Islamaphobes and racists everywhere.

The raising of borders and demonizing of a religion by the leader of the world's only superpower frames the war against ISIS in the language of the terrorist—that this is a battle of faith. It harms relations with partners in the war. It makes terror attacks more likely. Within hours of Trump's statement, ISIS and Al Qaeda called it a 'blessed ban' that would drive American Muslims and those elsewhere into their arms. They described the Trump presidency as evidence that the West *is* at war with Islam, and said their prophecy of the 'enemy' turning against Muslims was coming to pass.

ISIS believes an isolationist and fortress America will create a political and moral vacuum that will be filled by the fanatic. The mooted commitment to torture and black site interrogation has evoked Abu Ghraib and the photos that spawned ten thousand jihadis. It is as if the West has learned nothing.

Economic protectionism is a further misstep. It is no coincidence that all of the countries with the highest instances of young people being radicalized and turned into jihadis also see unemployment in this key demographic. Jobs, economic empowerment and regeneration are key to arresting the lure of extremism across the Middle East, Asia, Africa and Europe. Trade and fairer economic engagement by the richest nations is the surest way to stem the tide of further radicalization or mass migration.

In the new order, extremism is feeding extremism. Defeating ISIS is inextricably linked to defeating the politics of division that is taking hold in the West and parts of Asia. As this book has shown, to destroy the Islamic State there is no single solution: we must revoke their territorial writ, dismantle their financing architecture, disable the media and recruitment machine, inhibit the import of hardline Wahhabism into our mosques and schools and, most urgently of all, defend freedom, tolerance and the rule of law—democracy's DNA. We must guard against the tide of Islamaphobia crashing upon American and European shores. We must work with the majority of moderate Muslims around the world to ensure that Islam as a religion of peace prevails.

The excesses of the last war on terror under the Bush presidency helped create ISIS and its incursions into other parts of the world. History is now at risk of repeating itself under the Trump Presidency's anti-Muslim rhetoric, human rights crackdown and increasing protectionism and isolationism. Its timing could not be worse—2017 has closed with ISIS on the back foot, loosing terrain, seeing its finances targeted, suffering widespread desertions and contemplating the fragmentation of its so-called Caliphate. The Trump doctrine could reverse those gains by alienating many Muslims globally once more.

While driving ahead with efforts to topple ISIS's few remaining footholds in Iraq and Syria, there must be long-term engagement to build the peace. The first step must be to contain the unfolding humanitarian crisis as millions of refugees flee ISIS territories, and for the international community to bring the perpetrators of these war crimes to justice, to assist the many victims as they begin the process of recovery.

The second aim should be to rebuild the shattered towns and cities and infrastructures of civil society after the fall of the Islamic State's physical domain is complete. As ISIS is driven out, it is razing its kingdom to the ground, town by town, city by city, using IEDs to level hospitals, schools, oil facilities and other buildings. Theirs is a legacy of ruin that will cost tens of billions of dollars to fix.

Back in August 2014, at the apogee of ISIS's success and before the worst of the devastation had happened, the World Bank had estimated that the cost of rebuilding the parts of Syria damaged would be upwards of $200 billion

('The Syrian Marshall Plan', *Foreign Affairs*). In 2015, the Iraqi government reclaimed Ramadi, once a thriving city of half a million people that had been rendered uninhabitable with bridges, roads and other core infrastructure destroyed. The deputy governor of the Anbar province, where the city is located, said reconstruction of cities in his area would cost $22 billion (*The Arab Weekly*, 23 October 2016). Rebuilding Mosul, the former Iraqi ISIS capital that fell in the summer of 2017 after a brutal siege, will require tens of billons of dollars more.

The costs are enormous, but unavoidable. Geoffrey Aftandilian, a lecturer in Global Studies at Boston University and a former US State Department Middle East analyst for many decades, warned in an article for the *Arab Weekly* in October 2016: 'Leaving these damaged cities in the Sunni heartland of Iraq in a state of disrepair will feed Sunni resentment, which, if not addressed, will make the situation ripe for another group like ISIS to emerge. It behoves the international community, including Gulf Cooperation Council countries, for strategic and humanitarian reasons, to develop a reconstruction plan...and a mechanism to pay for it.'

The task of rebuilding shattered communities and economies is key not just to defeating ISIS in the long term but also to addressing the refugee crisis that is threatening European stability and fuelling the rise of right-wing politics in the West. The West and its allies are currently focused on finishing the job of taking back ISIS territory, but a strategy for reconstruction is also needed urgently. Reconstruction means creating safe and economically viable communities for refugees to return to; creating jobs for young people to be engaged in, thereby drawing them away from the lure of jihadi recruiters.

Just as there is an anti-ISIS Coalition to destroy the Islamic State's kingdom, so there needs to be a similar coalition between East and West to rebuild the territories devastated by ISIS and the war against it. There is a powerful case for devising a Marshall Plan style solution for the region. After the Second World War, US Secretary of State George Marshall put into effect the project named after him which helped rebuild Europe. Today a similar multinational commitment is required to prevent ISIS or its kind resurrecting in the region and using it as a base to export its terrorist ideology.

Rebuilding the lives of Iraqis and Syrians will take more than just vast sums of regional and foreign investment. People like Dr Saleh Dhumad, head of the Iraqi sub-committee at the Royal College of Psychiatry in London, are working to increase the level of psychological counselling for refugees and former captives of ISIS in the region. He believes investment is required for repairing the psychological damage and that this is a prerequisite to economic regeneration: 'The simple fact is many of these civilians will be traumatized, suffering from severe depression, and if you are suffering like this you cannot work, you cannot rebuild. People fear what will happen after ISIS—"What's next for us?" The wounds are so huge...These people have seen their lives destroyed, they have had family killed, they have been raped, all normality has been taken from them.'

At the grassroots level, NGOs and ordinary psychiatrists are working to heal the damaged psyches of civilians, particularly young children and adolescents. But they are doing so with very limited resources and little international support. Dr Dhumad is now working with me to raise funds to bring together a group of psychiatrists from around the world to deliver counselling to those in need in the camps, either directly or through training programmes for locals who can then disperse out into the communities.

There is a need not only to counsel refugees to overcome their traumatic time living under ISIS, but also to identify and assist those young children and people who have been exposed to radical ideology. 'I heard from the NGOs on the ground that there are children in the camps of northern Iraq who have been trained in slaughter. Small kids trained to use a doll to practise cutting off the head. This idea of killing is now planted in young minds. These kids are angry and aggressive all the time and right now there is nothing on the ground to help deradicalize them,' said Dr Dhumad.

After the fall of Mosul, Dr Dhumad visited the broken city and its environs to assist the international NGOs operating there. During that visit, a terrifying incident happened, involving a 10-year-old in one of the refugee camps that held former ISIS captive civilians. The child had not spoken since arriving and was withdrawn and isolated for many weeks. One day, aid workers discovered the boy in a room where they found he had hanged two smaller children. The event underlined their darkest fears—that the horrors of ISIS will echo through the next generation unless they are dealt with now.

The threat is no longer limited to parts of Western Asia ravaged by ISIS. As we have seen, with the Islamic State losing its strongholds in Iraq and Syria, it is seeking to implement Plan B: exporting terrorism into cities around the world, recruiting Muslims within these overseas communities to mount lone wolf-style attacks which are quick to organize, aimed at soft targets and almost impossible to prevent entirely. The aim, apart from spreading terror, is to sow division and discord in as many countries as possible. Which is why the counter-propaganda offensive against the Islamic State is even more important now.

As fiercely as the democratic world defends its ideals and freedoms, it must expose—intelligently and consistently—

the lie that the Islamic State is a religious call to Muslims everywhere and that this is a kingdom built on the laws of Allah. Behind the veil of propaganda lies a desire to forge a global *terrorist* state built on the enslavement of millions, including Muslims; and an economy founded on greed more rapacious than any dictator's, whether extracting value from a barrel of oil or the body of a young child. Respected, popular moderate voices, both Muslim and non-Muslim, must explain that nothing about the Islamic State is Islamic.

To a growing extent, this messaging fightback is being done, with governments, moderate Muslims, civil society and the media revealing the truth of what ISIS stands for. Questions are being raised within the Middle East and in the West about the nature of Wahhabism and its interpretation of sharia and Islam that is being taught in schools and mosques.

Social media companies, too, have woken up to their exploitation in the terrorist propaganda wars and are seeking to collaborate to silence the Islamic State's voice online.

But the greater task is addressing the perceived marginalization of those young people around the world who have been vulnerable to ISIS's siren call.

The responsibility lies both in the West and the East. And there is a promising whiff of change in the air after so much bad news for so long. In recent days, as I finished writing this book, Saudi Arabia's crown prince and heir apparent Mohammad bin Salman made a momentous announcement to the world, vowing to return his country to 'moderate Islam'. He asked for the world's support to transform the kingdom into an open society that empowered its people and drew investment. He said the Saudi state had been 'not normal' for three decades, and in an apparent reference to the rise of the global Wahhabi proselytization of the last thirty years, he said it had been a reaction to the Iranian Revolution of 1978-79.

This statement of intent marks the beginning of a

revolution in thinking. More than any country, Saudi Arabia, with its Muslim World League offices embedded into almost every capital around the world, has the power of influence to ensure that the moderate voice of Islam prevails. Now we must see if this seismic shift materializes and endures. If it does, it will be one of the most historic and important blows in the war against Islamist extremism

Equally, there are calls for the oil-rich nations of the Middle East to take the lead now in rebuilding the areas damaged by ISIS and the military offensive against it. With the richest of these nations, Saudi Arabia, showing signs that it has understood the dangers that lie ahead, it is likely that this may happen. Rebuilding the economies of northern Iraq and Syria would strengthen the wider trading region to deliver much needed jobs to Arab youth—economic statistics bear out that the countries which faced the greatest number of their population going to jihad were those where young Muslims faced high unemployment, low skills and lack of social mobility.

But together with these small, welcome signs of possible change, there are developments that appear to repeat the worst mistakes of the past.

Under siege in Iraq and Syria, and always seeking to exploit despair or brewing discontent among Muslim communities anywhere, ISIS is trying to establish bases in Libya and Yemen, which are both in the grip of chaos. Even as it does this, it has sensed an opportunity in another part of the world.

The current persecution of the predominately Muslim Rohingya community in Myanmar has evolved within months to become a major international crisis. Atrocities have been committed by the security forces of this majority Buddhist nation against the Rohingya people, leading to hundreds of thousands, including women and children, fleeing for their lives to neighbouring Bangladesh. The UNHCR has described it as 'a textbook example of ethnic cleansing'.

The marginalization of Rohingya Muslims has captured the interest of ISIS and there are now growing fears that it could target this part of the world next as a recruiting ground.

Meanwhile, millions who fled ISIS and the wars in Iraq and Syria, crossing over in boats and dinghies to Europe, risking death, are housed in poor camps as governments in Europe argue over who should take responsibility.

There is a moral duty among wealthy Western nations who helped destabilize Iraq in the first place to act now and be accountable. There is a need to properly integrate those refugees already displaced in foreign lands, just as the Jews were in other parts of the world after fleeing Germany in the Second World War and who went on to be great contributors to their adopted nations' wealth, civil society and culture.

Bombing the Islamic State into oblivion will not come close to 'mission accomplished'. The task of destroying ISIS's legacy is vast, multi layered and a generational one: military action, economic reconstruction, rehabilitation and de-radicalization on the ground, and above all, preserving democratic values and the principles of equality, multiculturalism and compassion that are the hallmarks of modern civilization. This is what is required to defeat ISIS, and prevent ISIS 2.0 rising.

The hollow kingdom of Islamist jihad is predicated on one thing alone: teaching a generation to love death more than life. But as the Jewish Holocaust survivor said, there comes a time when a man knows all there is to know of death. He needs to know life again: a family that is safe, a place to call home, the dignity of work, clean water in a stream, blossom on a tree and a society that is just.

ACKNOWLEDGEMENTS

The book could not have happened without the testimony of the many courageous people in Iraq and Syria who told their stories and fought for peace and tolerance in the region.

I would also like to thank a few people for their support over the years which has contributed to this book being written.

First and foremost, my publisher Ravi Singh and all of the talented team at Speaking Tiger. I am honoured to be part of the Tiger family. As always, Ravi's advice, friendship and intellect have been invaluable.

Thank you to Peter Wright, my esteemed former Editor at Britain's *Mail on Sunday* and Editor Emeritus of Associated Newspapers. Peter gave me the wonderful opportunity to cover many stories that helped lead to this book: from the Arab Spring and the uprising in Libya to sharia law in Britain and an exploration of madrassa-based education. I am grateful to MoS and its Managing Editor John Wellington for allowing me to reproduce some of that material in this book. Also, thanks to Keith Waldegrave, the legendary and unflappable MoS photographer I was lucky enough to work with on many of my assignments. The 'foreigns', as he called our jobs, would have been no fun without him.

A special word of remembrance for John 'Mozza' Morrison (1949-2017), former political editor at Reuters and my old boss and friend. John was one of the great foreign correspondents of his time in Moscow, Paris, Vienna and across Africa. He was an acclaimed author and playwright and also a dear friend who constantly encouraged my writing endeavours. He is missed greatly.

Thank you to Westgate Communications' Connie Bruin and Martin Bailey for all their hard work on my website. It has been a pleasure.

Lastly, all writers owe the highest debt to the loved ones who support us behind the scenes and generally put up with our annoying idiosyncrasies: in particular, thank you to my husband Andrew and my lovely son Felix.